First published in Great Britain in 2006 by
MAINSTREAM PUBLISHING COMPANY (EDINBURGH) LTD
7 Albany Street
Edinburgh EH1 3UG

ISBN 978 1 84596 175 6 (from January 2007)
ISBN 1 84596 175 7

A catalogue record for this book is available
from the British Library

Typeset in Sabon
Printed in Great Britain by
William Clowes Ltd, Beccles, Suffolk

EASY RYDER

urope's Magnificent K Club Triumph: Three In a Row!

Ian Stafford

MAINSTREAM
PUBLISHING

EDINBURGH AND LONDON

Seve Ballesteros and José Maria Olazábal –
the greatest partnership in Ryder Cup history.
(© Phil Sheldon Golf Picture Library)

EASY RYDER

**Europe's Magnificent K Club Triumph:
Three In a Row!**

Paul Casey plays the perfect bunker shot at the 16th during the Saturday morning fourballs. (© Darren Jack)

CONTENTS

Introduction   9

ONE   History of the Ryder Cup   17

TWO   The K Club   47

THREE   The Captains   59

FOUR   The Build-up   69

FIVE   The Players   97

SIX   Europe Take the Initiative _   121

SEVEN   Europe Pile on the Pressure   145

EIGHT   Europe in Dreamland   167

Conclusion   191

Ryder Cup Statistics   199

The 18th green at The K Club
in all its splendour.
(© Warren Little/Getty Images)

Paul Casey (right) celebrates with partner David Howell after his hole in one at the 14th wins their afternoon foursomes match on the second day. (© Harry How/Getty Images)

INTRODUCTION

IT ALWAYS FELT AS THOUGH THERE WAS GOING TO BE
something very special about the 2006 Ryder Cup, long before the
first ball was hit in anger on the morning of Friday, 22 September.
Everyone involved in the wonderful sport of golf just sensed it.
Perhaps it was because of the setting. The K Club in County Kildare
might not have been everyone's favoured choice beforehand, but it
had been created by Arnold Palmer, one of the true greats of the
competition, and the biennial event was to be held for the first time
in Ireland, one of the most fanatical golfing countries in the world.

We're off! Jim Furyk drives the first shot of the 2006 Ryder Cup. (© Mark
Pain)

The Irish factor was always going to make the tournament a success. Few love their golf more than the Irish, and few are more passionate. At the same time, not many people are more knowledgeable and respectful. There was no danger of any repeat of the unfriendly scenes witnessed at the 1991 Ryder Cup at Kiawah Island or of the controversial and unsporting events seen at Brookline eight years later. The Irish know how to enjoy themselves – and they would be given every opportunity to do so – but they also know how to behave.

Or perhaps the eager anticipation was because of the recent history of the event. After many years of American domination, Europe had hit back hard. Of the past ten Ryder Cups, the Europeans had, astonishingly, won seven, including the last two. They would be hoping to make it three wins in a row for the first time ever, whether competing as Great Britain and Ireland or as the expanded European team. But the USA were not going to take the recent European dominance lying down. At Oakland Hills in 2004, Europe had inflicted their biggest victory over the American team, winning by a margin of 9 points. The USA were humiliated, they were hurt and they were angry. They would be doing everything in their power to ensure the same did not happen in Ireland, but they would be up against a European team who were no longer in awe of their cousins from across the Atlantic.

Alternatively, the fervent build-up might have been because of the players who were going to be on show. America, after all, sported the world number three in Jim Furyk, the world number two in Phil Mickelson and arguably the best player the world has ever seen in Tiger Woods. Throw in such players as David Toms and the determined Chris DiMarco, both winners of majors, and the visiting team possessed some of the biggest stars in golf. So too, though, did Europe. The European Tour had become bigger, better, more competitive and more lucrative over the years. It was the belief of the European players that they now stood shoulder to shoulder with their American counterparts and that their tour was just as good as the one across the Pond.

Or the high levels of pre-tournament expectancy might have

been because of who the two captains were. Europe's Ian Woosnam and America's Tom Lehman were two men who had both worked their way up from nothing to reach the pinnacle of world golf as players, who had squeezed every last drop of their potential out of themselves, who had always been prepared to roll their sleeves up and get their hands dirty, and who loathed the thought of losing.

Whatever the reason, and despite the mammoth victory just two years' previously, the whole of Ireland, and indeed the whole of western Europe, waited with anticipation, trepidation and expectation for the Ryder Cup to begin for only the second time in its 79-year history outside Great Britain or America. To the Irish, the Ryder Cup has always been a bit special. Blessed with some of the world's most beautiful and challenging courses, the small country has always provided more than its fair share of golfers. Once a newly created European team started to make inroads into the American dominance from the early 1980s onwards, an Irishman has often been found close to the action. Europe have boasted some special players in the past 20 years or so, golfers such as Seve Ballesteros, Nick Faldo, Bernhard Langer, Ian Woosnam and Sandy Lyle, but more often than not it has been a lesser-known Irishman who has produced the final and most compelling piece of drama.

In 1987 at the course that Jack built at Muirfield Village in Ohio, Europe inflicted their first-ever defeat on the USA on American soil, a result largely due to the little-fancied Eamonn Darcy's gutsy win over Ben Crenshaw in the singles. In 1989 at The Belfry, it was a wonder shot from Christy O'Connor Jr. that demolished Fred Couples and handed a draw and a retention of the trophy to Europe. In 1995 at Oak Hill in New York, it was Phillip Walton's turn to win the Ryder Cup for Ireland and for Europe, when he defeated Jay Haas at the last. And in 2002, again at The Belfry, Paul McGinley sank a putt to halve his match with Jim Furyk and win the Ryder Cup once more for the Europeans, an achievement the little Irishman celebrated, famously, by throwing himself into the lake beside the 18th green.

Last time around, in 2004, it was Colin Montgomerie, a Scot, whose putt secured yet another victory for the rampant Europe,

Time to party: the partners of Europe's victorious team get down to it.
(© Mark Pain)

but a quarter of the team was made up of Irishmen in McGinley, Padraig Harrington and Darren Clarke. In the run-up to the 2006 cup, it transpired that the same Irish triumvirate would represent Europe again, but this time on Irish soil. What a welcome they and their teammates could expect from a fanatical crowd relishing the biggest sporting event ever to hit their island.

In fact, the Ryder Cup has now grown into one of the largest sporting occasions in the world. From its humble origins in 1927, when a St Albans-based seed merchant named Samuel Ryder paid for a trophy and launched the official Great Britain and Ireland versus America golfing extravaganza, the tournament has experienced its ups and downs. After a promising start, most of the downs were endured by the British Isles as America's golfers trounced their opponents every two years. Some of the biggest names in golfing history played their part in the Ryder Cup, from Walter Hagen to Ben Hogan, Sam Snead and Gene Sarazen, but it was all one-way traffic for the United States. By the late 1960s and '70s, the one-sided nature of the competition had become ridiculous. The USA were sporting teams consisting of such players as Jack Nicklaus and Arnold Palmer, Lee Trevino and

Billy Casper. Even when a newly created European team tried their luck for the second time in 1981, they came up against an American team boasting the winners of 11 majors.

But something was stirring. A new generation of European stars was emerging, and, thanks to the influence of captain Tony Jacklin, they began to give America a taste of their own medicine. The Ryder Cup needed this competitiveness to survive. It had been in grave danger of petering out at one point – but not after Europe started to win and win consistently. Suddenly, the Ryder Cup became big box office. Golfers began to care about it far more than they had done before. There were now controversial moments and talking points were created, as were some sublime moments of sporting history. Then the emergence of Tiger Woods introduced a whole new generation to the game and thus to the Ryder Cup. By the time the trophy was presented to Europe once again at the end of the 2004 competition, the Ryder Cup had surpassed everything else in golf to become the number-one event in the sport.

And so to The K Club in 2006. We knew it was going to be

Brothers in arms: García, Casey and Montgomerie, three European giants at The K Club. (© Mark Pain)

good. We knew the European team had many stars in form. And we knew, after Oakland Hills, that they would find themselves, for the first time ever, installed as favourites. But being the front-runners was a different ball game entirely for the Europeans. Would they be able to handle it?

We had no way of knowing what would happen next. We knew the crowd would be passionate, but never in our wildest dreams could we have imagined the unprecedented level of fervent but fair support the Europeans and Americans would receive each day from approximately 50,000 fans. We knew that both teams would be mindful of previous Ryder Cups, at which competitiveness had boiled over to provide unwanted, unsavoury moments, but we could never have guessed just how sporting and friendly the keen rivalry would be over the three heady days of golf. We knew the action would be good, but nobody could have forecasted quite so many birdies, so many long putts, so many outrageous slices of luck and two holes in one. And we knew the Europeans would be tough to beat, but nobody could have predicted just how dominant they would be over an American team bursting with star names.

Finally, and most poignantly, it was inevitable that the event would be emotional. Tiger Woods had lost his father to cancer in the spring. After taking a break from the game, the superstar golfer had returned to win the British Open at Hoylake, collapsing in tears when he secured the title at the 18th green. Chris DiMarco, who finished runner-up to his compatriot at the Open in July, had lost his mother that very week. Neither had had too much time to start recovering from the deaths of their loved ones, but the process for both of them was at least under way.

Not so Darren Clarke. When he should have been competing at the US PGA Championship in August, he was instead attending the funeral of his wife Heather, who had lost an 18-month battle against cancer, despite having fought bravely right up to the very end. It was a loss that affected so many members of the European Ryder Cup team. The popular Northern Irishman was left to pick up the shattered pieces with his two small sons. Three weeks later, he told Ian Woosnam that he was available for selection for the

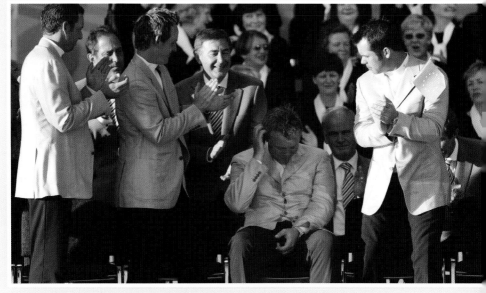

Thanks, Darren! An emotional Clarke receives a standing ovation from his teammates at the closing ceremony. (© Mark Pain)

fast-approaching competition. However, the Welshman, to his credit, did not choose Clarke out of sentiment. He eventually picked him because he believed the man had enough strength of character to come through, even if he had to play golf in the most daunting circumstances imaginable.

Woosnam was ultimately proved right, but not even he could possibly have guessed just how well Clarke and a team united behind the Northern Irishman would rise to the occasion. Twelve golfers represented Europe at The K Club, and all twelve, in differing ways, delivered. The dozen on-form European players, who produced startling golf for three days – performances borne out of the unity they always seem to discover at the Ryder Cup, the most sensational support from the crowd and a unique solidarity with their friend and colleague Clarke – were simply unstoppable. America, regardless of the fact that they had Tiger Woods on their team, never stood a chance.

Beforehand, Ian Woosnam would have been happy to amass just 14½ points, the least amount necessary to win the Ryder Cup for a third time in a row. The European players, however, would not be satisfied with that. They sensed that they were on the verge of creating golfing history, and they were not about to pass the opportunity up.

The morning fourballs saw Europe take a 1-point lead, despite the defeat of Montgomerie and Harrington, their lead-off pair. That might have been a major psychological blow for the European team in the past but not any more. They shrugged off the defeat and bounced back to take the session. By the end of the first day's play, following the afternoon's fourballs, Europe had increased their advantage to 2 points. It was a repeat performance on day two, with Europe taking both fourball and foursome sessions by an identical 2½–1½ score line. At the helm was the young Spaniard Sergio García, who saw off everything America could throw at him. The foursomes also witnessed a sensational hole in one by Paul Casey to win his match. After two days, Europe held a 4-point lead going into the final day's singles matches. They would only need 4 points to draw and retain the trophy, and an extra ½ point to win it outright, out of the 12 on offer.

On Sunday, 24 September, it seemed as though half of Ireland had come to The K Club to witness the final piece of drama at this compelling sporting event. Led by the irrepressible Colin Montgomerie, Europe surged towards victory, a sea of European blue dominating the scoreboard. It was left to Henrik Stenson to conjure up the winning putt, as his team went on to equal their biggest-ever winning margin and become the first team in the history of the Ryder Cup to win all five sessions. But the real drama centred around an emotional Darren Clarke, who sealed a magnificent performance in the tournament by winning his singles match to secure a maximum 3 points out of 3. When he cried on the 16th green, every sports fan in the world shed a tear with him.

The 2006 Ryder Cup was not Europe's first victory, and it will most certainly not be their last. But thanks to the marvellous support, the impeccable sportsmanship, the quality of the European players, the superlative golf produced, and the emotions that tested the stiffest of upper lips, there has never been a Ryder Cup like it.

The following pages retell its incredible story.

ONE

HISTORY OF
THE RYDER CUP

THE RYDER CUP HAS BECOME THE BIGGEST EVENT in golf, bar none. What began as a unique team game between the USA and a Great Britain team in a sport usually contested by the individual is now a biennial festival of golf which dominates the sporting screen and back pages around the world. Those who have played in it make no bones about it: nothing, not even putting for a major championship, comes close to the pressure and responsibility of playing for 11 other teammates. It is a highly unusual experience for the golfer who excels on his own and has only himself to blame for the other one hundred and three weeks of every two years.

Over the decades, some of the greatest stories in sport, let alone golf, have stemmed from the Ryder Cup. In its 79-year official history, the competition has seen more triumph and disaster, heartache and exultation, drama and pathos, controversy and sportsmanship, and passion and camaraderie than any other sporting event, all played out in front of galleries that number many tens of thousands and – increasingly so in recent years – global television audiences of hundreds of millions.

Who can forget the moment when Jack Nicklaus, the greatest golfer ever to play the game, conceded a putt to Tony Jacklin, thus sparing the Englishman the possibility of losing the match and the competition? In the recent history of sport, there is no better example of good sportsmanship. On the other hand, who can forget the sight of American players, caddies and even wives traipsing all over the 17th green at Brookline or the atmosphere at Kiawah Island, which resembled more a war scene than a golf tournament?

Just about anyone who was or is anyone in golf has played in the Ryder Cup. A list of some of the greatest names reads like a veritable *Who's Who* of the sport. Walter Hagen, Ben Hogan, Gene Sarazen, Sam Snead, Arnold Palmer, Jack Nicklaus, Lee Trevino, Tom Watson, Tiger Woods and many more have graced the tournament for America. Tony Jacklin, Nick Faldo, Seve Ballesteros, Bernhard Langer, José Maria Olazábal, Sam Torrance, Sandy Lyle and Ian Woosnam have all done likewise for first the Great Britain team and then, latterly, for Great Britain and Ireland and for Europe.

But perhaps the greatest days of the Ryder Cup are the present ones. The introduction of a European team to face the dominant Americans in 1979 eventually bore fruit and saved a festival of golf that was in grave danger of petering out. Long gone are the days when America simply needed to turn up to win. Indeed, before this year's Ryder Cup at The K Club, Europe, who always used to begin proceedings as underdogs – at least on paper – had won seven out of the previous ten competitions. These victories included scenes that will remain for ever etched on the history of golf: the lofted arms of Sam Torrance in triumph after sinking the putt to win the 1985 cup; the howl of anguish from Langer as he missed the most pressure-filled putt imaginable to lose the tournament six years later at Kiawah; the sight of what seemed like half-a-dozen Seve Ballesteroses exuding more energy than any of his players as he captained Europe to victory on Spanish soil; the most controversial scenes ever witnessed in golf two years later at Brookline; and the image of Colin Montgomerie, overcome with emotion after a difficult year away from the golf course, as it was left to him to sink the putt that won the Ryder Cup in 2004. It may just be coincidence, but the Ryder Cup has thrown up so many unlikely stories that one wonders whether the man upstairs happens to be a golf fan.

Yet it all began in the most humble of fashions when a British seed merchant named Samuel Ryder decided to supply a prize for an international golf competition that had already seen America play against Great Britain in two previous matches. When the Ryder Cup was first contested in 1927, Ryder was the happy provider of the now famous trophy that has been held aloft by some of the greatest names the game has ever seen, which is why his name has lived on long after his death. Back then, he foresaw a competition which would showcase the highest standards of goodwill, sportsmanship and elite golf in a team environment. Today, the competition is barely recognisable as the same one contested in Ryder's day, but the seed merchant from the Midlands of England would be satisfied, nonetheless, with how it has all turned out.

The original idea was actually the brainchild of an Ohio businessman called Sylvanus Jermain, ably supported by both Walter Ross, president of the Nickel Plate Railroad Company in Cleveland, and James Hartnett, the circulation manager for *Golf Illustrated* magazine. Having failed to raise enough funds to send an American team over to Britain, it was Hartnett who managed to persuade the US Professional Golfers' Association to foot the bill in late 1920. In June 1921, the first golf match between Great Britain and America took place at Gleneagles in Perthshire. Fittingly, Scotland, the home of golf, provided the initial venue for what would become the greatest and hardest-fought spectacle in golf.

The British team sported two of the greatest golfers of their day: Harry Vardon and J.H. Taylor. Although the Americans could boast Walter Hagen, the rest of the team – many of whom were British exiles – were some way below the standard of the British, who ran out comfortable winners by a score of 9–3. Few members of the public bothered to watch, and the press saw it as nothing more than an exhibition match. The *Glasgow Herald* was prepared to hand out commemorative medals, but that appeared to be that. The concept of the competition becoming a biennial event had not yet materialised.

Hagen, though, thought otherwise, and the idea never left his mind. It was just creating and then seizing the opportunity that proved troublesome, at least for another five years. Credit for the next meeting between the two great adversaries must go to the Royal and Ancient, however inadvertent its contribution, because the esteemed governing body of the Open Championship decreed in 1926, for the first time, that regional qualifying rounds should be staged before the Open. This resulted in Americans arriving early for the tournament, with time on their hands. They were all required to qualify at Sunningdale, and it was here, at the famous Surrey course, that they first met Samuel Ryder.

It was Ryder's suggestion that America should play Great Britain at Wentworth Golf Club as a warm-up in preparation for the Open. Ryder, a 68-year-old golfing fanatic, was the captain of his local golf club and had also been mayor of St Albans. He had previously enticed the best golfers of the day to events held at the Verulum Golf Club in St Albans and had organised an England versus Scotland match. Hagen, always up for a challenge, accepted Ryder's invitation immediately, only to be part of an American team thrashed 13½–1½. The Americans were spared this humiliating result becoming the first official Ryder Cup score because the General Strike back home had prevented many of their team members from travelling. Instead, their numbers were made up by a collection of Scots, English and even an Australian. Ryder decided to withhold the trophy as a result, agreed with the American and British captains to launch a biennial event starting the following year in America, and happily lent his name to the trophy after donating £100 towards it. He also ensured that the figure of Abe Mitchell would adorn the lid. Mitchell was Ryder's personal golf tutor and a man who would have played in the inaugural official Ryder Cup but for the fact that he developed appendicitis on the eve of departure. He would become known as one of the best golfers never to win the Open.

Ryder's involvement continued to be decisive. When *Golf Illustrated*'s appeal to raise £3,000 for the British team to sail to America fell £500 short, it was Ryder who made up the difference.

And it was Ryder who saw off his team at Southampton docks (minus Mitchell, who nearly died from his illness) as they set sail for Worcester, Massachusetts.

It was here that the first Ryder Cup officially took place. Thirty-four have followed, prior to The K Club in Ireland in 2006, and most panned out as at the Worcester Country Club – until, that is, European dominance set in decades later. For now, however, a combination of the late and dramatic loss of Mitchell, the long journey, adapting to American conditions and the Hagen effect proved too much for the visiting team. In a format which sported four foursomes matches and eight singles, America triumphed 9½–2½.

Two years later, the Ryder Cup 'officially' came to England and the Moortown Golf Club in Leeds. Hagen was still the main man for America, although he had been joined by Gene Sarazen among others. So confident was the four-times back-to-back winner of the US PGA Championship that when he heard he would playing against George Duncan, the Great Britain captain, he remarked, 'There's a point for our team right there.' Duncan overheard this remark and promptly thrashed Hagen ten and eight over thirty-six holes. Cheered on by the first real partisan crowd at a two-day Ryder Cup, Great Britain reversed a foursomes deficit to win the singles, taking the match 7–5.

And thus the Ryder Cup was established. Over the next few tournaments, a number of significant events would help to shape the famous competition. In 1931, for example, the tournament staged at the Scioto Country Club in Columbus, Ohio, coincided with a ferocious heatwave. The Great Britain team had no answer to sweltering temperatures often exceeding 100 degrees Fahrenheit, let alone the brilliance and charisma of Hagen, the first-ever golfer to earn $1 million from playing the game. After their team were thumped 9–3, the British PGA protested about the weather conditions, and it was agreed that the Ryder Cup would never again be staged during the American mid-summer, instead being put back to its now traditional month of September.

Perturbed by the nature of their defeat two years previously, the Great Britain team went to some lengths in order not to repeat the process when the competition returned to England in 1933, this time to the Southport and Ainsdale Golf Club on the Lancashire coast. In picking J.H. Taylor as their first non-playing captain, they chose one of the members of the 'Great Triumvirate', which also included Harry Vardon and James Braid. Then aged 62, Taylor was past playing, but he was still a strict disciplinarian, to the point of having his team endure early-morning runs along Southport beach. It seemed to work. Great Britain emerged as close winners, and, after four Ryder Cups, the honours were even. Ardent followers could not have wished for a closer, more competitive tournament, but despite this victory for the British, the tide was already turning inexorably towards America; it would be a quarter of a century before victory would again be tasted by Great Britain.

In 1935, for example, Great Britain went down 9–3, despite playing three brothers for the first and only time in Ryder Cup history. In what would prove to be Hagen's last Ryder Cup as a player, Ernest, Charles and Reg Whitcombe could not prevent the Americans from recording a comfortable victory. Two years later, in what was the last Ryder Cup for ten years, America became the first team to win successive competitions. One glance at the make-up of the American team tells you why. Hagen, at 45 years of age, had become the new non-playing captain, and he found himself in charge of a team that included the likes of Sarazen, Snead and Byron Nelson. Such a strong team proved far too much for the Great Britain players, who succumbed 8–4. Not only had America taken the trophy twice in a row, but they had also won for the first time on British soil, a feat that prompted President Franklin D. Roosevelt to make personal contact with captain Hagen.

Samuel Ryder had not lived long enough to witness this. He had died the previous year from a haemorrhage, at the age of 77, and was buried together with his beloved five-iron. The man had departed, but his trophy would continue to be fought for as fiercely as any other in sport right up to the present day. For this, credit must go to a wealthy American fruit grower called Robert Hudson, who sponsored the Portland Open each year and was a great supporter of the Ryder Cup.

While American golfers continued to thrive during the Second World War, with Ben Hogan coming to the fore as the main money earner, their British counterparts were either fighting in the war or failing to find any competition to enter at all. After the Allied victory, many of the British golfers virtually had to start all over again.

Under such circumstances, and with the country beginning its slow recovery from the war, the British PGA could not find the money either to send the team to Oregon or to launch an appeal. Step forward Hudson, who not only agreed to underwrite the British team but also entertained them royally. It was Hudson who paid for their transatlantic voyage on the *Queen Mary*, hosted an extravagant reception banquet in New York for them and accompanied them on the four-day rail journey to the north-west of the United States. Throw in all expenses paid, gifts provided and the caddies' tabs arranged, and Hudson's contribution to the Ryder Cup was massive. But why did he go to so much trouble? For the love of golf and the pleasure of seeing the event staged at his home course.

The American team, meanwhile, established a new selection process, which, more or less, remains the same to this day. At that time, the US PGA awarded points to any professional finishing in the top ten of a tour event. Team places were then decided based on the accumulation of points. It meant, of course, that the Americans were on fine form, and they dealt a humiliating 11–1 defeat to the British. Nothing went in the visitors' favour. Bereft of any meaningful golf for six years, they came up against an American team of golfing superstars, including Hogan, Snead and Nelson. The British had a few champions of their own, including Henry Cotton, Dai Rees and Max Faulkner, but most of the others fell well below the standards of the Americans. So astonished was Cotton at the longer distances achieved by American driving that he demanded to inspect the grooves on Hogan's club to determine whether they were legal or not. They were, as indeed were the rest of the American clubs. It would prove to be one of the great Ryder Cup controversies.

Hogan, clearly, had not forgotten Cotton's actions when the Americans returned to England in 1949, this time to play at the Ganton Golf Club near Scarborough. Now a non-playing captain, he queried the legality of the British clubs, stating that the grooves did not conform to the rules. The resident golf professional at Ganton, Jock Ballantine, thus spent the eve of the Ryder Cup filing down the home team's clubs. More resentment followed when the American team offered their British counterparts some of the huge cargo of food provided for them by Robert Hudson, who correctly thought that the British team could not afford such largesse in the recent aftermath of the war. The gesture was sincere, but it only served to dent British pride.

However, it would take more than a hiccup in diplomatic relations to deter Hogan. Seven months earlier, he had been almost killed when his car crashed head on into an overtaking coach. Hogan was in hospital for 58 days after suffering multiple injuries. Still on crutches when the Ryder Cup came round, he was clearly unfit to play, but his bloody-minded will to win ensured that he would captain the American team to a 7–5 victory, even if it meant a great deal of hobbling and a great deal of pain.

The British selection policy followed America's when it came to the 1957 Ryder Cup, staged at the Lindrick Golf Club in Sheffield. The players would be selected depending on how many points each golfer had scored in top-20 finishes in professional strokeplay championships. There was more optimism, too, for the home team. Despite the recent dominance of American golf, the visitors did not seem quite as strong as usual. Both Ben Hogan and Sam Snead declined to play, and the US PGA was apparently complacent enough not to apply pressure on them to compete. Britain, meanwhile, appeared a far stronger unit than the one that had succumbed so easily two years before. Apart from experienced campaigners such as Dai Rees and Max Faulkner, they also welcomed back the likes of Peter Alliss and Bernard Hunt.

Despite this, they fell behind 3–1 after the opening day's foursomes. The second day's singles remained, and if the competition was to follow almost every precedent, the Americans would storm home in the singles. To make matters worse, Faulkner asked not to play, because, in his own words, he was playing 'rubbish'. It proved to be an inspired decision as Faulkner spent the second day being the team's best cheerleader, and his efforts, coupled with a partisan home crowd, encouraged Britain to a 6½–1½ win in the singles and an overall score of 7½–4½.

The Ryder Cup had been regained for the first time in 24 years and all seemed to be well again in British golf. The truth was very different. America were on the verge of producing a new wave of golfing superstars, Britain would be forced to expand to incorporate the whole of Europe in 1979 in order to be at least competitive and the Ryder Cup trophy would not return to European shores for a staggering 28 years.

America exacted revenge for their 1957 defeat two years later in California, but the visiting British were just happy to arrive in Palm Springs after a dreadful Atlantic crossing, a gruelling journey across America to Los Angeles and then a short flight which saw the plane, caught up in high winds, drop 40,000 feet to an altitude of just 9,000 feet. With the horrors of the Munich air disaster and the deaths of so many talented Manchester United football players still fresh in their minds, it was little wonder that a number of the golfers dropped to their knees and kissed the tarmac of Los Angeles Airport when the plane was forced to turn back. Given the choice of flying again or taking a bus, captain Bernard Hunt chose the latter. Later, those who experienced the dramatic flight formed the 'Long Drop Club', handed out ties to members and hosted regular dinners.

The British loss in 1959 prompted calls for changes to the competition. The format was judged to be unfriendly to spectators, and some observers suggested America should play a Commonwealth team, which would allow the likes of South Africans Gary Player and Bobby Locke and Australians Peter Thomson and Kel Nagle to play.

The British PGA resisted such a move, insisting that the event should stick to Sam Ryder's original concept. However, by the 1961 cup at Royal Lytham St Anne's, it had been agreed that the old thirty-six hole matches would be replaced by two sets of foursomes on the first day, with four played in the morning and a further four in the afternoon, and sixteen singles matches on the second day, eight in the morning and a further eight in the afternoon.

The Americans would be without Sam Snead, who was omitted after playing in an unofficial pro-am tournament without permission from the PGA. In seven Ryder Cups, Snead had played thirteen matches, winning ten and halving one. It remains one of the greatest records of any player in the Ryder Cup. America, nonetheless, had too strong a team for the home side – including a certain Arnold Palmer, who was already twice winner of the US Masters, and US and British Open champion – and ran out comfortable winners.

More changes were afoot by the time the 1963 Ryder Cup was staged in Atlanta, Georgia. The match would now consist of two series of fourballs, two series of foursomes and two sets of singles, all over eighteen holes. Thirty-two points would now be on offer, as opposed to twenty-four previously, and the new structure demanded that the Ryder Cup be staged over three days, starting on a Friday. All it meant in the short term was that America could beat their opponents by an even greater margin. The 23–9 victory that year remains one of the most humbling experiences in European Ryder Cup history, and while the home team made more of a game of it two years later at Royal Birkdale, losing by a still decisive 7 points, they were dismissed by an even greater margin when a USA team that included Palmer, Billy Casper and Julius Boros, and was captained by the great Ben Hogan, won by 15 points in Houston in 1967.

The long-term future of the Ryder Cup was in danger once again. America were winning with ease and interest was waning. When they travelled to Royal Birkdale in 1969 with a team including Jack Nicklaus, Lee Trevino, Ray Floyd and Billy Casper, only one result seemed likely. But if the subsequent draw was a surprise, the decision taken by Nicklaus at the end of his singles match with Tony Jacklin would go down in sporting folklore.

Before Nicklaus made his most sporting of gestures, one of the greatest in history, the tournament had already been brimming with drama. Although America had won the previous five Ryder Cups, British golf was on a high after Jacklin had won the Open just two months before. Going into the last day's singles, the match was all square at 8 points each, a remarkable achievement for a British team who were such underdogs. The singles would continue in this tight vein. Brian Huggett believed he had won it for Britain when he converted a putt to beat Billy Casper, having just heard a tremendous roar from the previous hole, where Jacklin was playing Nicklaus. Falsely believing Jacklin had just won his match (he had holed an eagle putt to make it all square with one hole to play), Huggett broke down in tears after he sunk his putt, only to discover that it was still all to play for.

And so it all boiled down to the final hole of the final singles match on the final day, between the recently crowned Open champion and the already multiple majors winner. After they had both driven off at the 18th, Nicklaus enquired of Jacklin, 'How do you feel?'

Jacklin responded, 'Bloody awful.'

The American replied, 'I thought you might, but if it's any consolation, so do I.'

However, this concession was nothing compared with the one that came shortly afterwards. Nicklaus managed to sink his six-foot putt to leave Jacklin with a nasty three-foot putt to halve the hole and end the Ryder Cup as a draw. By now, Jacklin's nerve was shot through. As he studied the putt that lay ahead, Nicklaus picked up his marker, strolled across to his English opponent and handed it to him, thus signalling a concession of the putt. In what has become one of the most famous quotes in golf, Nicklaus told his astonished playing partner, 'I don't think you would have missed that putt, but, in the circumstances, I would never give you the opportunity.'

Today, this is seen as one of the greatest moments in Ryder Cup history, and Nicklaus is quite rightly lauded almost as much for this as for his remarkable achievement in winning 18 majors. However, that evening not everyone appreciated the gesture. Snead, who was now the non-playing captain of the American team, refused to talk to his young star for the rest of the night. Casper, too, was initially outraged. Nicklaus did not know what all the fuss was about. As America were already the holders, he knew that à draw would suffice for his team to retain the trophy. Besides, he reasoned that British golf, and the Ryder Cup, did not need to witness a recent Open champion lose the trophy with a missed three-foot putt. Jacklin subsequently wrote his opponent a thank-you letter. 'It really was a great moment,' he said shortly afterwards. Once the Americans had overcome their shock and understood the good that had come of it, they allowed Britain to keep the trophy for one of the two years before the 1971 Ryder Cup, which was a second unnecessary but greatly appreciated sporting gesture.

For all the euphoria of securing a draw, the British team were still the challengers in St Louis two years later. It was back to business as usual, and America won with relative ease. They followed this up with yet another win in 1973 when the event was held at Muirfield, the tournament being contested for the first time in an official capacity in Scotland and featuring a newly created Great Britain and Ireland team. Two years later, America made it 17 wins out of 21 Ryder Cups since the first official tournament in Worcester, Massachusetts. Great Britain's tally of three wins and a draw had become a pitiful record. In truth, no team in the world could have lived with the 1971 USA team. Captained by Arnold Palmer, it boasted such stars as Nicklaus, Trevino, Casper and Floyd, as well as Tom Weiskopf, Hale Irwin and Jonny Miller. The British journeyman golfer Brian Barnes had the rare distinction of beating Nicklaus – then the greatest golfer in the world – twice, once in the morning and once in the afternoon singles, but that was just about the only British and Irish triumph of note in an otherwise one-sided affair. The final score of 21–11 told its own story, as did captain Palmer's decision to attend an air show on the final afternoon rather than watch his own team canter to victory.

More tinkering with the cup's format took place before the 1977 tournament at Royal Lytham St Anne's. The event would be reduced to five foursomes, five fourballs and ten singles matches. This meant there was a maximum of 20 points to play for, resulting in a better chance of a less heavy defeat for the beleaguered British and Irish team. This was what transpired, although the result stayed the same. The only real bright spark in an otherwise forgettable competition was the outstanding debut of a young British rookie named Nick Faldo. Partnered by Peter Oosterhuis, Faldo managed to beat Ray Floyd and Lou Graham in the foursomes before dismissing Nicklaus and Floyd in the fourballs. Then, for good measure, Faldo defeated Tom Watson in the singles. It would not be enough to prevent another heavy defeat, but it signalled the start of an outstanding career for Faldo, both in the Ryder Cup and in strokeplay golf.

Faldo or no Faldo, enough was enough. Great Britain and Ireland would never compete again versus the United States. Instead, a newly created European team would take on America in 1979, and, once again, that man Jack Nicklaus was at the centre of the drama.

By now the most respected figure in world golf, Nicklaus realised that for the Ryder Cup to maintain longevity a more competitive element would be required. Whether it meant a world versus America competition or Europe versus his country, Nicklaus decided to mention the idea to Lord Derby, the then head of the British PGA, at Lytham during the 1977 competition. Not everyone agreed. Arnold Palmer, the man who preceded Nicklaus as the number-one golfer in the world, felt American dominance was not a good enough reason for wholesale change; but Derby was convinced by Nicklaus's argument and championed the restructure in time for the 1979 Ryder Cup at the famous Greenbrier course in West Virginia.

Only two players from outside Britain and Ireland were picked – the Spaniards Antonio Garrido and Seve Ballesteros – but it was a start, and in Ballesteros the new European team had unearthed a man who would become the best player in the world and one of the most significant in Ryder Cup history. All that was to come, though.

John Jacobs, the first captain of the European team, had enough on his plate attempting to beat the Americans on their home soil, but his job was made worse by the seemingly unruly behaviour of two British golfers, Ken Brown and Mark James. The firm friends brought a rebellious element to the three-day event, turning up late for a team meeting and then later for the opening ceremony, where they were accused of yawning during the national anthems. It was clear to most people that James and Brown were making no effort either to hide their contempt for the procedural facets of the event or to conform to dress regulations. To make matters worse, James was carrying a chest-muscle injury which would make his contribution on the course negligible. Both Brown and James would go on to serve the causes of European golf and of Europe in the Ryder Cup admirably, but when they returned home from America in 1979, both were fined for their behaviour. Europe, meanwhile, were heavily beaten, although the organisers still declared the new-look event, with the two teams playing for the now well-established 28 points, a resounding success.

By 1981, however, British, Irish and European golf was beginning its upward curve. At the forefront was Ballesteros, who had emerged as not only the best player in the world but also the most exciting to watch. When he was not pumping his fist with passion, he was finding the green from impossible situations following his customary average drives from the tee. But he had also become embroiled in a row with the European Tour over its refusal to pay appearance money to him and the other stars of European golf, even though they did just that to visiting Americans. Ballesteros boycotted the tour in 1981, and because the first ten places in the European Ryder Cup team were taken by the best performers on the tour, he was reliant on a wild-card selection. The committee decided that non-selection would be a fitting punishment and, ironically, chose Mark James instead.

Other future achievers in the European team included Scot Sandy Lyle, making his second appearance, and rookies Sam Torrance and Bernhard Langer, both of whom would make significant marks on the Ryder Cup in years to come. For now, though, the odds were stacked against them. Of all the great teams that have represented the USA, there is common consent that the 1981 team was the greatest of them all. A dozen that included Nicklaus, Watson, Trevino, Floyd, Miller, Ben Crenshaw and Tom Kite dismissed the still fledgling Europeans 18½–9½ at the Walton Heath Golf Club in Surrey. The chasm seemed to be widening, but it was about to be closed.

The biggest single turning point in Europe's upturn in fortune came with the surprise appointment of Tony Jacklin as the 1983 European Ryder Cup captain. It was a surprise because Jacklin had made it known how displeased he was with not being selected as a player two years previously, thus underlining his prickly nature. But Ken Schofield, the European Tour's chief executive, realised that being a Ryder Cup team captain amounted to a great deal more than a few encouraging words and some ill-conceived selections. The European approach needed to be professional, and in Jacklin they had found the right man.

The transformation was evident from the moment Jacklin insisted on first-class air travel to take his European team to Palm Beach in Florida for the 1983 competition. Schofield flew the players on Concorde, along with their wives, girlfriends and caddies. The European sense of self-importance shot up.

Jacklin's next success was to persuade Ballesteros to return to the fold. The Spaniard was encouraged by Jacklin's hunger, his eagerness to improve his players' lot and his innovations, such as a players' room at the team hotel for the private use of the players and wives only. But the 1969 Open and 1970 US Open champion did not get everything right. While old friend Jack Nicklaus, the American captain, promised to give everyone on his team a good game, Jacklin made it clear from the off that players such as Gordon Brand, sen., would be required only for the singles. Another newcomer that year was Ian Woosnam, who would enjoy a distinguished playing career and, of course, get the nod to captain the 2006 European Ryder Cup team at The K Club.

In the end, Europe would fall short by a single point in a tussle illuminated by the genius that was Ballesteros. Having effectively withdrawn himself from the 1981 cup, the Spaniard threw himself into the 1983 version, happily holding rookie Paul Way's hand as the unlikely duo scored 2½ points out of 4 in the foursomes and fourballs. He also conjured up a shot described by those present as one of the greatest of all time when he followed on from a poor drive off the tee with a wedged shot that left the ball close to the front lip of a fairway bunker. Ballesteros was over 250 yards from the pin and, by rights, should have used a high iron to advance the ball a little way up the fairway. Instead, he blasted the ball onto the green using a three-wood. He ended up halving his match with an astounded Fuzzy Zoeller, as America scraped home. Pride had been restored to European golf, but Jacklin was far from satisfied. He was hungry for a win, and he would not have to wait long to realise his dream.

There was a sense that something very special was about to happen even before the 1985 Ryder Cup got under way at The Belfry. Bernhard Langer had become the US Masters champion that spring, and Sandy Lyle followed that up by claiming the Open title in the summer. As well as the British players and Langer, four Spaniards were selected by virtue of their positions in the European Order of Merit: José Rivero, José Maria Cañizares, Manuel Piñero and the indomitable Ballesteros.

It was Seve who began the magic. Although Europe found themselves 3–1 down following the first morning's foursomes, Ballesteros dumbfounded Curtis Strange and Mark O'Meara by driving to the back of the 10th green after the Americans had laid up on the other side of the pond to leave themselves with a more conservative chip onto the green. Ballesteros and Piñero won the hole and went on to win the match. Europe won the afternoon exchanges of fourballs to find themselves a point behind after day one. They repeated their 2½–1½ fourballs score line the following morning in the fourballs, and then won 3–1 in the second day's foursomes to gain a 9–7 lead as the two teams entered the final day's singles.

It could, and should, have been a lead of just a single point but for Craig Stadler's incredible miss in the foursomes when playing with Curtis Strange. Playing Langer and Lyle, the man nicknamed 'The Walrus' somehow shot his two-and-a-half-foot putt wide on the 18th green to halve the match when an American win appeared odds on. It was only a ½ point dropped, but it doubled Europe's advantage and also ensured that the second day ended on a downer for the visitors.

America's plan to reduce the lead early on by placing their big hitters at the top of the singles draw did not pay dividends. Europe won two of the first three singles matches, and after Ballesteros had launched an astonishing comeback to halve with Tom Kite, and Lyle and Langer had both secured a point each, it was left to Sam Torrance to apply the *coup de grâce*. In doing so, he created one of the most abiding images in the history of golf.

It could so easily have not been Torrance. After sixteen holes, he found himself one down to Andy North, before levelling it on the penultimate green. Howard Clark, who was playing in the match after Torrance, had a chance to win the Ryder Cup by beating O'Meara on the 17th, but his putt caught the lip of the hole and stayed up. Therefore, with North having found the water at the 18th, Torrance was left with three whole putts to end twenty-eight years of American dominance. Never one to turn away the chance for drama, Torrance sunk the putt in one attempt, raising both arms and putter high above his head in triumph before the ball had even dropped. With his pencil stuck behind his ear and the first glimmer of a smile appearing on his face, Torrance's pose just about said it all. Mobbed by Jacklin, the players who had concluded their singles and the players' wives, Torrance knew he had just experienced one of the greatest moments of his life. Europe had won by the convincing margin of 16½–11½. It was the start of a European revolution.

One unenviable bogey had been quashed. Europe were back to winning ways for the first time since 1957. Now came a much stiffer challenge: to try to win for the first time ever on American soil. To add spice to the occasion, Jacklin was retained as captain, while America turned to Jacklin's great friend and rival Jack Nicklaus to lead the team in a non-playing capacity. Moreover, the tournament would be staged at Muirfield Village in Columbus, Ohio, on a course designed by Nicklaus in his home town and named after the venue where he'd taken his first Open title in 1966.

Incredibly, the Europeans arrived bursting with confidence. They now boasted five of the best players in the world in Ballesteros, Langer, Faldo, Lyle and Woosnam, and they were also giving a young Spaniard named José Maria Olazábal his first shot at the Ryder Cup. Olazábal would be partnered by Ballesteros, and the two would become one of the most feared partnerships in Ryder Cup history. In 1987, they won three out of their four foursome and fourball matches. The first day's fourballs proved particularly decisive, with Europe, having squared the morning foursomes 2–2, winning all four afternoon fourballs. They edged a further point ahead during the second morning's foursomes, before drawing the afternoon fourballs. It all meant that out of a possible 12 points on offer in the final day's singles, Europe needed just 3½ points to retain the trophy.

They made hard work of it. America, as they usually do, stormed back in the singles, winning 5½ out of the first 7 points. It took an unlikely name and the most obvious one to settle the issue. Ireland's Eamonn Darcy had failed to win a single point in three previous Ryder Cup appearances and ten matches, but his win over Ben Crenshaw stopped the rot for Europe, leaving Seve Ballesteros to apply the finishing touch. His point gained over Curtis Strange secured Europe's first away victory, on the 60th anniversary of the inaugural tournament played in 1927. Later, Ballesteros admitted that sinking his putt on the 17th green was his greatest moment in the Ryder Cup. His compatriot Olazábal celebrated by performing an impromptu flamenco dance on the 18th green, an act which annoyed the Americans at the time; this was nothing, however, compared with the way they would behave four years later.

Before then came the 1989 competition and only the second draw in the long history of the Ryder Cup. America's captain Ray Floyd made an early error of judgement when he stood up at the dinner on the eve of the tournament and declared that his team were the '12 greatest players in the world'. This was not well received by the European team, especially Nick Faldo, the current Masters champion, and Ballesteros. It was all the motivation they needed.

After losing the first morning's foursomes 3–1, Europe stormed back to whitewash the afternoon fourballs. Draws in the following day's foursomes and fourballs meant that Europe required five wins in the singles to win the cup for a third successive time. It was José Maria Cañizares who secured his team's 14th point when he beat Ken Green by one hole, but it is Christy O'Connor Jr. who is largely credited with ensuring the Ryder Cup stayed in European hands. The Irishman had been one of Jacklin's wild-card selections, a choice which raised eyebrows at the time. O'Connor was up against Fred Couples, and as they veered towards the end of their match, the scoreboard revealed that all the games behind, save for Cañizares's, were looking good for America. One up at the 17th, the Irishman watched as Couples launched the longest drive of the day towards the 18th green. O'Connor's response was solid, but it left him 230 yards from the pin and 50 behind his American playing partner. Playing first, the European took out a two-iron and proceeded to club the ball to within four feet of the hole. Knowing when the game was up, Couples responded by shanking his attempted nine-iron approach shot. He failed even to make the green and responded by conceding O'Connor's putt, the match and

35

the Ryder Cup. Cañizares ensured the job was completed moments later. The fact that America won the last four singles matches to secure a draw did not dent European pride. Jacklin announced his retirement as captain, having won the Ryder Cup three times in four attempts. His trusty lieutenant Bernard Gallacher would take over and would soon become engulfed in one of the most controversial and ill-tempered Ryder Cups of all time.

By 1991, America had not held the Ryder Cup for six years. That year's tournament was staged in the immediate aftermath of the Gulf War in Kuwait. The venue was The Ocean Course at Kiawah Island in South Carolina, and the American media immediately dubbed the contest the 'War on the Shore'. This was in keeping with the mood of nationalistic fervour in the United States at the time. The Americans were determined to win and ensure that the Europeans were not given a look-in. The tone was set by a local radio presenter who gave out details of the European team's hotel and encouraged listeners to disturb the players by launching a 'Wake Up the Enemy' campaign. Sadly, they did, in their droves. The Europeans were further enraged when they were forced to sit through a 'History of the Ryder Cup' film on the eve of the weekend, only to watch a succession of American victories.

Matters became worse once play got under way. America took the morning foursomes 3–1, their one defeat occurring when Paul Azinger and Chip Beck lost to Ballesteros and Olazábal in an ill-tempered affair. At the 10th, the Spaniards accused Azinger of cheating by playing with the wrong ball for the previous three holes. The subsequent ruling went with the Americans, but it threw them, and what had been a three-hole lead ended up as a defeat on the 17th.

Europe narrowed the deficit in the afternoon but then fell further behind the following day before bouncing back with a 3½–½ victory in the second afternoon's fourballs. It meant that both teams went into the final day's singles all square on 8 points each. Europe made the early running, with Faldo and debutant David Feherty beating Floyd and Payne Stewart. Azinger and Corey Pavin struck back, the latter whipping up even more partisan support by wearing a Desert Storm camouflage cap. The singles carried on in this vein. Ballesteros and Paul Broadhurst scored 2 more points for Europe, while Beck and Couples clawed 2 back for America. Crucially, the home team nudged ahead when Lanny Wadkins defeated Mark James. With Steve Pate having withdrawn through injury, leaving the unfortunate David Gilford without a match in the singles, all eyes focused on the final pairing of the day. Bernhard Langer needed to beat Hale Irwin to draw the Ryder Cup and retain it once again for Europe.

With four holes to play, Irwin was two up, but by the time the pair walked down the 18th fairway it was all square after Langer had holed nerve-racking putts at the 15th and 17th. During these holes, Irwin's ball had been thrown back onto the fairway by an American supporter. The competition was sinking to a new low. Now, it all boiled down to the final hole in the final match of the Ryder Cup. Irwin could only manage a bogey, and Langer was left with a six-foot putt to win the Ryder Cup. Ordinarily, the implacable German could have sunk the putt with his eyes shut. But this was no ordinary putt. While the eyes of the world were on him, and the eyes of the American team bore into his back in the hope of a miss, Langer noticed two spike marks in the line of his putt. It was enough to make the ball deviate, and the pain was etched on his face as he watched his putt slide wide of the hole.

The Europeans had lost the Ryder Cup by just 1 point, but no one blamed Langer. 'Nobody could have holed that putt,' a typically supportive Ballesteros announced later. 'The pressure was just unbelievable.' The German feared he would be affected for the rest of his life. Instead, he won the German Open the following week on the European Tour. It was one of the most impressive victories recorded by any golfer in recent times.

After Kiawah, Gallacher attempted to resign, but the players would not hear of it and persuaded him to stay on. Tom Watson was appointed as America's captain for the 1993 cup, and a raft of moves were taken by the British and American PGAs to improve relations post-Kiawah, such as imposing greater crowd control and publishing guidelines on controlling provocative views aired by the players.

Now it would be America's turn to inflict a wounding victory on opposition turf. In keeping with the sudden closeness of the competition, they went into the singles a point down, but a 5-point surge in the middle of the singles saw them home by a 2-point margin. In another closely fought contest, the most important development was that relations between the two sides were largely improved, exemplified by the way in which a victorious Davis Love III embraced Italian Costantino Rocca, who had seen his one-hole lead evaporate with two holes to play.

Gallacher decided to stick it out as captain one more time when Europe travelled to Oak Hill Country Club in Rochester, New York, in 1995. By the morning of the final day's play, the Scot could have been forgiven for wishing he had retired. Europe were 2 points down with just the singles to play, and America had a long tradition of winning the individual matches.

This time, though, things would be different. Howard Clark started the European comeback, beating Peter Jacobsen in a round the highlight of which was a fortuitous hole in one at the 11th. The Yorkshireman's six-iron drive from the tee resulted in the ball kicking from the shoulder of a bunker on the right and ending up in the hole. Wins for James, Gilford, Montgomerie, Faldo and Torrance followed, giving the unlikely figure of rookie Philip Walton the chance to win the cup by defeating Jay Haas. The Irishman made hard work of it but managed to hole the winning putt on the 18th green. The Ryder Cup was back in European hands as the blue team recorded only their second-ever victory on American soil.

In 1997, the Ryder Cup made yet more history by being staged for the first time in mainland Europe. Seve Ballesteros's back was by now causing him so much grief that his form had plummeted, and he was unable to play. Therefore, when Gallacher announced his retirement from the European captaincy and Valderrama in Spain was chosen as the 1997 venue, the choice of new captain was obvious.

The Ballesteros reign did not begin well, however. The Spaniard received a great deal of criticism, much of it justified, after he insisted that fellow countryman Miguel Angel Martin pass a fitness test on a recently operated-on wrist. Martin had earned automatic selection after showing good form in the early part of the season but had not played competitively for many weeks as a result of his injury. In truth, Ballesteros wanted Olazábal – who had not gained automatic qualification – in his team, and when Martin refused the fitness test, he was deselected.

America, meanwhile, arrived in southern Spain boasting six major champions, including a young man called Tiger Woods, the recent Masters champion who had just entered the professional ranks. On paper, the Americans looked to be strong favourites. But European team spirit, which increased as the Ryder Cup entered the late '90s, counted for much, as did the ubiquitous Ballesteros, who did his utmost to advise every single player on every single shot.

By the end of day two, Europe held a 10½–5½ points advantage, and even if America always came back strongly in the final day's singles, this was surely asking too much of them. Still, they tried their best and almost succeeded. Piling their big-name players up at the top of the singles list, they drew level, but a win for Langer, making amends for his miss at Kiawah Island, and a half from Montgomerie saw Europe stagger over the finishing line with their noses 1 point in front. The hero of the hour proved to be Rocca, who had been vilified for his defeat to Love two years before but was now praised for the manner in which he dealt out an emphatic four-and-two beating to Woods.

Europe had won the last two Ryder Cups and made their way over to the 1999 tournament at Brookline in Boston confident of making it a hat-trick of successive wins. Ballesteros had declined the chance to captain the side again, to the relief of most of the players, who had found his hands-on style rather too hands-on.

Instead, Mark James took over the reins, an ironic twist given that he was the bad boy of the 1979 Ryder Cup, and his appointment resulted in yet more controversy and in-fighting.

Much of this focused on the non-selection of Nick Faldo, based on his poor form and his failure to gain automatic qualification. His poor showing in the Order of Merit was in part due to his insistence on playing mostly on the American tour. It did not help that James and Faldo were far from being friends. Woosnam and Langer were also omitted, with James preferring youth to experience. At first, this policy appeared to be working. America, already ruffled by the controversy that their failed attempts to obtain appearance money had caused, slumped to a 6–2 first-day deficit. Although they fared better on day two, they remained 4 points behind with just the singles remaining. They seemed to be staring defeat full in the face and with it a second successive loss on home soil, their third beating in a row.

The final day of the Brookline Ryder Cup will remain for ever etched in the annals of golf. The shame of it is that it should have been remembered for the incredible fight-back the USA players launched. Stacking his big guns up front, captain Ben Crenshaw knew he needed a good start, and that is exactly what he got. He was doubtless aided by his decision to invite George W. Bush, the then Governor of Texas, to motivate the American team the night before the singles matches by reading from a letter written by William Travis during the siege of the Alamo.

It seemed to do the trick. The Americans rattled off the first six singles matches with wins, transforming a 4-point deficit into a 2-point lead. Padraig Harrington hit back with a win over Mark O'Meara, but when Steve Pate defeated Miguel Angel Jiménez all Justin Leonard needed to do was halve his match against Olazábal.

At the 17th green, Leonard, facing a 45-foot putt, went first. What happened next can only be described as one of the darkest moments in Ryder Cup history, if not the darkest. The ball, much to everyone's surprise, fell into the cup. Olazábal was now faced with a putt of around 20 feet to square the hole. If the Spaniard missed, Leonard would win the hole, take the lead with one to play and guarantee at least the ½ point the USA required to win back the trophy.

Before Olazábal had the chance to prepare for his putt, chaos ruled. While Leonard charged off the green in joy, many of his teammates, their wives and their caddies charged on to celebrate. Camera crews followed to record the American celebrations, while Olazábal stood alone and in obvious horror some 20 feet away. When the green was finally cleared and the Spaniard prepared to take his putt, he was forced to step away again because of chants from the crowd. It was an unedifying and intolerable situation, and Olazábal, not surprisingly, missed.

In the end, the American achievement of winning eight singles matches and halving one out of twelve was a deserved way to win the Ryder Cup, but this was largely forgotten as the recriminations began on both sides of the Atlantic. Sam Torrance, the next European captain, made his first priority a restoration of all that was good about the Ryder Cup. And he found a willing accomplice in Curtis Strange, America's new captain. However, it turned out that they would have three and not the usual two years to prepare for the return to The Belfry.

Everything was set for the 2001 Ryder Cup when two planes crashed into the Twin Towers of the World Trade Center in New York and a third plane hit the Pentagon in Washington on the fateful day that has become known as 9/11. The coordinated attacks were the worst terrorist atrocities ever to hit mainland America. In the circumstances, and with an understandable reluctance on the part of the Americans to fly anywhere, it was decided that the Ryder Cup should be postponed for a year. From then on, the event would take place in even-numbered years.

A couple of months after Brookline, Payne Stewart, who had admonished the crowd for heckling playing partner Colin Montgomerie, had died when a private plane he was travelling in lost cabin pressure. After such tragic events, it was more important than ever to return the Ryder Cup to its traditional sporting context.

For two days of the 2002 Ryder Cup, there was nothing between the great golfing adversaries. On the Saturday night, both teams were level on 8 points each. Then came a moment which has been spoken about ever since, a moment in which Torrance knew his team would win and Strange the very opposite. At the evening press conference, both captains announced their line-ups for the singles. The canny Torrance decided to play all his big guns first. 'I wanted to see a sea of European blue on that scoreboard,' he explained later. Strange, in contrast, saved Phil Mickelson and Tiger Woods, his two biggest stars, until last. His reasoning was that if it came down to the final two pairings, as the Ryder Cup had done every year since 1983, America would win. The problem was that Europe might have won the competition by then.

Torrance's hunch proved correct. Europe won 4½ points out of the first 6, with Colin Montgomerie, Bernhard Langer, Padraig Harrington and Thomas Bjørn all producing the goods. Then came a real shock: Ryder Cup debutant Phillip Price from Wales beat Mickelson, the world number two, on the 16th green to win by three shots – it was an astounding margin of victory.

Europe needed just 1 point to regain the trophy. Niclas Fasth seemed the man destined to secure it, especially when Paul Azinger's approach shot to the 18th green ended up in a bunker. Incredibly, and entirely in keeping with the drama of the competition, the American holed his bunker shot, Fasth missed his putt and the match ended up all square. Europe still needed a half to win, and all eyes turned to Paul McGinley. The Irishman was playing in his first Ryder Cup but was much respected on the European Tour. His opponent Jim Furyk almost repeated Azinger's feat by holing a nearly identical bunker shot on the 18th green. McGinley, left with an awkward ten-foot putt even before the enormous pressure was taken into account, found the target and celebrated by jumping fully clothed into the nearby lake. He had followed in the footsteps of Irishmen such as Christy O'Connor Jr., Eamonn Darcy and Philip Walton in providing a crucial shot to win the Ryder Cup.

The real hero of the hour, though, was Colin Montgomerie, who had taken over the mantle of Ballesteros to become Europe's unofficial leader. Partnering Langer and Harrington, he secured 3½ out of a possible 4 points in the foursomes and fourballs, and then established the theme of the singles by starting the day off with an emphatic five-and-four victory over Scott Hoch. This, surely, would be Monty's finest hour. But the scriptwriters had other ideas.

Two years later, the Ryder Cup came to the Oakland Hills Country Club in Michigan. Everything pointed to another close and epic encounter. In the end, it was anything but. Much of this can be explained by the way the two captains went about their business: Europe's Bernhard Langer got just about everything right; America's Hal Sutton was the opposite. Sutton's decision making was nothing short of an unmitigated disaster.

Part of his problem was deciding what to do with Tiger Woods, the best player in the world but one who possessed an inexplicably poor record in the Ryder Cup. Sutton's solution was to pair him with Phil Mickelson, thus creating an unbeatable and intimidating pairing. It proved to be a flawed idea – especially when Mickelson decided to change his equipment just a fortnight before Oakland Hills – and the fact that the pair hardly saw eye to eye was a badly kept secret.

While the American team entered the competition accused by their own media of having prepared poorly, the Europeans arrived in the United States confident and, with the likes of Luke Donald and Sergio García in the team, youthful. The only real dilemma Langer faced was whether to pick Colin Montgomerie, who finished a lowly 27th in the European Order of Merit, having shown little evidence of form after a messy and public divorce that year. Langer knew better than to discount him. Montgomerie's personality changed whenever he entered the lions' den of a Ryder Cup, and 2004 would prove to be no different. Langer picked the

Scot as one of his wild-card entries. It would be a crucial decision for both men.

Montgomerie began as he meant to continue, partnering Harrington to a win in the fourballs over the so-called American dream team of Woods and Mickelson. With Darren Clarke and Miguel Angel Jiménez then Sergio García and Lee Westwood following suit, Europe had a 3-point lead by lunchtime. By the end of day one, with Montgomerie and Harrington again winning in the foursomes, the European lead had increased to 4 points. America clawed back 1 point in the second day's fourballs, but fell even further behind in the final fourballs, which Europe took by three matches to one.

Despite the fact that the cup was being played out on American soil, Europe went into the final day's singles with 11 points under their belts, needing just 3 more points to draw and retain the trophy and 3½ to win it outright again. García secured the first point, beating the hapless Mickelson, Clarke added a ½ point, drawing with his friend Davis Love III, and Westwood saw off Kenny Perry.

It all meant that the stage was set for Monty. The best player never to have won a major, Montgomerie had become arguably the best player in the Ryder Cup. His match against David Toms was the sixth to be played in the singles, and when they reached the 18th green, he held a slender one-shot lead. His penultimate putt finished five feet short. With Toms ending with a par, Monty faced his five-footer to win the round and the Ryder Cup. He had been through the emotional wringer over the previous few months and was lucky to be playing in the Ryder Cup at all, but in sinking that five-foot putt, the Scot demonstrated exactly why his captain Langer had shown so much faith in him.

Even before the ball disappeared into the hole, Montgomerie dropped his putter to the ground and held his head in his hands in a rare show of relief and emotion. Europe had retained the Ryder Cup once again and had recorded their third win away from home, but they were not quite finished yet. Showing a new-found ruthlessness on the Europeans' part, French debutant Thomas Levet, the dapper Englishman Ian Poulter and the two Irishmen Harrington and McGinley all won their singles matches. Europe had won by the massive margin of 18½–9½.

The recriminations in the American camp were almost immediate. Hal Sutton took much of the flak, but Messrs Woods and Mickelson were not far behind. America had proved, once again, that while they boasted most of the world's top players, they could not transform a dozen supreme strokeplay players into a team. Europe could and had won their seventh Ryder Cup out of the last ten. At this rate, it would be Europe asking the USA to expand in order to provide stiffer opposition.

The stage was set for the 2006 Ryder Cup. America were hell-bent on winning back a trophy that was once predominantly their own; Europe had other ideas. Something had to give.

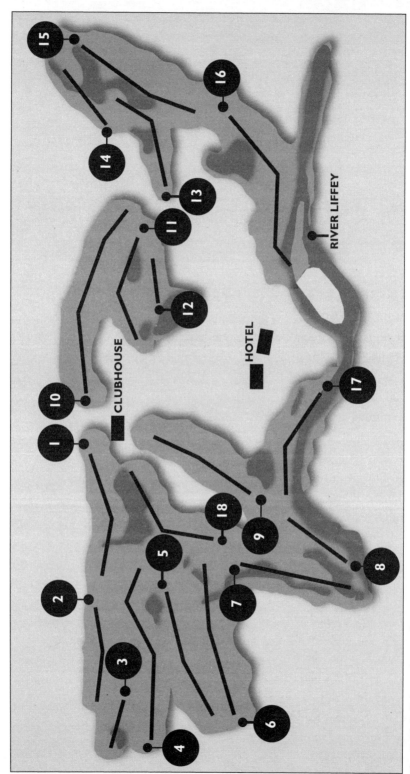

The K Club Palmer Course layout

TWO

THE K CLUB

THE 36TH RYDER CUP WAS AWARDED TO THE K CLUB back in 1999. It was a significant moment in the history of the event. In the preceding years, Irish golfers had played a major part in deciding the destination of the famous old trophy. Unsung heroes such as Eamonn Darcy, Christy O'Connor Jr. and Peter Walton had all made significant contributions to the cause in previous competitions as Europe had drawn level with and then overtaken American golf. More recently, Paul McGinley sank the putt to claim the 2002 Ryder Cup, and he has become a regular feature in the European team, along with Padraig Harrington and Darren Clarke. So it was not before time that the country with some of the most fearsome, beautiful and famous golf courses in the world staged the Ryder Cup. Indeed, after Valderrama in 1997, it was only the second time that the competition had been held outside Great Britain. In Irish terms, it was the biggest sporting event ever to hit the Emerald Isle.

The man behind The K Club is cardboard-box tycoon Dr Michael Smurfit, the Monaco tax exile and chairman and chief executive of Jefferson Smurfit, the Irish paper-and-packaging group. A 40-minute drive south of Dublin, the 550-acre estate, purchased by Smurfit's company in 1988, is adjacent to the picture-postcard village of Straffan in County Kildare. This is horse-racing country and especially horse-breeding country, with numerous stud farms littered around the environs, but right on the edge of Straffan can be found the magnificent Kildare Golf and Country Club.

Almost immediately, Smurfit went to work on creating what would become the 2006 venue for the Ryder Cup. Some £30 million was spent building an Arnold Palmer-designed, 18-hole golf course on the estate, and Smurfit and a partner bought the place outright for a fee of roughly £70 million in 2005. In the lead-up to securing the Ryder Cup, other European Tour events were staged at The K Club, most notably the annual Smurfit European Open. All golfers playing at such events at the course in the past have also enjoyed first-class accommodation in the rather grandiose Straffan House Hotel found at the centre of the estate. A second course, the Smurfit, was opened three years ago, providing a more 'linksy' style to complement the Palmer course.

It is fitting that the 2006 Ryder Cup was played on a course designed by one of the greatest golfers of all time and one of the most significant figures in the history of the Ryder Cup. A six-times winner of the cup for America, as well as the 1975 winning US captain, Arnold Palmer never actually tasted defeat in his seven competitions. Now, his course was to provide the setting for the eagerly awaited 2006 event.

Prior to the tournament, there were those who argued that if the cup was going to be staged in Ireland it should be played on one of the island's famous links courses, such as Portmarnock or Ballybunion, but Ryder Cup courses tend to follow a parkland tradition in respect of their design, layout and surrounding environment. The facts that the last time the competition was staged on a links course was in 1977 – at Royal Lytham St Anne's – and that in the whole eighty-year history of the Ryder Cup it has only ever been staged seven times on links courses back this up. Besides, such is the enormity of the cup these days that most golf courses are immediately ruled out because they simply cannot physically handle the event.

The K Club clearly could, however, and with its almost un-Irish characteristics – lush parkland with plenty of lakes – it comes close to the common American golf course or, indeed,

The Belfry in the West Midlands of England. With two par-5 holes riddled with water hazards on a course dominated by the River Liffey, which meanders its way south from Dublin, it was always going to provide a grandstand finish to golf's most spectacular event.

Beforehand, Dr Smurfit was expecting anything and everything. 'We're talking about the official 40,000 a day expected on all three days, plus a few more who will manage to leak in,' he admitted. 'The security will be extraordinarily high. People will try and hang-glide in, use false uniforms and other disguises. But we'll have to stop them, because we have to control the number of people, otherwise you'll get 100,000 here.'

Those who did gain entry were in for a real treat. The Palmer Course at The K Club not only poses many questions from a shot-making viewpoint but also judges characters. In typical Palmer fashion, the course has one recurring theme: will the golfer play safe or have the bottle, in the pressure-cooker intensity of the Ryder Cup, to go for his shots and potential glory or failure? Just to add some spice to the course, European captain Ian Woosnam used his privileged position to add some unique European touches to the course to play to his team's strengths and the Americans' weaknesses. This included narrowing some of the fairways and cutting some of the long rough around the greens.

Here, then, is the Palmer Course in all its glory.

Hole 1

'Bohereen' – Par 4, 418 yards: A relatively gentle way to begin proceedings, the first hole offers a nice wide fairway to aim for from an elevated tee. Irons, 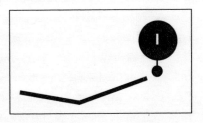 rather than drivers, are in order here, because a good start is imperative, and the bunker on the left-hand side of the fairway should be avoided, as should the dense trees to the right. From then, a wedge or a high iron onto the green is best, but not too far, so as to avoid the bunker on its back right. Players may choose to lay up short of the bunker, or they may go for broke.

Hole 2

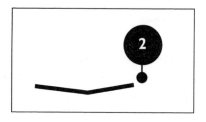

'The Tunnel' — Par 4, 413 yards: This is a seemingly less than testing straight par 4, but there is a catch. The fairway slopes from right to left, so many drives head down the right of the course, and there is a pot bunker 270 yards down on the left-hand side. As at the first, if a solid drive is executed well, a short iron or wedge should land the ball on the small and elevated green. This hole presents an excellent birdie opportunity.

Hole 3

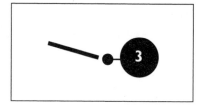

'The Island Beach' — Par 3, 170 yards: This is the first of four similar holes on the course, each of them short and sporting water in front of a wide green. Previous experiences of this hole at the European Open have shown how golfers, conscious of clearing the water, have shot well clear of the back end of the green. Good judgement, made trickier by the swirling wind that is always prevalent at this hole, is the key. The green also throws up another problem with its hog's back ridge running through the centre, a feature that can send poorly directed tee shots scuttling away from the hole. At its deepest, the green measures only 14 feet across from back to front, so the margin for error is small. If a player avoids such issues with a well-struck mid-iron shot, then a birdie opportunity awaits.

Hole 4

'Arnold's Pick' – Par 5, 568 yards: The first par 5 of the golf course, and the first hole that tests foursomes strategy. Although the hole is a par 5,

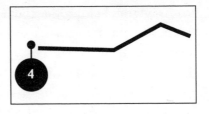

the green is reachable with a long drive and a second long iron, assuming the water some 350 yards from the tee is avoided. A 300-yard-plus drive will not only clear the mounds that can be found on the left side of the fairway but also provide a clear sight of the pin. The main problem here is that the fairway slopes from left to right, and the ball may end up in the rough on the right-hand side. This hole provides another opportunity for a birdie but also for plenty of practice with the sand wedge: seven bunkers surround the green.

Hole 5

'Square Meadow' – Par 4, 440 yards: Another chance of a birdie, providing the drive from the tee is both long and to the right, which is easier said than

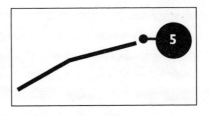

done considering that the fairway is uphill and often plays into a prevailing wind. A long drive is imperative: the shorter the approach shot, the better. The green throws up its own challenges, especially as it is at a slight angle and hides the bottom of the pin from the fairway. Players are often deceived into believing there is more green than there really is, and with fast run-off areas at the back, right and left, a par is an acceptable return.

Hole 6

'The Liffey Stream' – Par 4, 478 yards: The green, for once, holds few problems. It is the getting there that is the challenge! A

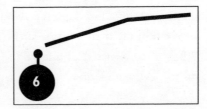

long par 4, this hole provides both thick rough and the Liffey Stream as hazards, and the chances are that if one does not get you, the other will. To give yourself an opportunity of landing safely on the green with a short-iron approach shot, you need to be bold and take out your driver on the tee. With the Liffey situated 68 yards out, the rough, if found instead of the fairway, will prevent you from taking on the water in two shots. If, however, your ball is nestled nicely on the fairway, you are still far from being home and dry. The chances are you will be on a sloping lie, and, with the Liffey continuing up the side of the green, any second shot that veers even slightly to the left will end up sleeping with the fishes.

Hole 7

'Michael's Favourite' – Par 4, 395 yards: This is a very difficult hole. Water runs down the whole of the right-hand side of the fairway, while two lakes, in front of and behind the small green, complete the watery feel to this hole. To complicate matters, Ian Woosnam increased the length of the 7th by an extra 40 yards, asking for the introduction of a new tee. And  approach shots are not easy, because the green is just 25 yards long from front to back. As a result, this is another hole that poses a question: do you go with a wood or a driver? A wood is the safer option in terms of giving yourself a better chance of avoiding the water, but it gives you only a narrow strip of fairway to aim for and a tricky long-iron shot into the small green. A driver, on the other hand, will leave you with a preferable short-iron approach shot, if you successfully find the wider patch of fairway. Get the driver wrong – and the wind will not help here – and you may find yourself in the water down to the right or the trees to the left. The 7th is also regarded as one of the most visually intimidating holes on the Palmer Course.

Hole 8

'Mayfly Corner' – Par 3, 173 yards: The second par 3 of the course and a pretty one, too. The hole was set up to provide plenty of birdies over the three days of the Ryder Cup, and plenty of wins, as well, because of its inherent dangers. The Liffey again plays its part, running down the right-hand side

of the green in an intimidating fashion. The safe option is to aim left, but the bunker situated at the front left will present a tricky, sloping shot back towards the water. If you play too defensively, this bunker may come into play; if you play too aggressively, the Liffey will be waiting. That said, more confident players aim straight for the pin with a mid-iron.

Hole 9

'The Eye of the Needle' – Par 4, 461 yards: This is another hole that was given a face-lift prior to the Ryder Cup. In particular, the tee was pushed back, which brought the large tree situated 281 yards down the middle of the fairway very much into play. Avoidance

is obviously the key here. To this end, it is best to direct your ball to the left of the tree, thus presenting a mid-to-short iron to the green. However, the main problem in terms of the first drive is the fact that the presence of the tree makes the area to the left narrow. The green does not present too many problems, although green-side bunkers are brought into play when the pin is placed at the back right.

Hole 10

'Mick Holly' – Par 5, 584 yards: This is a key hole for every type of play at the Ryder Cup. Before the tournament got under way, the players would have regarded

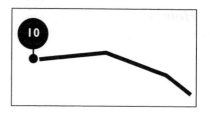

this seemingly straightforward par 5 as a definite birdie opportunity, particularly in the fourballs, and the best possible way to begin a charge up the back nine. If the longer hitter succeeds in driving the ball some 300 yards down the middle of the fairway, an eagle opportunity is available. However, if the fairway is missed, the door opens for the opposition. They can either use the same route, better executed, or opt for a shorter initial drive, followed by a choice between laying up to within 120 yards of the pin or an attempt to find a narrow strip some 75 yards from home, making the birdie chance that much easier. The permutations offered by this hole are fascinating.

Hole 11

'Lily Pond' – Par 4, 415 yards: This is another example of a typical Arnold Palmer hole, reflecting the style in which the great golfer used to ply his trade.

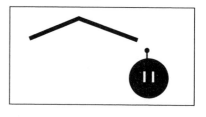

This is a risk-and-reward hole or, depending on your mentality, a risk-and-big-trouble challenge. Long hitters can drive the ball 300 yards over the trees on the corner of the right-to-left dogleg, thus leaving a relatively short approach shot onto the green. This plan has two additional benefits: by cutting off the corner, you run less risk of finding the two large bunkers on the right side of the fairway; and your approach shot is less likely to find the lake to the left-hand side of the green, just as long as you do not fade too far over to the right of the green and into the trees. This hole was set up to provide the pairs playing in the fourball matches with the chance for one to drive long over the corner and the other to play safe.

Hole 12

'The Domain' – Par 3, 182 yards: This hole can provide plenty of birdies, and also plenty of bogeys, depending on where the pin is placed. If the pin is on the right-hand side of the green, there are not too many  problems. The hole does play downwind, however, which means the bunkers to the right of the green capture many balls. The green was extended especially for the Ryder Cup in order to bring the water to the left into play. If the pin is placed to the left, the margin for error when aiming directly for the pin becomes massive. Playing safe to the right presents its own problems, too, because water awaits on the other side of the green.

Hole 13

'Laurel Haven' – Par 4, 428 yards: This is a potential birdie hole, especially in the fourballs format, but another one not without its dangers. Bigger hitters can comfortably clear the right-to-left dogleg corner, leaving a straight shot to 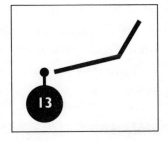 the pin with a short iron. But you can choose not to use a driver from the tee, so as to avoid the long rough to the right of the fairway. The next problem is a green flanked by two bunkers to the left and yet more water to the right.

Hole 14

'Church Fields' – Par 3, 213 yards: This is the longest of the course's par-3 holes, and a long iron is required to counter the prevailing winds from the right that are nearly always in evidence here. The green slopes towards the 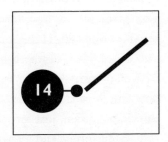 back, making a front pin placement tricky. If the pin is on the left near the water, the bottom of the flag cannot be seen. Drives to the left of the pin can end up in the stream, and drives to the right can find one of the two large and cavernous bunkers to the right and front of the green.

Hole 15

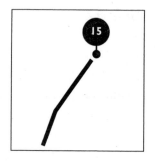

'Pheasant Run' – Par 4, 446 yards: The 15th is a tricky hole, to say the least, especially with the addition of 50 new trees to the left of the fairway. A prevailing wind hits you full on, making drives difficult. Veer to the left and you hit those trees; drift to the right and yet more water awaits. As the fairway slopes towards the water, drives here are often left of centre, which means the trees can be struck. The next problem is the green, to be found on top of a hill, making the approach shot hard to judge. The green itself slopes from right to left. This hole was always expected to provide plenty of drama, especially in relation to the match score.

Hole 16

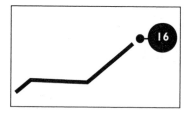

'Inish More' – Par 5, 555 yards: This par 5 provides a chance for golfers to reach the green in two from the back tee, thus setting up eagle and birdie chances. It also gives an opportunity for the player or partnership to go on the offensive. However, it is fraught with potential negative outcomes. The fairway has a series of mounds between 220 and 270 yards, which can pose problems from the tee, depending on how much of the corner the golfer is prepared to cut off from the dogleg. The next problem – and this is a big one – is that the River Liffey runs across the front of the green. Any badly hit approach shot will end up either in the stream or in one of the bunkers to the left of the small green. And even the putting surface, with its bumps and hollows, makes a birdie hard work. Players can certainly reach the green in two, but even then three putts are not rare.

Hole 17

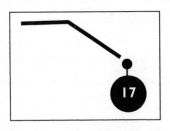

'Half Moon' – Par 4, 424 yards: The 17th was set up to be a hole at which the outcome of matches would inevitably be decided. It was here in the 2005 European Open that Denmark's Thomas Bjørn, leading the tournament at the time, hit his first three drives into water before finding the fairway en route to recording an eleven. Once again, the River Liffey plays a dominant role, meandering its way down the whole of the left-hand side of the fairway. The aggressive player needs to take on the corner and the river; the more conservative golfer will find the fairway easier with an iron but then leave himself a long and difficult approach shot. Avoiding the river is one thing; avoiding the new trees that Ian Woosnam had planted down the right-hand side of the fairway is another. The green itself, with its deep slope from right to left, poses more problems. Three and even four putts at this hole are common.

Hole 18

'The Hooker's Graveyard' – Par 5, 537 yards: This is a nasty test to end the course, and a real examination of a golfer's nerve. Matches can swing at this final hole, depending on whether the player(s) in a losing position decides to go for broke and whether he pulls it off. To take on the green in two requires a drive off the tee carrying more than 300 yards. Anything less than that and the ball is bound to find one of the many bunkers in the middle of the fairway. Even if a safe drive is achieved, another stern test awaits with a long approach shot. To the right of the green can be found a cluster of four deep bunkers, and there is water to the left and front. Any golfer believing that he is home and dry as he prepares to tee off at the 18th is deluded. The final hole on the Arnold Palmer course was created to guarantee last-gasp and potentially crucial drama.

THREE

THE CAPTAINS

Ian Woosnam

Ian Woosnam was appointed as the European captain for the 2006 Ryder Cup by the European Tour on 2 March 2005. The battle for the captaincy was a straight race between the fiery Welshman and Nick Faldo, a six-times major winner. Both had impressive Ryder Cup records as players, but it was Woosnam, the slight favourite beforehand, who won the vote. Faldo was compensated by the fact that he will be Europe's captain in 2008 when the Ryder Cup returns to America.

Woosnam was a popular choice. As a player, he is very much respected. The 48 year old has 44 tournament victories around the world to his name, a remarkable record which includes the US Masters title in 1991, his only major win. This was achieved in the midst of the European domination of the Masters, when Nick Faldo, Seve Ballesteros, Bernhard Langer, Sandy Lyle and, later, José Maria Olazábal all got to wear the famous green jacket at Augusta. Indeed, Woosnam is the only Welshman ever to win a major, as well as being a part of the team that won Wales the World Cup. Yet he considers the Ryder Cup to be as significant as anything in his career. 'Winning it as captain would be as big, maybe even bigger, than winning the Masters,' he admitted.

At 5 ft 4 in., Woosnam has enjoyed a remarkable 30-year career as a professional golfer. The artisan rather than the artist, his

59

powerful, punchy and bold play reflects his character. 'I've been a fighter all my life,' he explained. 'That's the only way I've ever approached my golf, trying to beat the best in the world.' He also possesses what Ballesteros described as 'the best swing since Sam Snead'. Shortly after his Masters triumph, he was ranked the number-one player in the world for eleven months. And he could, and maybe should, have become the Open champion in 2001, had his caddie not famously packed one club too many in his master's bag, thus provoking a two-shot penalty from which the Welshman never recovered. Twice, in 1987 and again in 1990, however, Woosnam won the European Order of Merit title. His Ryder Cup history is pretty good, too. Out of the eight tournaments he featured in, from 1983 to 1997, Europe won the Ryder Cup five times, and although his singles record fails to show a single victory, his overall record of playing in thirty-one matches, winning thirteen, losing ten and halving eight, while proving himself extremely difficult to beat in the foursomes and fourballs format, is highly impressive. Add seventeen World Cups, nine Dunhill Cups and fourteen other cup competitions, as well as the rather important fact that he was 2002 Ryder Cup-winning captain Sam Torrance's assistant, and few in golf were better prepared for the chance to captain a team in the Ryder Cup than Woosnam.

It was all a far cry from the farm in Llanymynech, North Wales, where Woosnam was brought up and from where he obtained so much of his trademark fighting spirit. His father Harry, who passed away three years ago, provided much of the golfer's inspiration and attitude. 'He drummed into me at an early age that the only way to be the best at anything was to work much harder than anyone else,' Woosnam recalled.

One of 'Woosie's' favourite stories involves his late father visiting a fighting booth while on holiday in Pwllheli, North Wales. 'There was this well-known Welsh champion in the ring, and when they asked for people off the floor to have a go, Dad jumped in there. One punch later, the champion was knocked out.' Woosnam junior would also enter the ring and, despite his diminutive size, would see off allcomers. 'In the end, nobody would fight me,' he remembered.

Later, his father sold his beloved dairy farm and switched to arable farming in order to help finance his son's fledgling golf career. Famed for his upper-body strength, Woosnam attributes this to all the work he did on the farm as a youngster, from stacking bales of hay to driving a tractor with no power steering. 'I developed great strength doing all that,' he revealed. He also used the farm to hone his accuracy with his irons, woods and drivers. Using sacking for a net, he spent many an hour driving golf balls in a farm shed. He hung from the ceiling a biscuit-tin lid that could be raised or lowered, depending on what club he was using, as a target to aim for. Woosnam also famously travelled up and down the country and across the Continent to golf tournaments in a beaten-up old camper van, often surviving on tins of baked beans. He had his scrapes and his adventures, and it certainly ensured that he lived a little along the way, but he also emerged as a leading player on the European Tour and then, ultimately, the world stage. And over 500 tournaments later, he was awarded the most prestigious position in European golf.

One of the first to call Woosnam once the European captaincy had been announced was American captain Tom Lehman. They know each other well, sharing a similar battle-hardened background in golf and a determination to fight for every inch. 'I know Tom pretty well,' Woosnam admitted. 'Certainly well enough to go out to dinner and have a good chat. Golf will be the winner at the Ryder Cup. We both agree on that.'

Woosnam, not surprisingly, was very proud to be the European Tour's pick as captain, especially with his golfing background. 'Being appointed in front of Nick Faldo has been brilliant for me,' he said. 'I didn't have an amateur career, and although I did have an international career, it wasn't like Sandy Lyle's or Faldo's. I've had to really work for it, and it's been very nice when you achieve it and, in this instance, be recognised for it.'

From early in his captaincy, Woosnam fired out the warning shots. 'I will be looking for all the players to make an effort to qualify,' he explained. 'If they can't be bothered to make the effort, then I don't see why I should be bothered to pick them. They will have to realise that it won't be a case of just because they may happen to be a great player they are in the team. It won't work like that. I've battled all my life. I expect them to battle too. I guess I'm going to be a battling captain.'

Another word he used to describe the potential style of his leadership was 'excitable', which was no surprise to anyone: 'I will do what I do best, which is to be instinctive and natural. If the players are happy, then they will play well. In the end, I can only do so much. Really, it's about the players. If they play great and win, then I'm a great captain. If they don't and they lose, then I'm a bad captain. But I'll try and be aggressive, in keeping with the way I played my golf.'

He certainly learned a thing or two about the Ryder Cup when acting as Torrance's right-hand man at The Belfry in 2002. Perhaps his most significant contribution was to suggest that Colin Montgomerie, playing out of his skin, should start the proceedings in the singles for Europe. Torrance, who had wanted Sergio García to play first, agreed, and Montgomerie led what became a blue-coloured European charge to victory at the top of the singles leaderboard.

Before the tournament began, Woosnam also knew exactly what his players would go through, having played eight times himself in the pressure-cooker environment of Ryder Cup golf. 'I always put a lot of pressure on myself, because I knew I was playing for a team,' he suggested. 'Maybe that's why I never won a singles match. I was too desperate to win, sometimes, and too desperate to be a team man, instead of concentrating on my own golf. My biggest mistake as a player in the Ryder Cup was in 1989 when I was the last man out in the singles, against Curtis Strange. We'd already won the trophy, and I was one-up with three holes to play. Curtis suggested conceding the game as the cup was won and lost, but I wanted to play on. What happened? Curtis made three birdies in the last three holes and beat me. I should have kept my big mouth shut! I'll be making sure nobody makes the same mistake this time round.'

When Woosnam was asked what his predictions were for the 2006 Ryder Cup at The K Club, he replied, 'Only that it's 50–50, even if some have Europe down as favourites. We're looking to win three back-to-back Ryder Cups for the first time in history, and we have a good team, but the Americans will be desperate to put things right after what happened at Oakland Hills two years ago, and in their captain they have a man who will pump them up. Whatever happens, it will be close and will probably go right down to the wire again.'

Woosnam's selections for his back-up team were typical of the man's desire to do it his way. He picked Des Smyth and Peter Baker as his two vice-captains, with Sandy Lyle and David 'D.J.' Russell acting as assistants. Smyth is not one of Europe's bigger names, but he did win four European tournaments and featured in the Ryder Cup twice, in 1979 (when the team became Europe for the first time) and in 1981, losing on both occasions. He now spends some of his time playing on the US Champions Tour, where he has twice won tournaments, as well as on the European Seniors Tour. Perhaps the major reason for his selection was his nationality. Smyth is Irish, and Woosnam felt, quite rightly, that as there was an influential Irish presence among the players, there should also be one within the management team.

Baker, meanwhile, has been friends with Woosnam for over 20 years, the pair having first met on a Shropshire golf course close to Woosnam's Oswestry home and Baker's home town of Wolverhampton. A member of the 1993 team that lost narrowly at The Belfry, Baker managed to beat the 2006 American vice-captain Corey Pavin in the singles that year. He also partnered Woosnam successfully in both fourballs matches, winning twice. 'I will help out Woosie in any way I can,' he promised. 'If he wants my input, he will get it.'

Supplementing the captain and his vice-captains were D.J. Russell, a popular European Tour player who now plies his trade on the seniors tour, and Sandy Lyle, the 1985 Open champion and 1988 Masters winner. Lyle was making a return to the Ryder Cup for the first time since 1987, having played for the European team on five occasions, winning twice.

Tom Lehman

America knew who their captain was to be some time before Europe had appointed theirs, and in announcing Tom Lehman in November 2004 to take over from Hal Sutton's disastrous reign, the US PGA invited controversy from all sides. The fact that Tiger Woods, the world's number-one player, had openly campaigned for his friend Mark O'Meara to be in charge hardly suggested togetherness in a team whose unity, or rather lack of it, had often been a problem in the past. But this was nothing compared to the reaction on the other side of the Pond, where European golf, still scarred from the invasion of the 17th green at Brookline in 1999, saw Lehman as one of the chief culprits.

Seven years on and Lehman was a changed man, both physically – he had lost two stones in weight – and also in his genuine remorse over one of the Ryder Cup's sorriest incidents. 'I am aware of what people think of me in Europe,' the 47 year old admitted four months before the start of the three-day event at The K Club. 'Do I wish this wasn't the case? Yes, I do. I broke my own code that day, for sure. I can't control people liking me or not, but I do care about it. If we could just freeze-frame the 17th hole, that would be great, wouldn't it? Justin [Leonard] can make his putt then celebrate, while the rest of us clap our hands and pump our fists but remain seated. If I could lead my life again, then this is what I'd like to happen.'

Before the tournament got under way, the opportunity that Lehman had as America's captain was not lost on the man from Minnesota. 'My primary goal as captain is to win the Ryder Cup,' he explained. 'But I also understand that being captain gives me a chance to change perceptions about me. I hope that if my team and I can conduct ourselves properly, then people may see me in a different light. I didn't cheat on anyone or anything like that. I just behaved badly at a golf tournament. I now intend to do my best to win over the people in Ireland.'

In truth, Lehman was nothing less than impressive after he received the captain's nod. Although he and Ian Woosnam had their differences following the events at Brookline, these had long since been patched up, perhaps partly because they are from similar backgrounds and have similar characters. Lehman struggled to make it on the US Tour in the early '90s, driving to and from tournaments in a battered car, and he was seen as nothing more than a journeyman golfer when he tried his luck in tournaments in Asia, South Africa and the original Hogan tour. By 1996, however, he was good enough to win the Open and became a popular and respected figure in Europe. One year later, he was ranked as the world's number-one golfer, albeit for just seven days. He played in three Ryder Cups between 1995 and '99, losing twice before the infamous Brookline victory in 1999, and has an overall playing record of won five, lost three and halved two out of ten matches.

Throughout these heady days, Lehman stayed true to his upbringing. It was little wonder that Dockers, the hard-wearing, no-nonsense clothes company, chose him to endorse their brand. 'I couldn't imagine spending more than $50 for a pair of pants,' Lehman once famously said.

But Lehman was not the favourite to take over the 2006 captaincy. Instead, it was O'Meara who was thought to be the more likely candidate, that is until the man with Irish origins stated that the players should be paid for appearing in the Ryder Cup, a comment that was far from well-received. One of the first courses of action Lehman took when he accepted the responsibility of the American captaincy was to set up a meeting with Woods, the O'Meara advocate. 'It was important for me to let Tiger know I have no problem with his feelings about Mark,' he explained. The meeting seemed to do the trick. 'The PGA of America picked the captain, they picked Tom and Tom is going to be a great captain,' Woods announced.

For all his achievements in the sport, Lehman does not rank as one of the great golfers in his country's long and successful history in the game. Indeed, with just five tournament victories to his name, he joined only four others who have captained America in the Ryder Cup with less than ten tournament wins in their careers. But his passion for winning the 2006 cup and his humility, despite Brookline, were made obvious in the months and then weeks running up to The K Club. 'There is no one more passionate about the Ryder Cup and playing for a team than me,' he insisted. 'I intend to motivate the players and inspire them to bring out the best. Frankly, we have had issues as a team in the past, and now is the time to talk about them as a team. Communication will be imperative in my team. Last time round, at Oakland Hills in 2004, America weren't beaten, they were humiliated. Nobody likes getting beat, but to lose in the manner we did two years ago really hurts, and I wasn't even playing. It's hurting those who did play there a whole lot more. I'm telling you, the pain of 2004 is going to be a major advantage for us. It's safe to say that the guys are extremely motivated to put that wrong right.'

It was also safe to say that Lehman was very keen to end America's sorry run of defeats: the team had lost in the previous two competitions and in seven out of the last ten Ryder Cups. 'As much as I've enjoyed the individual challenges of golf, you can't replace being in a locker room as part of a team,' he said. 'That's why it's my view that in terms of passion and fan appeal the Ryder Cup goes far beyond the majors. It's the biggest thing in golf.'

Getting this across to the Americans had clearly been a problem in recent times. 'There's no doubt you need an "X factor" to be a successful team,' Lehman explained. 'Dare I say it, but we had it at Brookline. Even when we were four-down, we knew we were going to win. In general, the Europeans have had it more than us in recent years, and they have the momentum.' A lack of team ethos did not come into it, though, argued the new captain. 'We just haven't played very well. Hole a few putts and team spirit tends to come flooding back. What I will say is that there's no doubt the Europeans seem to enjoy playing in the Ryder Cup more than we do. You only had to watch the action two years ago to see this. Americans tend to feel the pressure more. This time that's not going to happen. We're going to really enjoy it.'

That said, Lehman was full of respect for the European team, whichever dozen players were ultimately selected. 'There's absolutely no doubt that they will provide stiff competition. You can get fooled by players such as Darren Clarke and Lee Westwood, Paul McGinley and the others. They're great guys, great company and they seem to like being around each other, on and off the course. But these same guys can deliver a Glasgow kiss on you. And Ian Woosnam did not achieve what he has in the game without being fiery and passionate. If both sides get it right, it's going to be some three days of golf.'

Lehman's selections for his two vice-captains underlined the degree of fight and passion the Americans were bound to produce at The K Club under his leadership. In Corey Pavin and Loren Roberts, the captain could not have chosen two more passionate Americans or stronger supporters of him personally. Pavin and Lehman go back a long way. In the 1995 Ryder Cup, they were paired together and beat Nick Faldo and Colin Montgomerie in the first morning's foursomes. Pavin was the reigning US Open champion at the time. He went on to partner Roberts in the final fourballs, beating Faldo and Bernhard Langer, although it would prove to be his last of three Ryder Cups as a player. It was Pavin, of course, who wore the army cap at the 1991 event at Kiawah Island, endorsing the whole 'War on the Shore' atmosphere in the wake of the Gulf War. Roberts played in just the 1995 cup but got to know Lehman well enough to be confident of the man's ability at the helm of the 2006 American team. 'If there's ever a player you would confide in, Tom would be the one,' he insisted. The American team, hell-bent on avenging the previous two Ryder Cups, would soon be glad of a captain they could rely on.

FOUR

THE BUILD-UP

THE FINAL COUNTDOWN TO THE 36TH RYDER CUP
began immediately after Tiger Woods clinched the 2006 US PGA
Championship title, his twelfth major and his second of the summer,
following his imperious triumph at the Open Championship at
Hoylake in July. The Open was his third tournament win in a row
– he would go on to record five – and it meant that he now lay
just six majors behind Jack Nicklaus's all-time record of eighteen
majors, after leaping over Walter Hagen into second place in the
league table of professional major winners.

What made Woods' second successive majors win the more
remarkable was that in the spring he lost his father and mentor
Earl, who died after a long battle with cancer. After taking time
off from the game, Woods, quite understandably, played poorly on
his initial return. But, after a summer of success, he was back to
his very best, and his best was way too good for anyone else in
the world.

Tragically, Woods' fellow American, and Ryder Cup colleague,
Chris DiMarco suffered the loss of his mother in the week of the
Open Championship. However, he still managed to finish as runner-
up to Woods, before tying for 12th position at the US PGA. Both
performances served as a great testament to his character. From a
European point of view, Sergio García and Luke Donald finished
tied for third, with Donald beginning the final day sharing the lead

with Woods. Ian Poulter, a stalwart of the victorious 2004 Ryder Cup team, ended up in tied-ninth position. He had found his form, but it was too late to make the 2006 team.

The US PGA was the final qualifying competition for Americans in their race to make the Ryder Cup team. Woods, naturally, was top of the earners on the US Tour by a considerable margin, increased even more by his victory at Medinah. He was also, irrefutably, the best golfer in the world, playing the best golf. But, intriguingly, his Ryder Cup record was poor. The general explanation for this was that he was a supreme individual sportsman who struggled in a team environment and that his partners in the fourballs and foursomes found playing alongside him almost harder than facing two determined Europeans.

One day on from the conclusion at Medinah, Tom Lehman named his 12 to take on Europe at The K Club. Ten players, by virtue of the points they had gained during the previous two years on the US Tour, were already known, and the ten presented an unusually unbalanced group of players.

At the top sat Woods, with almost twice as many points as the next man, Phil Mickelson. It was these two, as the world's top-two-ranked players, whom the previous American captain Hal Sutton had so disastrously paired together in 2004. Neither had ever done himself justice in his previous four Ryder Cups. Jim Furyk, ranked third in the world, came next, completing an impressive top three, followed by Chad Campbell, David Toms and Chris DiMarco. So far, so good.

Lehman's problem, however, was with the next four names that he revealed at the Medinah Country Club. Numbers seven to ten read Vaughn Taylor, J.J. Henry, Zach Johnson and Brett Wetterich, the latter the only Ryder Cup man never to have made a halfway cut in a major. All four were the rawest rookies imaginable. It hardly improved matters that Wetterich had provoked the strongest of criticisms from Woods' former coach Butch Harmon. 'Wetterich isn't the kind of guy you want on your Ryder Cup team,' he said whilst commentating on Sky Sports. Harmon was especially incensed by what he saw during the second round at Medinah, when Wetterich took four shots to escape from the rough at the 9th on his way to shooting a 77. 'He literally gave up,' Harmon said. 'He just walked along and made a few swings. He made a pass at the ball, completely whiffed it, then he chunked it, then he hit it again. Being an American, I'll be rooting for my side, and I don't want Wetterich on it if that's the way he acts.'

Lehman was quick to defend all his rookies. 'They are in the team because they are in the top ten, which proves that they must have been playing good golf,' he argued. 'They all deserve to be here.' But one look at the team sheet prompted Woods to make his captain a promise, according to Lehman. 'Don't worry about the rookies,' Woods told him. 'I'll take care of them.' And like a good captain should, Lehman stood by his star, adamant that Woods would play a vital role. 'If anyone else questions Tiger's commitment to this team, I'm going to go crazy,' he announced.

Lehman's next problem was whom to select as his two wild-card entries. In truth, the pool of potential players was not too deep. John Daly was too much of a risk, Fred Couples was injured, Davis Love III had some pretty terrible Ryder Cup baggage and Corey Pavin, Lehman's assistant, was considered too old. 'There are not a lot of Americans winning tournaments any more,' Lehman admitted, with incredible frankness. 'A list of guys who had won would be a very small list.' His two choices, Scott Verplank and Stewart Cink, underlined this sorry fact. It had been two years since Cink had last won a tournament and five since Verplank had topped the leaderboard at the end of a fourth day.

'Stewart has played steady golf throughout his career,' Lehman said of Cink. 'He hits the ball great, is a strong putter and a great chipper of the ball.' He was equally fulsome about Verplank. 'One of the things we need are guys who putt well, keep the ball in the fairway and will never quit,' he said. 'That's Scott.'

At least Cink, with two appearances, and Verplank, with one, had Ryder Cup experience, which is more than could be said for the four rookies. Then again, Europe had played a number of rookies two years previously at Oakland Hills and had recorded their biggest margin of victory in America in the history of the Ryder Cup.

Matters hardly improved for Lehman and his team two days later when Rick Reilly, one of America's leading sports writers, who pens pieces for the acclaimed *Sports Illustrated*, tore into the US team. 'Have you seen the US Ryder Cup team?' he asked. 'It has all the intimidation power of the Liechtenstein navy. It would have a hard time beating the Winnetka Country Club Ladies B team. It is the single worst team we have taken to a Ryder Cup, and that's saying something considering the last batch got pummelled.'

Lehman was incensed. 'When we get to Ireland, that article will be the first that I stick on our team-room wall,' he responded. 'He's certainly got me fired up, I can tell you, and I'm sure he will have my team fired up as well.' Chris DiMarco concurred. 'I think we're all intent on stuffing a few words back down people's throats,' he declared.

At least one thing had gone right for the beleaguered American captain, a small but significant victory that would help to create a united American team and provide the togetherness so lacking in previous Ryder Cup events. On the day that he announced his team for the Ryder Cup, Lehman stated that the American's would be making a trip over to The K Club the following week to play some golf, go fishing and 'drink some Guinness'. However, his two best players, Woods and Mickelson, were not available for the trip, with both having prior engagements. One week later and Lehman had persuaded both his stars to alter their diaries and join their teammates in a bonding exercise on the Emerald Isle. 'The key for us is to get our best players fully committed to the cause, rocking and rolling, so they can put their points on the board,' a clearly happier Lehman explained, having persuaded the US PGA to invest £250,000 in chartering a jet to transport his team from Cleveland to Dublin.

When it came to the 48-hour visit, which began on 28 August, the heavens opened, as is their wont in Ireland in late summer. It failed to dampen Lehman's mood, however, after seeing all 12 of his teammates play some golf at the Ryder Cup venue. 'I'm thrilled,' he reported. 'Coming here as a team was necessary. It shows their motivation and commitment to the team. Some went to a lot of trouble to be here. I take my hat off to them.'

DiMarco and Furyk were certainly pleased to see Woods and Mickelson, the big two, make the trip. 'We know who our leaders are, and it's great that they are here,' said DiMarco. Furyk added, 'Tiger and Phil are going to step up, and they are going to be our leaders.' This was pretty modest coming from the world number three. Jim Furyk may not possess the most technically pleasing of swings, but he has proved himself to be a serious player on the global golfing circuit. 'I consider myself to be one of the veterans,' he admitted. 'It's about knowing what to expect. When you are in the lead for the first time or go out on the Sunday trying to win the tournament, you can go out there not knowing what to expect. A lot of those times you push too hard and do things you normally wouldn't. It's just about getting comfortable, and that is what the veteran players can do. We try and let the rookies lean on us, make them comfortable and let them know that everyone on the team has earned the right to be there. They don't owe anyone anything, and they just can go out there, play golf and have some fun.'

After the failure of Mickelson and Woods to ignite as a partnership in 2004, Furyk found himself partnering the world number one for the US win in the 2005 Presidents Cup against the 'Rest of the World' team. 'Tiger was just like a machine,' Furyk recalled. 'I just had to sit back and watch the show. We always tend to play better in the Presidents Cup. Our team tends to be a little more loose, and we have more fun. And I play better when I'm enjoying myself. We tend to tighten up as a whole at the Ryder Cup. I think you can look at the guys' faces in the locker room and on the bus on the way to the course, and everyone looks so uptight. We don't want that to happen this time.'

Things were hardly going smoothly for the Europeans, either, although Darren Clarke's personal circumstances made the forthcoming tournament pale into insignificance in comparison.

After a long and brave battle against cancer, Clarke's wife, Heather, finally succumbed to the disease in August, leaving the popular Northern Irishman devastated. In the spirit of golf, the sport immediately rallied around Clarke, one of the most respected and liked figures in the game. Initially, a number of Clarke's closest golfing friends stated that they would pull out of the US PGA Championship to attend Heather's funeral. Clarke would have none of it, and sent the likes of Lee Westwood, Padraig Harrington and Thomas Bjørn packing over to America. Harrington announced that all his earnings from the week would be donated to research into breast cancer, while both Westwood and Bjørn admitted to not having the stomach for the tournament. Paul McGinley was also told to play in the States but flatly refused, in part because his wife and Heather had been very close.

The tributes came pouring in, not only from Europe but also, pleasingly, from America, where a number of the players expressed their hopes that Clarke would be able to pick himself up in time to play in the Ryder Cup. 'Darren would be a great guy to have on their team if he can handle it emotionally,' said Davis Love III, who had just missed out on making the American team himself. 'He's a great guy, and I hope he plays.' It certainly became one of the game's talking points. Because of the personal commitment Clarke had been required to show at home over the course of the previous year, he had failed to make automatic qualification for the European team. But despite his obvious distress, he appeared to be one of the favourites for selection as one of Woosnam's two wild cards. Sandy Lyle, a member of Woosnam's backroom staff, confirmed this. 'Darren is very important to the European team,' said the former Masters and Open champion. 'He's one of our very best players and has a great record in the event. But he's also an incredibly big personality whose competitive streak and ability to motivate his teammates raises morale and helps bring out the best in others.'

As the BMW International Open in Munich – the last tournament offering points to the Europeans before the team was announced

– began, only seven players were guaranteed selection. While David Howell, Colin Montgomerie, Sergio García, Luke Donald, Henrik Stenson, Robert Karlsson and Paul Casey could play safe in the knowledge that their seats were already booked on the flight to Dublin, there was an almighty scrap for the three remaining places. The favourites to take the remaining spots were Harrington (all but guaranteed a place save for the most unlikely sequence of events), McGinley, the man whose putt won the 2002 Ryder Cup, and José Maria Olazábal. Of these players, Olazábal was by some distance the most at risk of losing out, with the likes of Paul Broadhurst, Johan Edfors, John Bickerton and Thomas Bjørn all breathing down his neck. Despite this, the Spaniard opted to miss the BMW International Open, citing tiredness. Instead, he would spend the week shooting quail in Toledo. 'I'm tired, and I need a rest,' he explained. 'If I went to Munich, I'd only have one week off before the Ryder Cup. If I don't keep my place on the team, it will hurt a lot. If I don't get a wild card, it will hurt even more.'

Colin Montgomerie, for one, was mystified by Olazábal's gamble: 'I know Olly has said he's tired, but he's got a long winter to be tired. If I were in his shoes, I know where I'd be. If Olly doesn't make automatic selection as a result of this, I'll feel sorry for Woosie, because it could make his wild-card decisions that much harder.'

Clarke, who made it known that he wanted to be considered for a wild-card place in the team, entered the Madrid Open in the week prior to the Ryder Cup in order to get some practice in. He would record four very reasonable rounds of 68, 72, 69 and 72 to finish in a share of 32nd place. It was a satisfactory return to competitive golf. Westwood, the favourite for the second wild-card berth, began well in Munich, having thought about withdrawing because he was suffering from tonsillitis. Woosnam's urging that he should play persuaded him otherwise. 'My legs felt like jelly,' he reported after a first day's 68. 'I asked a lot of myself, not just by playing, but by trying to impress at the same time. I'm very proud. It's made the journey worthwhile.' Westwood also revealed that a personal loss in his family had affected his year and had played a part in his own patchy form. 'The death of my gran in March hit me hard,' he admitted. 'I missed seven cuts in a row after she died. Then there was the situation with Darren's wife, Heather, which has been on all our minds.'

Meanwhile, Thomas Bjørn spoke of the pressure he felt trying to impress Woosnam. 'It's hard under normal circumstances, but the Ryder Cup and all it means just adds to it,' he confessed in Munich. 'Every corner you turn there is someone who wants to talk about it, and you want to make the team so badly it is bound to affect your play. The one person who must be happy is the captain because he is in a good position, given how many good players are chasing wild cards. As for myself, the one consolation is that, come Sunday night, if I don't make the team, I can draw comfort from the fact that I know Europe is going to have a really strong team.' These words would come back to haunt him.

Woosnam was delighted to see so many of his players performing in Munich. In the end, it was the Swede Stenson, third on the Ryder Cup points table, who took the title after sinking an eagle at the first extra hole to defeat fellow European teammate Harrington and the South African Retief Goosen. Five of Woosnam's team finished in the top seven. Harrington recorded the 29th second-place finish of his career, David Howell came fourth, having missed a three-footer to make it into the play-off, and Montgomerie and Luke Donald tied for sixth. Monty's placing was the more remarkable considering he had nipped back on the Saturday night to a Robbie Williams concert at Hampden Park, Glasgow, where he showed off the Ryder Cup from the stage to a packed audience. Paul Casey, meanwhile, performed respectably, tying for thirteenth position. 'The performance of the Ryder Cup guys has been absolutely fantastic,' Woosnam responded afterwards. 'It's been a great week for them as individuals and for the team.'

It was not all good news, however. Paul McGinley missed the cut in Munich, and, according to his friend and fellow Irishman Harrington, was stressed despite results going his way to guarantee him an automatic spot in the European team. 'It's a mental thing with Paul,' Harrington explained. 'He's gone through nine months of hell. He's at his best when he's determined, but there's a fine balance between being determined and trying too desperately.'

Olazábal, meanwhile, was so incensed by Montgomerie publicly querying his decision to miss Munich that the Spaniard contacted the BMW International Open to let his feelings be known. A peacemaking mission between the two stars would be required in good time for The K Club!

Prior to the big announcement, Woosnam admitted that deciding on the two wild-card selections was causing him considerable anxiety. 'It's the toughest thing I'm ever going to have to do,' he revealed. 'I've got a lot of good friends out there, players whom I know are desperate to make the team. At the end of the day, though, I've got to pick the players I think are going to be best for the side.'

He was also aware that the Americans appeared to be getting their run-up to the Ryder Cup right. Melissa Lehman, the American captain's wife, was even planning a Dublin pub crawl for the team's wives. McGinley sounded out a warning, having played alongside Tiger Woods for the first two rounds of the WGC-Bridgestone Invitational in Akron, Ohio, the previous week and having witnessed the world's number one dining out with the four American Ryder Cup rookies in a local restaurant. 'This US team is up for winning,' he said. 'It's very important that we don't underestimate them, especially as they are headed by the best golfer in the world, playing the best golf of his life.'

On the Sunday evening, following Stenson's victory at the BMW International Open, Woosnam finally announced his Ryder Cup team. The ten automatic selections were already known. Montgomerie, Donald, Howell, Casey, Harrington, Stenson, Karlsson, García, McGinley and Olazábal would be joined by Clarke and Westwood, the last two being Woosnam's wild-card choices.

It looked, on paper at least, to be the strongest European team in the long history of the Ryder Cup. No European team prior to this one had contained eleven members who'd won at least one tournament around the world since the previous match (Westwood was the odd man out). In total, Europe could boast seven of the world's top eighteen players, compared to Lehman's five in the American team.

McGinley, just about the only European lacking form, spoke of his joy in making the team. 'It's a huge relief,' he admitted. 'I've been under a great deal of pressure, and I feel a great weight has been lifted. Now I can get ready for one of the biggest weeks of my life without worrying or having to look over my shoulder. It's going to be a fantastic week, and I would have hated not to have been a part of it.' He did admit, however, to some anxiety over his recent form. 'I've used up a lot of mental energy, which you do when you're not playing well. It's important that when I get to The K Club, I'm ready to play my part. I hope that matchplay will suit me. I've played a lot of matchplay, and I have a good record. I'm looking forward to the Ryder Cup, but I can't expect the Irish crowd to lift me to play well.'

In truth, McGinley was not really the issue; Darren Clarke was. All eyes immediately turned to the Northern Irishman, who had been at his wife's bedside when she had passed away exactly three Sundays previously. It had been his friend and manager Andrew 'Chubby' Chandler who had talked him into making himself available for selection. 'Life will never be the same again for Darren, but what passes for normality will happen when he gets back on the golf course,' said the former tour professional. 'He knows it will be very emotional, particularly given the increased profile wives have at the Ryder Cup, but he put himself forward because he genuinely believes he can bring something to the team, both on the course and in the locker room.'

In a prepared statement, Clarke responded to his selection. 'It is going to be a magnificent week,' he said. 'I wouldn't want to have missed it – and neither would my lovely wife, Heather.'

In his Irish friend McGinley, Clarke had a strong ally. 'The last two years have been a massive learning curve for Darren,' said McGinley. 'He's dealt with one of the toughest situations you have to deal with, not just for himself when his wife was dying, but having to guide his two young kids through a minefield of emotions, too. He has come out the other side a better person for it and is a lot stronger, too. I have no fears of him dealing with it emotionally. Darren gets a lot of respect from our team and also from the Americans. I would think that Tom Lehman isn't too happy with the picks that Woosie made in Darren and Lee Westwood.'

Woosnam had no doubts. 'Believe me, Darren is ready to go, and I don't think it was a risk to choose him,' he said. 'He's raring to go. This is the first time ever that we will start as favourites, and now we've got to make sure we keep doing what we've been doing for the last 20 years. But I feel for the guys who haven't made the team. We have got so many great players in European golf that it was always going to be a difficult decision.'

The Welshman tried to contact Westwood but left his decision so late that the wild-card choice was already on a plane flying home from Munich. 'I only made the decision in the last few minutes, and Lee had flown off,' Woosnam explained. After Westwood finally received word of his inclusion in the European team, he was understandably delighted, especially after rising from his sickbed to play at the BMW International Open. 'I am so glad I made the effort to go to Germany,' he said. 'I would definitely not have played had it been any other week than the last one before Ryder Cup qualification. Everybody loves their golf in Ireland, and it's going to be an occasion not to be missed. I am pleased and honoured to be a part of it.'

The man who suffered the most as a result of non-selection was Thomas Bjørn. During the final afternoon in Munich, rumours swept the golf course that the Dane, who had a higher world ranking and better position in the European Order of Merit than Westwood, had received the nod from Woosnam. Later, when he discovered the truth, he did not try to hide his disappointment. 'Devastated doesn't even come close to expressing how I feel,' he reacted. More would follow after a night's sleep.

Woosnam, however, defended his decision to plump for Westwood.

'Lee has won tournaments around the world, he got 4½ points out of 5 two years ago and he has twice won at The K Club,' he explained. 'That was sufficient for me to go for him.'

The following day, Bjørn made his true feelings known. It made uncomfortable reading for Woosnam and the European team, and probably came as great news for Lehman and his American dozen. What irked the Dane more than anything was discovering his failure to make the European team on television in his hotel room in Munich. 'Ian Woosnam's captaincy has so far been the most pathetic that I have ever seen in my life,' he began, just for starters. 'I wish all 12 players the best of luck, I really do, but I'm hoping they win despite their captain. He has really gone down in my estimation. He is certainly no friend of mine. He has put a lot of players through a lot of misery simply because he is incapable of doing the right thing. There are plenty of people who are very uneasy about the Woosnam captaincy.'

It was certainly strange that Woosnam, who had been upset about the lack of communication in 1997 when Ballesteros was European captain, had spoken neither to Bernhard Langer, the previous winning captain, to pick his brains, nor to Olazábal for six months. Nor had he ever played with Luke Donald until the Munich tournament. It also came across as harsh bordering on ruthless that Woosnam had failed to inform either Bjørn or the other hopeful rookies, including Johan Edfors and Carl Pettersson, of his decision. 'I'm another one who Woosnam hasn't spoken to for six months,' added Bjørn. 'Let me say first of all that no one has more respect for Lee Westwood than me. He is a great golfer, a great guy and I'm proud to call him a friend. But the facts are there for everyone to see. He hasn't scored better than me in a single category, and so I have to come to terms with a decision that makes absolutely no sense. This is the hardest thing to deal with in my career because of the terrible way it has been handled and because it just doesn't add up.'

Woosnam admitted that Bjørn was 'not a happy camper' when they met up. 'I hope we can have a few beers when it is all over.' On the evidence of Bjørn's mood, this appeared unlikely, even if

Walter Hagen
(right) and J.H.
Taylor, the US and
Great Britain and
Ireland captains,
with Sam Ryder
(centre) at the
1933 Ryder Cup
in Southport.
(© Phil Sheldon
Golf Picture
Library)

The victorious American team at the first official Ryder Cup in Worcester, USA, in 1927.
(© Phil Sheldon Golf Picture Library)

Eric Brown selects a club at the 1957 Ryder Cup in Lindrick, helping Great Britain and Ireland to their first win in eight attempts. America would not be beaten again until 1985. (© Phil Sheldon Golf Picture Library)

American star Billy Casper in the rough at Muirfield, 1973. (© Phil Sheldon Golf Picture Library)

The great Arnold Palmer admires
his shot at Muirfield, 1973.
(© Phil Sheldon Golf Picture Library)

Captain Tony Jacklin and the inspirational Seve Ballesteros on their way to a narrow defeat
in Palm Beach, 1983. (© Phil Sheldon Golf Picture Library)

The waiting is over – Europe finally win. Sam Torrance celebrates after sinking the winning putt at The Belfry, 1985. (© Phil Sheldon Golf Picture Library)

One of the greatest partnerships in Ryder Cup history: Nick Faldo and Ian Woosnam help Europe to their first-ever win on American soil, at Muirfield Village in 1987. (© Phil Sheldon Golf Picture Library)

The most-pressured putt in golf. Bernhard Langer misses and loses the 'War on the Shore' at Kiawah Island, 1991. (© Phil Sheldon Golf Picture Library)

Colin Montgomerie, the scourge of the Americans, is carried off the course by Italian Costantino Rocca after winning at the 18th hole at Oak Hill, 1995. (© Phil Sheldon Golf Picture Library)

An artist at work: Seve Ballesteros captains Europe to victory in Valderrama, Spain, in 1997. (© Phil Sheldon Golf Picture Library)

The most-controversial episode in Ryder Cup history: the US team storm the 17th at Brookline in 1999 after Justin Leonard sinks a 40-foot putt. José Maria Olazábal, waiting to play, observes in horror. (© Phil Sheldon Golf Picture Library)

Colin Montgomerie and the late Payne Stewart playing singles at Brookline. The American apologised to the Scot for the crowd's behaviour. (© Phil Sheldon Golf Picture Library)

Paul McGinley wins the Ryder Cup at The Belfry in 2002 and later jumps fully clothed into the lake at the 18th to celebrate. (© Phil Sheldon Golf Picture Library)

Tiger Woods and caddie Steve Williams stride purposefully along at the 2002 Ryder Cup.
(© Phil Sheldon Golf Picture Library)

The Irish triumvirate:
Darren Clarke, Paul
McGinley and Padraig
Harrington with
the Ryder Cup after
playing their part
in Europe's biggest-
ever win, at Oakland
Hills in 2004. (© Phil
Sheldon Golf Picture
Library)

the following day the Dane had calmed down sufficiently to issue a retraction. 'Having had a day to reflect on my comments, I would like to apologise for the hurtful and personal nature of my remarks to Ian Woosnam,' he said. 'I realise I have made a mistake and have unreservedly apologised to Ian for my comments, which were made in the heat of the moment. I am a passionate guy who believes the Ryder Cup is one of the world's greatest sporting events, and I was desperately disappointed not to make it into the team. I realise that is 100 per cent the captain's choice, and in Lee Westwood and Darren Clarke I believe he has picked two great players. All I want now is for all the media, players and golf fans to get behind the team for the matches in Ireland and for my comments to be forgotten.' Bjørn was fined what was referred to as a 'substantial' sum by the European Tour, who would no doubt have been appalled by the outbreak of war within the ranks of their players.

Ironically, it was also announced that the European Tour had signed on Jamil Qureshi, the magician-turned-golf-psychologist, to help Woosnam and his assistants get their message across during the Ryder Cup. It was ironic because Qureshi's main clients on the tour were Bjørn and Westwood. Despite this, he was approached by Woosnam and his assistant Peter Baker during the BMW International Open, with Colin Montgomerie also present. 'The biggest thing about a Ryder Cup is the number of potential distractions in terms of crowd, coverage and the sheer scale of the event,' Qureshi said. 'Some will feel more stressed than others, and I'll be around not just for the captain and his helpers but also for the players. Some thrive on this kind of pressure, but others find themselves limited by it.' Although Tom Lehman had won all the plaudits in the build-up to the Ryder Cup, Qureshi believed that Woosnam would be in his element come the action. 'He's someone who will be first out of the trenches, and he'll be full of passion and enthusiasm for his task,' he explained.

Nine days before the start of the Ryder Cup, Clarke made his first public appearance in Madrid, where he was making his comeback at the city's Open after eight weeks away from the game. He appeared emotional but defiant and even injected some humour into the proceedings. When it came to dealing with the Ryder Cup, Clarke was frank. 'I'd be a liar if I said that I think I'll be able to get through the whole week without feeling uncomfortable, but I'm prepared for that,' he admitted. 'There was always going to come a time when I would have to stand up and get on with my life. I'll get myself through it, don't worry about that. At some stage, I had to grow up, and this is the perfect time to do it. I have responsibilities now, and I have to do the right thing, both for myself and for my boys.'

Clarke revealed that the Ryder Cup had been in his thoughts throughout his troubles. 'It's been in the back of my mind all year. It became obvious early on that I would have to be a captain's pick. There was clearly a lot of thinking to be done concerning my willingness to play, and I didn't want to make a rash decision after Heather passed away. I had to make sure in my own mind that I would contribute, because the last thing I'd want is to let my teammates down. Is it too soon? Well, it's been almost two years since Heather was first diagnosed. I knew what was going to happen at some point, as people do when faced with these terrible things. I was thinking of it the more ill that Heather got, and I'm sure I have come to the right decision. That's why I gave Woosie a call, and I'm glad he felt able to give me a wild card. I told him I was ready to play five times in three days if necessary, and I think that was all he needed to hear.'

It was clear, too, that the American team were all pleased that Clarke would be playing. Clarke admitted that Tiger Woods, who had lost his father to the same disease just a few months earlier, had telephoned on several occasions and sent text messages of support. 'We're all going to be desperate to win next week, but the bottom line is that it will be a week of golf among friends,' said the Northern Irishman.

Another player of whom great things were expected was David Howell. Having been part of the European team that went to Oakland Hills in 2004 as underdogs and returned home with the biggest margin of victory ever recorded on American soil, Howell expressed his concern about being a member of a European team labelled clear favourites. 'That's maybe for the first time ever, and it's a big problem,' he argued. 'It's not a situation we are used to. They have the world's most dominant player and have lots of major winners, whereas we have one [Olazábal].' Howell has also come to terms with being recognised as one of the world's leading golfers, as confirmed by his world ranking of 12, after many years of grind, in contrast to fast-rising contemporaries such as Justin Rose and Luke Donald. 'I've been on the tour for eleven years and I've been finding my way for the first five. I was no Rose or Donald, but I was probably a better player than I thought I was. Five years ago, I set out to attack this game and see just how far I could get, and the truth is it's a lot further than I thought. Now I'm as confident as anyone when I'm playing well. Being ranked 12th in the world has taken some adjusting to, and, at times, my game has improved more than my mind will let me believe. But the stats don't lie. Now I just have to live up to expectations.'

He would lose to Montgomerie in the World Matchplay at Wentworth the week before the Ryder Cup, but this result paled into insignificance when compared to the fact that Tiger Woods, fresh from winning five back-to-back tournaments (including his 50th tournament title at the Buick Open), lost in the first round to fellow American Shaun Micheel. Losing to Micheel, who finished runner-up to Woods in the US PGA having won the major in 2003, is no disgrace, but it was not the best news for American captain Tom Lehman. Micheel had not made his team, while Woods, the master of strokeplay, once again revealed his aversion to matchplay. On top of that, three of the semi-finalists – Colin Montgomerie, Robert Karlsson and Paul Casey – made up a quarter of the European team.

Casey went on to beat Micheel in the final by the wide margin of ten and eight. Capturing the biggest win of his career, as well as the biggest pay cheque (£1 million), just five days before the start of the Ryder Cup was impeccable timing on Casey's part. The list of scalps he took at Wentworth was also impressive. In beating Retief

Goosen, Mike Weir, Colin Montgomerie and finally Shaun Micheel, the 29 year old never went further than the 33rd hole all week and, in doing so, lowered the previous record of fewest holes played to win the World Matchplay by 4, from 128 to 124. The previous record holder happened to be a certain Ian Woosnam. Casey also somersaulted to the top of the European Order of Merit as a result of his victory. His thoughts, however, immediately turned to the Ryder Cup. Two years previously, he was a rookie and unheralded during Europe's victory romp, with 1 point from two matches. He then made matters worse by admitting he 'properly hated' the American team during the three days of competition. It hardly endeared him to American golf, and his play suffered as a consequence, but, two years on, with apologies made and accepted, Casey is an altogether different prospect. 'I was full of trepidation last time,' he conceded. 'I didn't know what to expect, but I absolutely loved it. This time I'll go there really excited about playing. I'd love to play in all five matches.'

Woods, meanwhile, opted to stay at the house given to him for the week at Wentworth rather than fly home before departing for Ireland. After playing tennis on the Saturday, he went to Stamford Bridge to watch Chelsea beat Liverpool in the Premiership. Most of his American teammates left home for Dublin on the Sunday night, except for Furyk, who was already at The K Club.

Despite his semi-final loss to Casey in the World Matchplay, Montgomerie was letting it be known that he was up for the Ryder Cup. There has never been a time when the Scot has not been, but these were still disturbing words from an American point of view. Without any doubt the best player currently on the circuit never to have won a major, Montgomerie has become, arguably, the greatest player in the history of the Ryder Cup. Certainly, Ian Woosnam rated him highly before the tournament got under way. 'Monty is like an ambassador for our team,' said the Welshman. 'I've got my vice-captains and my assistants, and he is going to be another guy I can sit back and talk to about what's going on. I can take his advice. He's a man of great wisdom, a lot of class and a lot of talent.'

This time round, Montgomerie had two personal goals: to win at least 4 points to overtake Nick Faldo's record tally for a European golfer of 25 points; and to be a part of a European team that had won three successive Ryder Cups for the first time ever.

'Can you imagine anything better than winning the Ryder Cup three times in a row and in Ireland of all places?' the 43 year old asked. 'I think that would be the most fulfilling moment I've ever had in golf.' It would also be a fitting end to Montgomerie's Ryder Cup career in Europe. He has stated that he hopes to play under Faldo in America in 2008 but has admitted that it will most probably be his last Ryder Cup, assuming he makes the team. 'That would be nine,' he counted. 'That's enough for anybody.'

In the meantime, Europe were looking to get the best out of Monty, both on and off the course. It was at the end of his first Ryder Cup, the War on the Shore at Kiawah Island in 1991, that he first came to understand the team ethos of the competition. 'Up to that point I had no idea what it meant,' he said. 'But when you see defeat reducing men of the stature of Seve and Bernhard to that state, well, you can't help but be caught up in it.'

Montgomerie has never lost a singles match in any of his seven Ryder Cups – a remarkable statistic. Neither, however, has he faced Tiger Woods. It would be a clash of real Ryder Cup heavyweights, the golfing equivalent of Muhammad Ali versus Joe Frazier. Monty, for one, was up for it. 'I'd love to play him this time,' he confessed during the build-up to the cup. 'This might be my last match, so why not go out playing him?'

His Ryder Cup story alone is remarkable enough, let alone all his ups and downs in strokeplay, his succession of second-place finishes in majors and his extraordinary eight European Order of Merit titles. 'A lot of what I've learned in golf stems from watching people like Seve, Faldo and Langer in the Ryder Cup,' he explained. 'In my second match, Nick asked if he could be my partner. I can't tell you what a boost it was to have the world's best player at the time saying that.' In 1999, at Brookline, Montgomerie became a figure of fun for the pumped-up American crowd. It got so bad, and so personal, that his father left the course and watched the rest of the competition on television. 'His love affair with the Ryder Cup was shattered that day,' said Montgomerie junior. Three years later, captain Sam Torrance asked him to start the final day's singles, and Montgomerie went on to beat Scott Hoch five and four as Europe thundered home to victory. 'That was the best I have ever played in a Ryder Cup, and I can't tell you how proud I was to have played that day.'

In 2004, Montgomerie bettered his 2002 performance, first by beating Woods and Mickelson when partnered with Harrington to wreck America's 'big gun' tactics, and then by holing the putt to secure another European victory. 'You look at the last two Ryder Cups and everyone has contributed at least a point,' he explained. 'That's what we have to do again this time. If we do that, then even Tiger at his best will struggle to get the trophy off us. If everyone is pulling in the same direction, it doesn't really matter that the opposition have the best player who ever lived. I'll be doing everything I can to make my team win. That's how much it means to me.'

The best player who ever lived continued to speak of his feelings for Darren Clarke. In fact, Woods may well have played some part in Clarke's decision to play for Europe in the Ryder Cup. 'I don't know whether I persuaded Darren to play or not, but we had a number of phone calls in which I told him what I felt about him as a person and as a player. I told him that he deserved to be on that team, and if Woosie wanted him to be one of his wild cards, then he should take it. It's not because of what he's gone through or is going through. But just from a player's perspective, he's too good not to be on the team.'

That said, nobody was more aware of the personal turmoil Clarke had gone through than Woods. 'I wanted to keep my distance when Darren was grieving, but because I went through something similar earlier in the year I felt that if I could help in any way to make him feel better, I would. You expect to lose a parent at some point in your life, but you don't expect to lose someone you thought you'd be spending the rest of your life with. That's the difference between the two of us and why what he's going through is so much harder. Darren was helpful to me earlier in the year. We played together at the Players Championship in March for the first two days, and it was a really nice pairing for the both of us. Heather was not doing well at the time, and my dad was doing really bad. So it was nice to be able to talk while we were playing about things we were dealing with. There was a sense of calming.

'The good thing for Darren is that he'll have 11 teammates and all the spouses around. It will be hard in a way, but also comforting. Each person grieves differently. The hardest thing for me was getting out there and playing because it was my father who introduced me to the game of golf. Every fundamental and basic I know in golf came from my dad. So every time I reverted back to stance, alignment, position, all these basics that I do, I thought about Dad every single time. With Darren, I think the hardest times will be at night. You're not going to have that person to share things with any more.' Woods went on to say that he would give his European opponent 'a big hug' when they met at The K Club and also asked if he could sit next to Clarke at one of the official dinners. 'I will make every effort to help Darren in any way I can,' he promised. 'We all will.'

Clarke's great mate and former Ryder Cup partner Lee Westwood had every confidence that his fellow wild-card selection would once more deliver in Ireland. 'I've heard Tiger say that the only time he feels free of stress is when he is on a golf course, even if there are 20,000 people watching,' he said. 'I think Darren will feel the same in Ireland this week. My only concern is Darren seeing the rest of us with our wives. Heather really loved the Ryder Cup, and she would definitely have wanted Darren to play in Dublin. Even when she was incredibly ill, she used to tell him to go and play. She was an incredibly strong woman. Darren will need some support, but, with friends on both teams, he'll get it.'

Not least from Westwood, who was hoping in advance of the tournament that he and his friend could form their indestructible partnership in the Ryder Cup once again. 'I'd expect to play with Darren as I have in the past in fourballs, where we have won four of our six matches. I've experienced most of Darren's moods on the golf course. I know how to read him. We can be natural with each other. You need to have an understanding of each other. All the great partnerships in recent Ryder Cup history, from Olazábal and Ballesteros to Woosie and Faldo, have had that.'

Westwood would have been encouraged by the verdict of his former captain Sam Torrance, who offered his views the weekend before the Ryder Cup. In the opinion of the only man ever to sink the winning putt in a Ryder Cup and then go on to captain a victorious European team, Woosnam's men would win the 2006 Ryder Cup with relative ease. 'You can never write off any American team, especially one containing Tiger Woods,' he said. 'But when you look at our team, we have strength all the way through and so many different combinations and partnerships who would gel well together and be successful. Woosie's in a great position because he has so many adaptable players who can play alongside anyone. When you look at the Americans, you're not so sure.'

In particular, Torrance was referring to the American rookies. 'J.J. Henry got into the American team on the back of a couple of good weeks, Wetterich has never even made the cut in a major championship, Taylor is an unknown who lacks experience and Johnson will need to step up a couple of levels in class to shine.' They would also have to deal with a partisan and raucous Irish crowd, which Torrance believed would be a major asset to the European team. 'It's going to be pandemonium,' he said. 'For the Europeans, it will be like having a hole start. For all these reasons, I have no hesitation in predicting with the utmost confidence that Europe will retain the Ryder Cup and chalk up three successive victories for the first time. For me, this is the strongest team we have ever fielded.'

Woods had tried everything he could prior to the start of the Ryder Cup to make the four American rookies feel more at ease. After taking them out for 'some nice steaks', Woods explained to them what the atmosphere at The K Club was going to be like. 'They won't have played in front of fans like that,' Woods said. 'It's very different playing in a Ryder Cup compared to a regular tour event. Then the fans are cheering for 156 different individuals. In Ireland, it will be very different. All these guys love college football, pro football and basketball, so they understand the atmosphere being that way, it's just that they have never played in it before. But as I have always said, last time I checked, lowest score still wins.'

Monday, 18 September was the day when Ireland finally got to greet the 24 players and the members of the managements from both sides as the European and American teams arrived at Dublin airport. From just about the moment The K Club was awarded the 2006 Ryder Cup, the country had been awash with excitement. Everywhere you travelled you were reminded of the forthcoming competition, from promotions at petrol stations, where golf balls were being given away, to billboard advertising. But now, with the sight of two teams lining up on the steps of their plane – posing for the photograph that is so often taken when sports teams travel abroad – Ireland knew the time had come.

The style experts certainly had a field day with the American choice of attire. Led by Tom Lehman, the Americans, minus Woods and Furyk, who had already arrived, appeared sporting autumnal-tweed bomber jackets with leather elbow patches, pale-blue shirts, ties, thick woollen tank tops and light-brown trousers. They looked as if they had just leapt out from the pages of a P.G. Wodehouse novel. The outfits were made by Ralph Lauren and, according to Lehman, were designed to give 'a Great Gatsby look'. The American captain was certainly happy with the outfits. 'Rather nice, don't you think?' he asked. 'It has earthy tones, and it is a tweed. It has some depth to it and some history, and that is what I like.' Europe, meanwhile, could not have been attired more differently. Looking more 'Cool Britannia' than Great Gatsby, the players wore zip-up grey tops, but only Woosnam had his zipped right up to his neck. Over these tops, the players wore dark suede jackets cut to the hip, plus tan suede shoes.

Safely ensconced at The K Club, members of both teams aired

their views on the upcoming tournament, with the start of the Ryder Cup just four days away. First to talk was Padraig Harrington, one of the Irish triumvirate for whom the coming week meant so much. 'Playing here at The K Club with an Irish crowd behind you will make this week very special,' he said. 'We all remember the scenes at The Belfry when Paul [McGinley] sank the putt to win the Ryder Cup in 2004. We ditched him in the water. I guess the Irish crowd might love it if me, Paul or especially Darren does it on Sunday. If that happens, they'll probably have to fish all three of us out of the water this time.'

Speaking about Ian Woosnam, who had finished a poor second to Tom Lehman in terms of Ryder Cup preparation according to the media, Harrington was full of praise. 'Woosie has been involved in many Ryder Cups, and he wants to do it his way,' he explained. 'He needs to feel responsible and in control. I'm comfortable with that. Bernhard Langer was brilliant last time round, even to the extent of advising me which club to use before every par 3. Woosie won't try to match that. He's going to wear his heart on his sleeve, put his arm around players and encourage them that way. It's a different form of captaincy.'

The Irishman expected to play a leading role this time round, just as he had two years before at Oakland Hills when he and Montgomerie set the tenor of the match by defeating Woods and Mickelson in the opening fourballs. 'We knew Tiger and Phil would lead the charge, so we had a team discussion, and it seemed as if everyone wanted me and Monty to take them on. I think it had a significant impact on the players behind us to see how we kept the blue numbers up on the board that whole match. We got an early lead and simply didn't let them back in. You need a captain in such a partnership. I had a higher world ranking than Monty, but there was no doubt who was the captain. Any time I play with him, Monty's the captain.'

Harrington was convinced that America, despite being tagged the underdogs, would be a much stiffer proposition than they were in 2004. 'It's important to get the partnerships right. America didn't last time, but they've realised this now, and they're going to be hard to beat. They'll be helping each other out more than last time, and their rookies will be particularly receptive. Europe has gained so much in the past from rookies flourishing alongside senior players, and that's what the Americans now want. Having lost the last two, they'll be well up for this one. And Tiger has a real point to prove. Even if he lost early at Wentworth last week, The K Club is very different. I can guarantee that he likes it. It's a magnificent Ryder Cup venue because of the amount of danger, trouble, water and sheer excitement. It will look spectacular, and it will play spectacular. It's a big hitters course.'

José Maria Olazábal followed on from Harrington, and if his words were to prove accurate, then we would be assured of the most sporting Ryder Cup ever. His last piece of Ryder Cup action was to watch the American team members invade the 17th green at Brookline in 1999, trampling all over his putting line. Seven years later and the Spaniard had moved on from those disgraceful scenes. 'If we are going to live with that in our hearts for the rest of our lives, then all I can say is that we're going to lead pretty poor lives,' he announced. It was a statement which met with wholehearted approval from just about everyone involved in the Ryder Cup. Olazábal may have blotted his copybook slightly by deciding to pull out of the BMW International Open in Munich, thus placing his guaranteed slot in the team in jeopardy, and his public annoyance at Montgomerie's dismay at such a decision hardly helped either, but on the first day in Ireland he was the perfect statesman, possessing the look of a European captain in waiting. 'So Tom Lehman jumped up and down a bit,' he continued. 'Don't we jump up and down a bit when we win? I expect him to jump up and down some more if his team win at The K Club. We really need to move on.'

And Olazábal was well aware that his impromptu Spanish dance immediately after helping his European team record their first-ever win in America, at Muirfield Village in 1987, had annoyed the Americans at the time. 'I feel pretty ashamed about that,' he confessed. 'Don't you have a lot of energy when you are 20 years old? But I look back at those images and realise how many players are no longer with us. I think of Seve Ballesteros and the partnership we formed that year. I'm not sure the Ryder Cup will ever see one like that again. It wasn't just like an older player taking a younger man under his wing. I had known him since I was 13 years old. He was more like a brother than a partner.'

The fact that Ballesteros is unable to perform anything like his former stupendous self due to a chronic back condition is not lost on Olazábal, who suffered from a back ailment and foot injury neither of which looked likely to be cleared up. It took a visit to Hans-Wilhelm Müller-Wohlfahrt, the famous homeopathic doctor to the stars, in Munich 11 years ago to cure him. 'I thought for a time that I would never be able to play golf again,' Olazábal admitted. 'Then to play was a bonus, to compete was even better and to win another Masters title . . . well, there are no words to describe that. Now, seven years on, to be good enough to play in another Ryder Cup . . . I'm a very fortunate guy.'

Age, experience and his own problems had clearly mellowed the excitable Spaniard. 'I'm a different person now,' he promised. 'I've seen sick children who still find the energy to smile at you, and you can't but think of that and wonder, "Aren't we lucky to be able to shoot 80?"

'What I do now is think about those bad times I've been through and focus on what I need to do to play well again. It helps me to find the peace to recharge the batteries and go again. It feels now like I'm starting all over again.' Even the argument with Montgomerie was dealt with when Olazábal arrived in Ireland. 'I've already kissed him on each cheek, twice,' he revealed. 'And I can promise you one other thing, too. If we win, there will be no samba.'

Another reason why Olazábal's peacemaking speech seemed so appropriate was the sight of Darren Clarke making an emotional return to Ireland at the start of the final week of preparations for the Ryder Cup and speaking of a positive that had emerged from the tragic death of his wife. 'It's been good getting closer to my two boys,' he admitted. 'I've had to look after them a bit more than

I used to do. It's been a difficult thing. Since Heather passed away, I'm happy with my relationship with my kids. It's my boys who make me tick. Towards the end of Heather's life, I didn't get the chance much to practise golf. Nor did I have any interest to do so. I would come home from the hospital and go and hit some balls, mainly to get my mind away from things. Heather passed away, and I took a little time off. After a few days, I got back into hitting balls again, because I knew that if Woosie were to offer me a pick, I would need to get myself back into decent shape again. It's nice to know that I have so much support. It's going to be very good for me. A lot of people understand the position I'm in. I've had a very emotional time of late, but I'm here to play golf. I want to play, I want to compete and I want to help my teammates. There may be more important things going on in the world than trying to win this week, but, in the end, we're all professionals, and we'll all want to win. As soon as we stand on the first tee, we'll be wanting to beat each other, but we also know it's not a matter of life and death, which is what a few of us have gone through.'

One man who was particularly pleased to see that Clarke had made it to The K Club was Tom Lehman. 'Darren's presence is a significant asset,' he said. 'I think having him here means a great deal, not only to him personally and to his teammates but also to the US team and all of the fans. I think it will just make this Ryder Cup much better. When it comes right down to it, we're all human beings, and when you see a man who has endured the kind of tragedy Darren has, you have an incredible amount of empathy for him.'

Another man took time on the Monday before the beginning of the tournament to recollect the misery of watching European golfers celebrate winning the Ryder Cup on American soil in 2004 at Oakland Hills. Chris DiMarco revealed that, while the rest of the US team sloped off in disappointment, he made a point of staying to take it all in. 'I wanted to burn that image in my mind's eye of the Europeans celebrating on American soil,' the New Yorker admitted. 'Don't get me wrong. The team and their fans were within their rights to enjoy such a great victory. But imagine what that was like for a proud American? I forced myself to stay because I wanted to remember it all for when the Ryder Cup came round again.'

This might explain why DiMarco talked about the 'hatred' of the Ryder Cup when speaking during the 2005 Presidents Cup, but he insisted his words were misconstrued, and he made a point of explaining himself personally to members of the European team. 'I was referring to the fact that some fans go to the Ryder Cup and think it's a football game, hating the opposition. I know there is only respect between the two teams.'

DiMarco was a major asset to the American team. In strokeplay, he had been disappointing, despite his world ranking of 15. But in matchplay, he was an altogether different force and had forged an impressive partnership with Phil Mickelson, at least judging by their Presidents Cup performances, the pair having dropped just a ½ point in four matches. 'Something about playing for America brings out the best in me,' he explained. 'I think about the Ryder Cup all the time. I'll be playing in one of those tour events where the test is just a case of how far you can smash the ball and then smash it again, and I'll start thinking about the Ryder Cup. I'm thinking about it even now whilst I'm talking.'

There is no doubting that DiMarco is a world-class golfer in his own right, as his second place at the 2005 Masters and his runner-up spot behind Woods at Hoylake at the Open a couple of months before the Ryder Cup proved. Yet he comes into his element playing team golf, which is probably why he was the sole American with a winning record at the 2004 Ryder Cup and why he sank the putt to win the 2006 Presidents Cup. 'I'm playing for my country, and if you can't feel honoured playing for your country . . . well, Jeez. You see, golfers don't get the opportunity to take part in the Olympics, so the Ryder Cup is kind of what it is for us. We play in such an individual sport for 51 weeks of the year, and then we come together. Gee, it's so special to have teammates.'

He also insisted that the Ryder Cup meant the same for every single member of the American team but that he showed his commitment a little more. 'I don't know if that is the Italian in me,' he said. 'It's just the way I was brought up. I had two older brothers who were always beating me up, and I always felt I had to get my two cents in. I owe those two a lot for the way I am. All I know is that something happens to me when I play golf under the American flag.'

Later in the week, Tom Lehman revealed that he had already made up his mind concerning the pairings for the opening fourballs on the Friday morning. 'I decided on them in the last couple of weeks,' he admitted. He also disclosed that he could not guarantee that all 12 of his players would get more than a match in the singles. 'In a perfect world, everyone would play at some stage in the first two days. But what if everything's going great and the four pairs I send out on Friday keep on winning?' His European counterpart, on the other hand, was still trying to reach such a decision. 'I have some pairings for Tuesday and Wednesday practice, and I'm going to have a look at how everyone is playing and talk to the lads,' Woosnam said.

Lehman also made an amusing revelation concerning the American team's needs on the culinary front. His planning, meticulous from the day he received the vote to take charge, had included ensuring that a week's supply of tortilla chips arrived with the team. 'We live in Arizona, it's the land of Mexican food,' Lehman explained, referring to his own family. 'When we were over here the last few years it was very difficult to find good chips and salsa. So we decided to bring our own corn tortillas. We're having the real deal. I must have loaded 200 bags of them into my travel bag, each bag weighing five and half pounds. So I figure it weighed 500 pounds.' It helped to explain why the American flight was delayed by some three hours before departing from Washington. 'We had a lot of one-way stuff,' Lehman said. 'It was just massive amounts of luggage. When the airline personnel saw the bags piling in, their brows got more and more furrowed. But I tell you this about those chips: we're going to eat those babies.'

Turning more serious, Lehman suggested once again that the Americans would be on their best behaviour. He had watched, for example, how the Europeans had scored a public-relations coup over the American team in 2004 by willingly signing autographs for the fans, something the home team had refused to do. This time, Lehman promised, his players would be more fun and more user-friendly with the galleries. It was because he knew how important it was to keep the Ryder Cup in perspective. 'There's billions of folks in this world who do not care who wins the Ryder Cup,' he pointed out. 'We're not dealing with world peace. We're not dealing with Aids in Africa. We are playing a contest, a game, which is an important game, and everybody is passionate about it. They want to win, but, at the end of the day, it is just a game.'

As he was speaking, the Irish rain was tumbling down on The K Club, something that the Europeans felt might be to their advantage: they were more used to bad weather than the Americans, who plied their trade in hard sunshine most weeks. Lehman begged to differ: 'We have a bunch of guys who grew up in parts of the world where there was wind and rain. [We have] a guy from Connecticut and a bunch of guys from Florida. I don't think wind and rain affect anyone any more. Everybody has to play in it, so it is just a matter of who has the mental toughness to deal with it to the end.'

Ultimately, it would all boil down to mental toughness. Both teams possessed it in spades. It would not be long before we would discover who would crack first.

FIVE

THE PLAYERS

EUROPE

Colin Montgomerie

Age: 43
Birthplace: Glasgow, Scotland
World Ranking: 14
Career Earnings: £16,728,731
Career Wins: 39 (1 in 2006)
Major Championships: 0
Ryder Cups: 7 (1991, '93, '95, '97, '99, 2002, '04)
Played 32, won 19, lost 8, halved 5
Ryder Cup points won: 21½

COLIN MONTGOMERIE IS THE MAN AMERICANS MOST fear, at least when it comes to Ryder Cup golf. Famously, he has never won a major, despite countless near misses, and he is universally recognised as the best player in the world with none of the big four titles to his name. Put him in the European team uniform, however, and the man becomes possessed. His best-known and most formidable record is his unbeaten run in seven out of seven singles matches. Four years ago at The Belfry, captain Sam Torrance asked him to lead the way in the singles for Europe, his win over Scott Hoch setting up a day when the scoreboard became smothered in the blue of Europe. He is almost as intimidating in the fourballs and foursomes, too, winning most of his matches, whether it be with Nick Faldo, Paul Lawrie, Bernhard Langer or Padraig Harrington. Off the course, Montgomerie is worth his diminishing weight in gold. A consummate team man, in the past he has acted as unofficial chief motivator and a shoulder to cry on. He is, quite simply, the heartbeat of the European team, and his career, unless he suddenly wins a batch of majors in his twilight years, will be defined by the Ryder Cup.

Like most golfers past their prime, Montgomerie is beginning to find it harder around the greens, but not when it comes to the Ryder Cup. 'It's what Monty does in the dressing-room that is almost as important as the points he makes,' insisted Paul McGinley. 'He's a good judge of character. He knows exactly when to say the right thing.' This view was endorsed by Padraig Harrington, who expressed his desire, before the cup got under way, to partner the Scot again after their success at Oakland Hills two years before. 'The key is to keep Monty happy,' he explained. 'If you keep his spirits up, you get someone who is almost unbeatable.' The Europeans would, therefore, attempt to keep their man happy over the Ryder Cup weekend.

Sergio García

Age: 26
Birthplace: Castellón, Spain
World Ranking: 8
Career Earnings: £14,261,425
Career Wins: 16 (0 in 2006)
Major Championships: 0
Ryder Cups: 3 (1999, 2002, '04)
Played 15, won 10, lost 3, halved 2
Ryder Cup points won: 11

IF MONTGOMERIE IS THE BEST PLAYER NEVER TO HAVE won a major, then Sergio García comes pretty close behind him.

However, the Spaniard has one major advantage over the Scot: he is still only 26 years of age and has the time that is fast running out for Monty to secure that coveted and elusive first major title.

And while Montgomerie is the heart of the European team, García provides the fight. Unpopular with the Americans because of his brashness bordering on arrogance, García has taken over the fearless, chest-thumping persona that once belonged to his compatriot Seve Ballesteros in the Ryder Cup. García, more than any other European, was most likely to wind up the opposition.

The 2006 Ryder Cup was his fourth, but, because of his age, he was still regarded as one of the juniors in the team. The truth is that he provides inspiration to the rest of the team, although in a different way from Montgomerie. His record in the Ryder Cup is testament to this. With a win record of 66 per cent, he has backed up his pumped fists with results and, in doing so, spread his own humour and winning mentality like an infection throughout the team.

García's putting may remain suspect, but, like Ballesteros and José Maria Olazábal, his love of the Ryder Cup is unremitting. In 2004, he won both fourball matches, which he played with Luke Donald, and dropped just a ½ point with Lee Westwood in the foursomes. He also defeated world number two Phil Mickelson in the second singles rubber of the final day, steadying the ship after Paul Casey had lost the first singles match to Tiger Woods. García was a certainty for the 2006 Ryder Cup and would have been a definite wild-card selection if he had not already automatically qualified.

Padraig Harrington

Age: 35
Birthplace: Dublin, Ireland
World Ranking: 18
Career Earnings: £13,473,695
Career Wins: 15 (0 in 2006)
Major Championships: 0
Ryder Cups: 3 (1999, 2002, '04)

Played 12, won 7, lost 4, halved 1
Ryder Cup points won: 7½

IF EVER A RYDER CUP SEEMED IN ADVANCE TO BE suited to a single player, then it was the 2006 event at The K Club. It looked as though Padraig Harrington, the player in question, had everything going for him. Born in Dublin, he was sure to enjoy unprecedented support wherever and whenever he went on the Palmer Course and was the favourite to hit the opening shot of the tournament and to partner Colin Montgomerie, with whom he had played so well two years before. Thanks to a contract with the Irish Tourist Board, Harrington was also the face of Irish golf. However, by his high standards, he had not quite reached the lofty heights of previous years in 2006. That said, Harrington is as strong as anyone in matchplay, possesses a good short game and never contemplates quitting. Bizarrely, he has never won a tournament on Irish soil, but he is long off the tee and has an excellent touch around the greens, so he was always going to be well-equipped to tackle The K Club.

José Maria Olazábal

Age: 40
Birthplace: Fuenterrabia, Spain
World Ranking: 19
Career Earnings: £13,261,929
Career Wins: 30 (0 in 2006)
Major Championships: 2
Ryder Cups: 6 (1987, '89, '91, '93, '97, '99)
Played 28, won 15, lost 8, halved 5
Ryder Cup points won: 17½

BEST KNOWN IN THE RECENT HISTORY OF THE RYDER Cup for all the right and wrong reasons, Olazábal, or 'Olly' as he is universally known on the circuit, formed the best partnership in Ryder Cup history with his compatriot Seve Ballesteros, defeating all and sundry before performing Spanish dances in victory. But when he was last seen in the competition, playing against Justin Leonard at Brookline in 1999, he could only stand and watch whilst waiting to putt as the Americans celebrated Leonard's incredible 40-foot effort by dancing on the green and, in Tom Lehman's case, stepping all over the Spaniard's line. His love affair with the Ryder Cup ended that day, but his enthusiasm returned along with his form in 2006, and he was able to gain the tenth and final automatic berth in the team.

Olazábal's two Masters triumphs, the second after a foot injury almost curtailed his career, meant he had something every other member craved: a major title to his name. And with so much experience, including six Ryder Cup appearances, Olazábal is able to handle any pressure that comes his way. His problem is his unreliability off the tee. Nevertheless, his quiet dignity and evident desire to win act as a nice buffer to García's more in-your-face antics.

Luke Donald

Age: 28
Birthplace: Hemel Hempstead, England
World Ranking: 9
Career Earnings: £7,159,236
Career Wins: 5 (1 in 2006)
Major Championships: 0
Ryder Cups: 1 (2004)
Played 4, won 2, lost 1, halved 1
Ryder Cup points won: 2½

ANOTHER PERFECT MAN TO HAVE IN YOUR RYDER CUP team, Luke Donald enjoyed great form in 2006, best demonstrated by his joint-third finish at the US PGA Championship. Regarded as incredibly consistent, Donald is exactly the kind of reliable player both teams required. Going into the tournament ranked as high as number nine in the world, Donald is unflappable as a golfer, just about the premium requirement for someone playing in a Ryder Cup environment. Because of this, Donald was one of the pre-tournament favourites to be selected by Ian Woosnam to play five matches. In the past, he has enjoyed great success in the fourball format with English compatriot, contemporary and great friend Paul Casey, combining well in both the Walker Cup and the World Cup, which the pair won for England in 2004. With García, he won both foursomes matches he played in the 2004 Ryder Cup. The possessor of one of the purest swings on the circuit, Donald has shaken off his rookie tag of 2004 and is one of the stalwarts of the European team. His reliability was good in 2004, and is good in general in fourballs because his style allows his partner to attack.

David Howell

Age: 31
Birthplace: Swindon, England
World Ranking: 13
Career Earnings: £6,546,020
Career Wins: 5 (2 in 2006)
Major Championships: 0
Ryder Cups: 1 (2004)
Played 2, won 1, lost 1
Ryder Cup points won: 1

DAVID HOWELL CAN LOOK BACK AT THE 2004 RYDER Cup as a major turning point in his career. It was at Oakland Hills that the quietly spoken golfer hit what was voted the European Tour's 'Shot of the Year'. Since then, through sheer hard work, determination and character, he has become one of the world's top players and a heavyweight on the European Tour. With increased assurance, he has even taken on and beaten Tiger Woods in a head to head in China. Howell is no longer an underachiever, and his confidence, previously a problem, is now sky high.

Howell played at The K Club as the British PGA Champion, by virtue of the fact that he won the 2006 BMW Championship, formerly known as the Volvo PGA Championship. His form dipped after winning the title in May, partly because of continuing back problems, but was happily rediscovered following a fourth-place finish at the BMW International Open in Munich. He was part of a winning partnership with Paul Casey at the 2004 Ryder Cup. Arguably the best putter in the European team – if not both teams – Howell was not one of the bigger names but would still prove hard to beat.

Paul McGinley

Age: 39
Birthplace: Dublin, Ireland
World Ranking: 53
Career Earnings: £5,930,878
Career Wins: 9 (0 in 2006)
Major Championships: 0
Ryder Cups: 2 (2002, '04)
Played 6, won 2, lost 1, halved 3
Ryder Cup points won: 3½

PAUL MCGINLEY WAS A CONCERN FOR THE EUROPEAN team prior to the tournament because his 2006 form had been poor by his standards. He managed to scrape into the team automatically on the back of a magnificent last third of 2005, in which he made the final of the World Matchplay and then won the Volvo Masters to make him one of the form players in the world. McGinley's new-found achievements in strokeplay were expected to continue but instead he has spiralled downwards ever since.

Poor form, plus knee surgery early in 2006, dented his confidence, although he entered Ryder Cup week more encouraged, safe in the knowledge that the strain of making the European team to play on his home patch was over. He also spent the last few days prior to the start of the competition working with leading coach Bob Torrance, father of 2002 winning European captain Sam. Like a few other players, McGinley seems to be lifted when faced with the challenge of the Ryder Cup. He is a consummate team player, and prior to the tournament commentators were expecting his form to take a dramatic leap forward, boosted by the knowledge that he was playing in a team including two other Irishmen and in front of an expected 40,000 partisan Irish fans a day. He would also do well to focus on his cup-winning putt in 2002, and the subsequent celebrations which saw him thrown into the nearby lake.

Paul Casey

Age: 29
Birthplace: Cheltenham, England
World Ranking: 17
Career Earnings: £4,679,039
Career Wins: 6 (2 in 2006)
Major Championships: 0
Ryder Cups: 1 (2004)
Played 2, won 1, lost 1
Ryder Cup points won: 1

PAUL CASEY WOULD HAVE BEEN MUCH HAPPIER WITH himself after dismissing some of the world's best to win with consummate ease the World Matchplay title at Wentworth just five days before the start of the Ryder Cup. This confidence boost would have made him more comfortable rubbing shoulders with some of the great names of European golf after his form and reputation suffered following some ill-advised comments about 'hating' Americans during the 2004 Ryder Cup competition. Casey claimed to have made up with everyone upset by such views, although it gave the Americans an extra incentive to beat him. He has homes in Arizona, close to Tom Lehman (whom Casey apologised to following his comments), and in Surrey.

In 2004, he partnered David Howell with some success; the European team were hoping for more from him in Ireland. Known to be an aggressive player who collects birdies and bogeys, Casey's style of play is suited to the fourballs, in which his poor shots can go unpunished and his good shots can win the hole.

Henrik Stenson

Age: 30
Birthplace: Gothenburg, Sweden
World Ranking: 11
Career Earnings: £3,466,017
Career Wins: 6 (2 in 2006)
Major Championships: 0
Ryder Cups: Rookie

THE K CLUB COULD HAVE BEEN A CAUSE OF EITHER inspiration or desperation for the Swede. Back in 2001, Stenson was so disgusted with his game that he walked off the course after just nine holes of the European Open. The chances of him making the Ryder Cup team five years later appeared non-existent. But that was then. In the past two years, Stenson has been transformed into one of the world's best players, helped by coach Peter Cowen. Of the 24 players on show at The K Club, Stenson was arguably the most improved golfer of them all. He has recorded an impressive list of high-place finishes in tournaments all over the world, helped by his huge drives from the tee. This length is best deployed in the fourball format, where scoring birdies is so important.

Although he was a rookie going into the tournament, he was a rookie enjoying supreme form, as his win at the BMW International Open in Munich – the final qualifying event on the European Tour before the Ryder Cup team was announced – showed. Stenson had already proved himself in matchplay golf and was carrying on the proud tradition of Swedish golfers in this event.

Robert Karlsson

Age: 37
Birthplace: St Malm, Sweden
World Ranking: 36
Career Earnings: £4,758,964
Career Wins: 7 (2 in 2006)

Major Championships: 0
Ryder Cups: Rookie

ROBERT KARLSSON, LIKE HIS FRIEND STENSON, WAS a Ryder Cup rookie from Sweden. However, the Americans, unlike Stenson, would be looking at Karlsson as a possible weak link. In 2004, he came extraordinarily close to losing his European Tour card altogether. And at 37 years of age, he arrived on the Ryder Cup scene rather late in his career.

He has quite a few plus points in his favour, however. At 6 ft 5 in., and over 14 st., he possesses possibly the longest drive of anyone who played in the 2006 tournament: the big Swede can always be expected to produce fireworks with his big hits. Karlsson also warmed up nicely for the Ryder Cup by reaching the semi-finals of the World Matchplay at Wentworth, proving that he was a mean matchplay golfer. The Americans would have known very little about him before his display at Wentworth, where he finally lost to Shaun Micheel. The bad news about Micheel was that he was American. The good news was that he failed to make the American team. Despite this result, doubts continued to hang over Karlsson as the competition approached.

Darren Clarke
Age: 38
Birthplace: Dungannon, Northern Ireland
World Ranking: 24
Career Earnings: £13,907,068
Career Wins: 17 (0 in 2006)
Major Championships: 0
Ryder Cups: 4 (1997, '99, 2002, '04)
Played 17, won 7, lost 7, halved 3
Ryder Cup points won: 8½

AS A RESULT OF THE SAD DEATH OF HIS WIFE IN August 2006, Darren Clarke became the main focus of the media's attention in the build-up to the Ryder Cup, having first announced his willingness and availability to play in the event and then been selected by captain Ian Woosnam to be one of his two wild cards. Despite his huge stature in golf – both physically and in terms of his achievements – more uncertainty surrounded the man from Northern Ireland than any other member of the team, and that included the two rookies. Would one of the stalwarts of the Ryder Cup be able to discover top form after such a long lay-off from golf, save for his comeback tournament in Madrid the previous week? More to the point, would he be able to handle the emotions he would feel at an event featuring players' partners and wives? If anyone could, it was Clarke, who entered the competition aware that his could be one of the all-time heroic performances and knowing that if there was anywhere he could escape from his recent traumas, it was the golf course. With the huge Irish crowd completely behind him, and wholehearted support from his teammates (and even the sympathetic Americans), people thought that Clarke might provide the inspiration the Europeans would need if they were to win. And he had a decent Ryder Cup record, having been a member of three winning European teams in the previous four tournaments.

Lee Westwood

Age: 33
Birthplace: Worksop, England
World Ranking: 51
Career Earnings: £10,108,090
Career Wins: 27 (0 in 2006)
Major Championships: 0
Ryder Cups: 4 (1997, '99, 2002, '04)
Played 20, won 11, lost 8, halved 1
Ryder Cup points won: 11½

LEE WESTWOOD WAS IAN WOOSNAM'S SECOND WILD-card choice, much to the dismay and anger of Thomas Bjørn. The Dane's unfortunate reaction to Westwood's selection may have placed some unwanted pressure on the former European Order of Merit winner, but if anyone could deal with it, Westwood could. He had not been in the best form but did show encouraging signs of improvement just prior to the start of the Ryder Cup. Besides, recent form does not usually count for much once play begins in the pressure-cooker intensity of this Euro–American golfing festival. Westwood has proven time and time again that when focused, as he invariably is during the Ryder Cup, he is one of the world's very best golfers. He has an unnerving ability to perform at the highest level in the Ryder Cup, regardless of the way he is playing in the build-up to the tournament. The fact that he needed a wild-card pick was a concern and indicative of his patchy form, but America would still rather not have seen Westwood in the European team.

Westwood's close relationship with Darren Clarke was an undoubted bonus, as well; Woosnam could not pick one without the other. They had proved to be a successful partnership in previous Ryder Cups, but having the understanding figure of Westwood close by was a necessity because of Clarke's exceptional circumstances.

USA

Tiger Woods

Age: 30
Birthplace: Cypress, California
World Ranking: 1
Career Earnings: $64,412,324
Career Wins: 62 (7 in 2006)
Major Championships: 12
Ryder Cups: 4 (1997, '99, 2002, '04)
Played 20, won 7, lost 11, halved 2
Ryder Cup points won: 8

TIGER WOODS IS THE NUMBER-ONE-RANKED PLAYER in the world by a long distance, the second-greatest golfer of all time by virtue of his twelve major championships and is almost certain to overtake Jack Nicklaus's all-time mark of eighteen majors in the near future. After losing his father to cancer in the spring, he bounced back in emphatic style by winning both the Open and the US PGA Championship in 2006, and with seven other tournaments won in the eight months of that year prior to the start of the Ryder Cup, he was quite clearly the best golfer in the world going into the tournament. In strokeplay, he was, when the mood took him, nigh on unbeatable over four days. And in 2006, once he had recovered from his personal loss, the mood had taken him.

His particular strengths are his short game and his unparalleled nerve, despite the eyes of the world being firmly and continuously fixed on him. He seems to have everything, closing in on Nicklaus's record and the billion-dollar mark in total earnings, and has even found time to become firm friends with his tennis equal Roger Federer.

Yet even with Woods there is a but, and the but concerns his sorry and unfathomable record in the Ryder Cup. For any player to have lost considerably more matches than they have won in the competition is a poor record. For Woods to be in this position – when he has been the number-one player in the world almost continuously throughout the past ten years – is unbelievable. The irony is that in his younger, amateur days Woods was at his best in matchplay. But his Ryder Cup record, plus his first-round exit in the World Matchplay in September 2006, suggested that much had changed since his non-professional days.

However, the assertion that he was not a team player had clearly begun to rankle with both Woods and his captain Lehman. The fact that Woods took it upon himself to take America's four rookies out to dinner suggested that this time he meant business, both for himself and his team, and demonstrated a change in the Woods psyche when it came to the Ryder Cup. Meanwhile, prior to the tournament, the Europeans hoped that his one minor weakness, a waywardness off the tee, would be punished along The K Club's narrow fairways.

Phil Mickelson

Age: 36
Birthplace: San Diego, California
World Ranking: 2
Career Earnings: $39,514,038
Career Wins: 29 (2 in 2006)
Major Championships: 3
Ryder Cups: 5 (1995, '97, '99, 2002, '04)
Played 20, won 9, lost 8, halved 3
Ryder Cup points won: 10½

NUMBER TWO IN THE WORLD AND THE WINNER OF three majors and twenty-nine tournaments in total – although he would probably have won a lot more if it had not been for a certain Tiger Woods – Phil Mickelson was America's second heavyweight player in their line-up. He can seek solace in the fact that if Woods is the best player in the world, Mickelson is the best left-handed golfer. As with Woods, however, his Ryder Cup record does not back up this fact. It may be better than his nemesis Woods', but not by much, and it was his embarrassing singles defeat to Welsh journeyman Phillip Price that really got the Europeans going on the final day in 2002 to win back the Ryder Cup they had lost at Brookline. Worse still was 2004 US captain Hal Sutton's strange decision to pair Woods and Mickelson together. When they lost the opening fourballs to Montgomerie and Harrington, it ushered in a European steamroller. Yet Mickelson, when the force is with him, can almost match Woods in terms of talent, excitement and shot-making. His short game is arguably the best in the world, and he hardly lacks experience.

Matchplay should also suit his game even more than strokeplay. Major championships have been lost by Mickelson's aggressive style of play, but in the matchplay of the Ryder Cup, attacking the flag wins games rather than losing them. Pre-tournament commentators speculated in the week leading up to the event that he would be paired with Chris DiMarco, because they had enjoyed a successful

110

partnership at the 2005 Presidents Cup. On paper at least, it would be a formidable partnership.

Jim Furyk

Age: 36
Birthplace: West Chester, Pennsylvania
World Ranking: 3
Career Earnings: $30,070,766
Career Wins: 12 (2 in 2006)
Major Championships: 1
Ryder Cups: 4 (1997, '99, 2002, '04)
Played 15, won 4, lost 9, halved 2
Ryder Cup points won: 5

JIM FURYK IS THE THIRD MEMBER OF AMERICA'S 'BIG Three'. With a not very impressive record in the Ryder Cup, Furyk was yet another big name determined to shed his reputation as a matchplay underachiever in the run-up to the tournament. Prior to 2006, he had an unbeaten record in the singles, seeing off the likes of Faldo, García and Howell and halving with McGinley in 2002.

It was in the pairings that Furyk had foundered. In his four previous appearances in the competition, Furyk could boast just 2 points gained out of a possible 11 in the fourballs and foursomes. However, just as Mickelson and DiMarco clicked during the Presidents Cup, so too did Furyk and Woods.

Before the competition got under way, observers predicted that Furyk's role at The K Club would be immensely important. Not only had he to bring his own 'A' game to the golf course, but he had to do everything in his power to ensure Woods brought his. If he succeeded, then Woods would be unstoppable, and Furyk would not be far behind.

Furyk's notoriously straight hitting off the tee, despite his ugly swing, is well-suited to a course such as The K Club, with its narrow fairways. His short game is pretty good, too, which makes his poor record in previous Ryder Cups almost as mystifying as those of Woods and Mickelson.

David Toms

Age: 39
Birthplace: Monroe, Louisiana
World Ranking: 16
Career Earnings: $25,625,161
Career Wins: 12 (1 in 2006)
Major Championships: 1
Ryder Cups: 2 (2002, '04)
Played 8, won 4, lost 3, halved 1
Ryder Cup points won: 4½

ON HIS DAY, TOMS IS AS GOOD A GOLFER AS ANY IN the world, as his US PGA Championship triumph in 2001 proved, but there were health concerns surrounding him in the build-up to the 2006 cup. Not only had he withdrawn from the Open with back problems, he also had what was termed a minor heart operation in 2005. On the plus side, he has a consistent if sometimes boring game and a big-match temperament, as he proved when he was, by some distance, the best visiting player at The Belfry during the 2002 Ryder Cup. He is also big-hearted, as the huge amount of money he helped to raise for the victims of Hurricane Katrina in New Orleans revealed.

However, it was Toms who made the slightly ridiculous remark that if America had brought their 'A' game to the 2004 Ryder Cup, they would have won. Given that they were beaten by 9 points in what was the heaviest recorded home defeat ever suffered by the USA, it seemed an inappropriate comment to make and one that paid little attention to just how well the Europeans had played.

Toms had run into some form before the cup began, having tied for eighth place at the WGC-Bridgestone Invitational in August 2006. But while his steady game results in fewer mistakes, his average-length hitting from the tee often makes it hard work for

The River Liffey dominates the Palmer Course and claimed many golf balls during the 2006 Ryder Cup. (© Darren Jack)

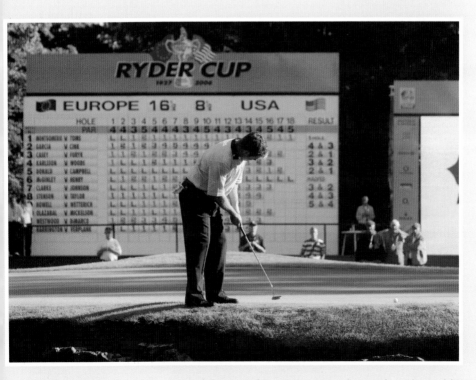

A sick Lee Westwood on his way to defeating Chris DiMarco in the singles, cheered by the sight of a scoreboard dominated by European blue. (© Mark Pain)

Zach Johnson considers another tricky shot for America. (© Mark Pain)

Darren Clarke goes wild after chipping in a birdie at the 16th to beat Woods and Furyk in the Saturday fourballs with partner Westwood. (© Mark Pain)

When it rains it pours. Tiger Woods wishing he was back home in the Florida sunshine. (© Mark Pain)

It was Williams or the nine-iron. An amused Tiger Woods looks on as Steve Williams tries to retrieve the nine-iron he's just dropped into the lake. (© Donald Miralle/Getty Images)

'Yes, yes, no!' Phil Mickelson (in blue) looks on in horror, while US captain Tom Lehman rests his hands on his head in dismay. (© Darren Jack)

The putt that won the Ryder Cup: Henrik Stenson has the honour as he beats Vaughn Taylor at the 15th. (© Darren Jack)

The most passionate man at the Ryder Cup. García plays to the crowd once again. (© Darren Jack)

'Cool Hand Luke'. Donald accepts the crowd's acclaim. (© Mark Pain)

Three happy Irishmen: Clarke, McGinley and Harrington with the Ryder Cup on Irish soil. (© Mark Pain)

Stenson and Karlsson, with the Ryder Cup, discover that life as a Swedish rookie is good. (© Mark Pain)

The man of the moment: Darren Clarke kisses the Ryder Cup. (© Mark Pain)

Captain Ian Woosnam attacks the first of many celebratory bottles of champagne.
(© Darren Jack)

him to challenge the top of the leaderboard. He is useful in the fourballs format, allowing his partner to go for broke.

Chris DiMarco

Age: 38
Birthplace: Huntington, New York
World Ranking: 15
Career Earnings: $18,611,371
Career Wins: 3 (0 in 2006)
Major Championships: 0
Ryder Cups: 1 (2004)
Played 4, won 2, lost 1, halved 1
Ryder Cup points won: 2½

CHRIS DIMARCO WAS ALWAYS GOING TO BE A KEY figure in the American team, for a number of reasons. No mean golfer himself, as his high world ranking and second place in this year's Open proved, DiMarco is in his element when playing for his country in a team event. And it did not go unnoticed that he was by far the best player on the US side when they were humbled at Oakland Hills in 2004.

His role, over and above his individual performances at The K Club, was twofold. The first was to get Phil Mickelson going. DiMarco and Mickelson proved they were a successful partnership when they won the 2005 Presidents Cup, with DiMarco, fittingly, sinking the winning putt of the match. However, his second role was even more important: DiMarco is to America what Sergio García is to the Europeans, and he was earmarked to be his team's chief rabble-rouser, chest-thumper and motivator, partly as a consequence of his New York Italian upbringing. In the past, DiMarco has annoyed the hell out of the Europeans, just as García gets under the US team's skin, but he doesn't care a jot. Woods may be the unofficial leader among the players on the course, but back in the team room at the hotel and in the locker room at The K Club, it would be DiMarco doing the shouting. The chief criticism of the American team over the past few Ryder Cups has been their lack of team spirit in comparison to the Europeans. It was apparent in the build-up that DiMarco, the self-appointed cheerleader, would do his utmost to ensure this wasn't a problem again. But the risk was that his efforts would detract from his own game. Certainly, his lack of length from the tee suggested he would be less of a threat as a player, especially on The K Club's demanding closing few holes.

Chad Campbell

Age: 32
Birthplace: Andrews, Texas
World Ranking: 22
Career Earnings: $12,187,881
Career Wins: 3 (1 in 2006)
Major Championships: 0
Ryder Cups: 1 (2004)
Played 3, won 1, lost 2
Ryder Cup points won: 1

CHAD CAMPBELL HAS PROMISED MUCH MORE THAN he has delivered so far in his career. The Texan's game from tee to green is admired worldwide, and his ball striking, in particular, is straight out of a textbook. His problem is sometimes with his short game, a potentially major failing when it comes to the Ryder Cup.

In 2004, Campbell endured two nightmare days in the pairings. Then, on the final afternoon, he destroyed Luke Donald in the singles, his short game finally living up to his long game. On a depressing afternoon for American golf, his performance was a very bright spot on an otherwise dark day. Prior to the 2006 tournament, he was considered to be a potential danger to the European team at The K Club, but only if he clicked. And judging by his display at Oakland Hills, this was a big if.

A glance at the US Tour statistics reveals his putting is poor and his accuracy off the tee even worse, despite his superlative striking of the ball. But he is ranked 22nd in the world, and with earnings well into eight figures, the man's done pretty well for himself. However, he has hardly lived up to his selection five years ago by America's biggest golf magazine as 'the golfer most likely to be the next big thing'. His form going into the tournament was not good either, although the Ryder Cup often throws the form book out of the window.

Zach Johnson

Age: 30
Birthplace: Iowa City, Iowa
World Ranking: 42
Career Earnings: $6,524,492
Career Wins: 1 (0 in 2006)
Major Championships: 0
Ryder Cups: Rookie

THE FIRST OF AMERICA'S FOUR ROOKIES, ZACH JOHNSON was regarded as one of the many weak links in a team that was billed as serious underdogs in the run-up to the tournament. However, being a rookie is not necessarily a bad thing: David Howell, Paul Casey, Luke Donald and Ian Poulter were all rookies in 2004 and played their part in Europe's demolition job over America at Oakland Hills. The problem with Johnson and his fellow rookies was that their recent form had not troubled the US Tour professionals much, let alone the Europeans they would be facing in the Ryder Cup. Throw in the fact that the competition was being staged at The K Club in front of 40,000 screaming Irish fans each day, and the portents were not exactly good for Johnson before the first ball was struck. Some good results in recent tournaments had lifted his confidence, but after a few top-ten finishes earlier in the year, he had done nothing since.

But maybe having no 'previous' going into the Ryder Cup was a good thing: no experience is arguably better than knowing what it is like to be beaten regularly. And perhaps hearing captain Tom Lehman state that he deserved to be in the team by virtue of his automatic qualification would calm Johnson's nerves, and being Tiger Woods' dinner guest settle his stomach. However, The K Club was always going to be a baptism of fire.

Vaughn Taylor

Age: 30
Birthplace: Roanoke, Virginia
World Ranking: 60
Career Earnings: $4,652,561
Career Wins: 2 (0 in 2006)
Major Championships: 0
Ryder Cups: Rookie

VAUGHN TAYLOR WAS RAISED IN AUGUSTA, GEORGIA, where he now lives, having previously studied at the local university and having spent four days each year watching the very best compete at the Masters. He made it to the Masters himself in 2006 but failed to extend his stay to the weekend. Playing in the Ryder Cup granted him an automatic invitation back to Augusta in 2007, but Vaughan also wanted to prove the doubters – and there were many – that he and his fellow rookies could hack it in such an intimidating and intense atmosphere.

On the plus side, The K Club was expected to suit his style of play. He keeps the ball largely straight and narrow, and so hoped to stay on the fairways more often than some of his better-known but less accurate colleagues. Better still, Taylor's short game has always been top notch, which would serve him well both in the pairings and in the singles. On the minus side, though, he had already confessed before the start of the Ryder Cup that he was anxious even thinking about the nerves he expected to feel playing at The K Club. It wasn't a good sign.

J.J. Henry

Age: 31
Birthplace: Fairfield, Connecticut
World Ranking: 64
Career Earnings: $6,105,179
Career Wins: 1 (1 in 2006)
Major Championships: 0
Ryder Cups: Rookie

ROOKIE NUMBER THREE ON THE AMERICAN TEAM,
J.J.'s real name is Ronald, but he uses his childhood nickname.
The fact that he won his first-ever title in 2006 proved that he was
in slightly better form going into the Ryder Cup than his fellow
rookies, even if the Buick Championship sported a weakened field of
entries. The bad news was that it took him six years to achieve the
mark, and there was nothing in his demeanour before proceedings
began to suggest that he would be able to handle the intimidation
of The K Club.

Like so many others, Henry is a big hitter, which works well in
the fourballs format if he plays alongside a steady partner. On the
other hand, his putting is average at best, a weakness which could
affect every aspect of his Ryder Cup three-day weekend. Aside
from his Buick triumph – which was enough to win him automatic
selection for the US team – Henry had shown little in 2006 to
keep the Europeans awake in the nights before the competition
got under way.

Brett Wetterich

Age: 33
Birthplace: Cincinnati, Ohio
World Ranking: 68
Career Earnings: $2,994,048
Career Wins: 1 (1 in 2006)
Major Championships: 0
Ryder Cups: Rookie

THE FINAL ROOKIE OF THE AMERICAN FOUR, BRETT
Wetterich was criticised by Butch Harmon in 2006 for all but
giving up at a golf tournament in America. Tiger Woods' former
coach even went as far as to say that he didn't want the guy on
the US team. But Wetterich had earned the right to be there by
virtue of his tenth-place finish in the US Tour list. In 2004, he
played his golf on a minor tour. In 2005, he was at the PGA Tour
qualifying school. Now, in 2006, he was playing for his country at
the Ryder Cup. It suggested that he had some fight, ambition and
a work ethic, which might have stood him in good stead for The
K Club. He also possessed a huge and often accurate drive.

However, he possessed the lowest world ranking on either side
and had failed to make the cut at any major. The biggest concern
surrounding Wetterich was his experience – or, rather, lack of it
– having never before played in matchplay. The Ryder Cup was a
tough place to start.

Stewart Cink

Age: 33
Birthplace: Huntsville, Alabama
World Ranking: 23
Career Earnings: $18,321,363
Career Wins: 4 (0 in 2006)
Major Championships: 0
Ryder Cups: 2 (2002, '04)
Played 7, won 2, lost 4, halved 1
Ryder Cup points won: 2½

STEWART CINK WAS THE FIRST OF TOM LEHMAN'S
wild-card selections, and a surprising one at that – although the
American team captain was hardly swamped with a choice of
winners, as he himself pointed out. Cink last won a tournament in
2004 and endured a poor Ryder Cup that year at Oakland Hills. He
lost both the Ryder Cup singles matches that he played in prior to
2006, to Thomas Bjørn in 2002 and to Paul McGinley in 2004.

Cink is another player who is wayward off the tee and suspect on the greens. The only real positive going into the tournament was that he rediscovered some form by taking Tiger Woods to a play-off in Akron, Ohio, one week after receiving the nod from Lehman. More of the same was required at The K Club.

Scott Verplank

Age: 42
Birthplace: Dallas, Texas
World Ranking: 37
Career Earnings: $17,860,494
Career Wins: 4 (0 in 2006)
Major Championships: 0
Ryder Cups: 1 (2002)
Played 3, won 2, lost 1
Ryder Cup points won: 2

SCOTT VERPLANK WAS LEHMAN'S SECOND WILD-CARD selection and, like Cink, another surprise pick. Whereas Cink had not won a tournament for two years, Verplank had gone five years without adding to his win tally. He also possessed arguably the shortest drive of all 24 players on show at the Ryder Cup, which all but ruled out eagle attempts at The K Club's par 5s.

But despite this shortcoming from the tee and his lower world ranking, Verplank appeared to many people to be the better of the two wild cards, at least when it came to the Ryder Cup's matchplay format. A steady, patient player who can slow down and upset more attacking Europeans in the process, his 2006 stats on the US Tour suggested he could be a threat for America after all. Any man who could boast coming fifth in the list of fairways hit and sixth in the putting list could almost certainly contribute to the American cause, especially in the fourballs. Verplanks's other attribute is his strength of will, something the US team knew they would have to draw on. A little-known fact is that Verplank is a diabetic and has brushed aside a potentially career-threatening condition to perform as well as he has done.

Verplank and Cink may have been the wild cards, but, unusually, more would be expected of them going in to the Ryder Cup weekend than of the four rookies on the American team.

SIX

EUROPE TAKE
THE INITIATIVE

THE SERIOUS BUSINESS WAS SUPPOSED TO GET INTO full swing on the Tuesday before the big weekend, the first official day of practice, but both sets of teams were still determined to prepare with a smile on their faces. An unknowing spectator might have been forgiven for believing the cup had been brought forward five days, judging by the wild celebrations performed on the 18th green by Darren Clarke and Lee Westwood. Instead, the partnership were merely making the most of a fourballs win over the two other Irishmen in the team, Padraig Harrington and Paul McGinley, and a victory in a fifty euro bet, after recovering from two-down.

Harrington later revealed how the thousands of posters depicting his face endorsing Irish golf were driving his wife to distraction, especially when she saw her husband's mug staring out at her from a toilet door. 'I think she'd just about got used to seeing posters featuring me all over town, but then she went to the bathroom and there was one on the back of the toilet door. I think it's fair to say she found that very off-putting.'

If all this attention and expectation was placing Harrington under more unwanted pressure, he failed to show it, instead pointing out that after three Ryder Cups, and a steep learning curve in the Walker Cup in 1991 on home soil, he was used to it. 'I was totally overawed by it all back in 1991, and there were clearly things wrong with my preparation that week that I can learn from now. I was only 19 back then. Now I've played in three Ryder Cups, so I know what to expect.'

Back then, the popular Irishman hoped he would become, at best, 'a journeyman golfer'. But his strong matchplay performances persuaded him that he really could play golf at a high level and could progress in the sport – much to the eventual benefit of the European Ryder Cup team. 'I turned pro on the strength of what I did playing matchplay in Ireland,' he explained. 'I never lost a singles match and given that all the players I was beating were turning pro I thought, "Why not me?" Even now I think my focus is so much better at matchplay than at strokeplay. I love the fact that it really is one shot at a time and that you've only got one opponent to worry about rather than one hundred and fifty-five. I think I'm a good scrambler, too, which is very distracting for the opposition. Put it this way: if every tournament was matchplay, I'd be a much better player.'

Naturally, he was aware of the rich seam of Irish success in the cup. 'I remember Eamonn Darcy's four-foot putt on the 18th at Muirfield Village,' he recalled. 'It was an unbelievable one to hole. Then we were off and running, weren't we? There was Christy O'Connor Jr. at The Belfry, Philip Walton at Oak Hill, McGinley at The Belfry again. Maybe it's because the Irish love team events and thrive on them. Everybody in Ireland follows Ireland in all team sports, and that inspires us. Personally, I love events and play in any I can. The camaraderie, the *craic* as we call it, is right up our street. No wonder so many of our mob have done so well in the Ryder Cup. So it's absolutely right that the Ryder Cup should come here when you think of the contribution the Irish have made over the years. Everyone is so proud, although I don't think anyone thought it would be this big.'

The Americans were in a similarly jocular mood, especially Jim Furyk. When the world number three was asked why Tiger Woods enjoyed partnering him, his reply was instant. 'He probably likes watching my swing, I would think,' he responded with a deadpan expression on his face. Woods, on hearing this, retorted, 'Yeah, because I'm always wondering how he makes contact.' Furyk's swing might be completely individual in its flailing style, but the golfer was not complaining. 'It separates me from the rest of the players,' he explained. 'From 200 yards out, I get recognised. I see people in my galleries trying to imitate my swing with umbrellas. I like that.'

Judging by their success in the 2005 Presidents Cup, Furyk appeared to be the answer when it came to partnering Woods. 'Maybe some guys are intimidated by playing with him,' he suggested. 'When you're paired with him, you get to see what a day in the life of Tiger Woods is like, and it's quite different from most of us as far as attention. I guess you either enjoy it or not. It makes sense to enjoy it and ride it out and be part of it. At the end, I'll go back to being Jim Furyk.'

During the build-up to the tournament, the chances were that Furyk and Woods would head America's bid to win back the Ryder Cup, starting with the fourballs on the Friday morning. It also seemed likely at that stage that they would be facing Colin Montgomerie, a man the Americans openly admitted they were going to target. 'He's the guy who has put the biggest dent in our points over the years,' admitted Stewart Cink. 'If I were to pick one out we've targeted, it would be their best "Ryder Cupper" over the past decade.' Montgomerie, true to nature, had a response ready and waiting. 'I take it as the highest compliment, but I have to tell them that in the eight Ryder Cups I've played in this is the strongest team. I'm just one of twelve.'

J.J. Henry was another player appreciative of Woods, after the world number one had taken him and his fellow rookies out to dinner. 'The biggest thing I got out of the meal is that all four of us earned our way onto the team,' Henry explained. 'We played our way in, and Tiger emphasised that. That was a neat way to set the tone for our trip to Ireland, and it tells you how much Tiger really cares.' The superstar golfer also picked up the tab. 'It was an all-cash place, and Tiger took out a couple of hundreds,' Henry confirmed. As far as he was concerned, there was no reason why he and the other rookies should not contribute to the week. 'We've no memories of failure,' he argued. 'So we've come in with fresh minds.'

Tom Lehman could not speak more highly of another rookie in his team, Vaughn Taylor. 'This guy grew up in Augusta on municipal golf courses, had never been to a private club and has had to earn everything he has achieved in golf,' said the American captain. 'I mean, he is a tough, tough individual who is very hard on himself. I'll take him anywhere. I'm not sure that you can rate how much guys hate to lose. I would say it would be pretty tough for a guy to hate to lose more than Vaughn Taylor.'

The same went for Colin Montgomerie. Every European captain for the past 16 years has made Montgomerie his first port of call. The reason is simple. The Scot is the sheer embodiment of team golf. 'I never hole a putt for me in the Ryder Cup,' he explained. 'My individual record here is meaningless, absolutely meaningless. I don't care about it. I'm holing putts for Sergio, for Padraig, for Paul or Darren, or whoever it might be. I'm not on a personal crusade. I'm just here for the team members, and they feel the same about me, too. That's why the putts tend to go in.' He paid tribute to Bernhard Langer, the previous European captain, for resurrecting his career through the Ryder Cup. 'I was 41 at the time, and the last few years had not been good, on or off the course,' he admitted. 'That selection by Bernhard saved me in many ways.'

This time round, Montgomerie could not see anything other than a close contest. 'We're looking forward to trying to make history, trying to win the Ryder Cup three times in a row. But I think this is going to be very tight. Tom Lehman has not put a foot wrong. He's determined, as all the American team are, to try and win this trophy back. I think it will come down to someone's putt on Sunday, the way it has done over the past 20 years.'

Ian Woosnam was happy after the first day's practice. 'On Friday, it's important that I go out as strongly as possible,' he said. 'It's important the guys are honest with themselves and with me. We had a team meeting last night. I did my bit, made an inspirational speech and had a few beers, and in the camp everybody's happy with everything.'

That night, everyone enjoyed the eve-of-cup gala dinner, during which the teams were entertained by Irish singer-songwriter Van Morrison. In the morning, however, things turned a little sour for the American team. The weather had become decidedly worse as the tail-end of Hurricane Gordon began to buffet the east coast of Ireland. Reports suggested that the front could hang around long enough to disrupt the opening ceremony on the Thursday and even the following day's play. In the meantime, Lehman made his first gaffe of the campaign when his team decided to miss morning practice, instead having a lie in and a team chat before venturing out after lunch. Once on the course, they opted not to drive off from the tees because of the weather and concentrated on practising their short games. More than 40,000 golf fans had battled their way through the adverse weather to get to The K Club, and they were so annoyed by the American team's pitch-and-putt tactics that they booed and jeered. 'It was my mistake,' Lehman admitted later. 'We shouldn't have left all those fans waiting in the stands. We should have hit some more tee shots. I apologise.' They received a loud if slightly ironic cheer when they finally teed off from the 9th.

Quick to score a pre-weekend psychological point, Woosnam instructed his men to go out and play, regardless of the weather. 'One of the main reasons why we went out is because a lot of people had paid a lot of money to see the golfers,' said the Welshman. 'I'm so pleased all my team went out and played. It's my belief that if you have a great swing, you can play in anything.'

Montgomerie won more plaudits after responding to some gentle ribbing from the gallery by inviting a local woman to hit his approach shot at the 17th. Admitting to being a 22-handicapper, she hit a good, if short, seven-iron, before running back behind the ropes. Montgomerie gently admonished her, 'You never cleaned the club!'

Sergio García also enjoyed himself. 'It was as tough as it was enjoyable,' he insisted. 'The temperature was OK, and a quick nine holes was just the thing. It was amazing how many people were out there. As for Woosie, he's been great. He's stepped up and said everything he needs to say. He's been chatty and funny, and he's adding to our confidence.' García also reiterated Montgomerie's team ethos: 'I would sooner lose five times in five games and for us to win the match, than for me to win five times in five games and for us to lose it.'

Tiger Woods, on the other hand, was not too happy when an Irish magazine linked his wife Elin, and other American Ryder Cup wives and partners, to a porn website. The Dublin-based publication had superimposed Elin Nordegren's head on to a topless model. 'My wife, yes, she has been a model, and she did do some bikini photos,' an angry Woods explained in a media conference. 'But to link her to porn websites and such is unacceptable. My wife and I are in it together. We're a team, and we do things as a team. And I care about her with all my heart. I'm very disappointed.'

It was probably not a wise move to make Tiger angry, especially when he was so clearly concerned about his past record in the Ryder Cup. 'I want my Ryder Cup record to be better,' he admitted. 'That's what I'm working for here. It's always hurt losing points in cup play. It's frustrating because you feel like you've not only let yourself down, but you've let down your teammates who are trying to win this cup for their captain and their country. As far as setting the tone this year, I'd like to do that. I want to get points for my team, and when I'm put up there it is my responsibility to get those points. If I play one match or five, the responsibility is there.'

Woods was also prepared to pay tribute to his captain. 'The relaxed atmosphere in the camp is a little bit different at this Ryder Cup because of Tom's personality. Each team takes on the personality of its captain, and Tom's very serious but also very mellow at the same time. I think that's how we are as a team. We are a unit, and that's how we're going to play.'

Phil Mickelson, with whom Woods had been disastrously partnered two years earlier, was big enough to talk about his unhappy experience at Oakland Hills, when the then American captain Hal Sutton had decided that the world number two would only see action on the Saturday morning as a cheerleader. 'Throughout anybody's time in sport, you are going to have highs and lows,' he explained. 'It's just part of dealing with life as a professional golfer. You have success and failure. Because this is not a team sport, where half the guys win and the other half lose, you are failing more often than not. Tiger and I just didn't play well. You learn by trial and error, and we thought it was going to come out very positive. You have to be willing to take risks and to fail at times.' Whatever Mickelson felt about Sutton, he was clearly impressed with his captain this time round. 'I think Tom's a terrific captain,' said the left-hander. 'We are hoping to put forward our best performances for Tom because he deserves it.'

Rookie Brett Wetterich was in much better spirits following his triumph in winning the 'skimming stone challenge', in which the 33 year old bounced his approach shot across the water at the 8th on another weather-affected practice day. In a complete break from tradition and etiquette, the team played nine holes as a twelve and seemed determined to enjoy themselves. Afterwards, Scott Verplank described Wetterich as a 'goofball'. The rookie accepted this in good nature. 'Maybe I had a couple of beers in me,' he conceded. 'The more I get to know the guys, the more my personality comes out. I never really socialised much with those guys at all, mostly because I was in the first group teeing off or making the cut, never really on top. But I'm starting to feel more comfortable around them. Before I'd never go up to them and chop them in the shoulder or something like that.' He also revealed his surprise at being inducted into his high school's Hall of Fame. 'It's been weird because I don't think my high school really liked me too much. I spent a lot of time in the principal's office.'

Whether Wetterich would be smiling after he had hit his first tee shot as a Ryder Cup rookie remained to be seen. But two of his opponents knew what he was going through. 'It's a bit like what you feel when you are trying to hole a pressure putt at the 72nd hole in a tournament,' said David Howell. 'What helped me last time was watching others hitting from the first tee. Only one of them caught the fairway, and that certainly calmed us down. We felt we couldn't do any worse.' García concurred, adding that the last thing a rookie wants is 'a partner who gives you weird looks if you miss a shot. Jesper Parnevik, when I played with him in 1999, did everything he could to keep me happy.'

The Thursday afternoon saw the official opening ceremony and, amid great excitement, the announcement of the Friday-morning fourball pairings, all played out in front of a crowd of 50,000. The forecast had been for poor weather, and on the Wednesday evening a gale had blown furiously enough to force a few power cuts. However, the gods had been kinder for the afternoon ceremony and for the two teams, their wives and celebrity spectators such as US basketball legend Michael Jordan and German tennis superstar Boris Becker. Once the celebration of all things Irish had been played out on a stage inside a large golf ball – including music, dancers, and speeches from Irish president Mary McAleese and European and American PGA officials – it was the turn of the captains to say their words and introduce their teams. But not before the national anthems of the USA, Great Britain and Northern Ireland, Spain, Sweden, Ireland and the European Union had been played.

An emotional Lehman went first, his voice breaking at times as he described his pride at seeing the flags being raised to the top of their poles and on hearing the anthems. Woosnam followed, looking considerably shorter in comparison to his American counterpart as he stood at the podium. This, almost more than the actual tournament, was what the little Welshman had been dreading, but, save for a few stutters, he came through with flying colours. And his players were brimming with smiles as each member of the team was introduced, every one being greeted by a huge cheer from the large crowd. Their moods had been high all day, ever since their photo shoot that morning, when Woosnam's bag man Martin Rowley had been unable to hold his kneeling position and had tumbled over, causing others to follow suit. The sight of the caddies toppling like

Getting their hands on it. Europe retain the Ryder Cup in 2006. (© Mark Pain)

On course for victory: Ian Woosnam observes. (© Mark Pain)

Losing hurts – just ask US captain Tom Lehman. (© Mark Pain)

The gallery looks on as Paul Casey plays a tricky approach shot. (© Mark Pain)

Stewart Cink and J.J. Henry secure a rare $\frac{1}{2}$ point for America. (© Mark Pain)

Seve Ballesteros greets José Maria Olazábal, his former Ryder Cup partner, on the 10th tee at The K Club. (© Mark Pain)

Lee Westwood and Colin Montgomerie have to make do with a $\frac{1}{2}$ point on the 18th against Phil Mickelson and Chris DiMarco in the Friday foursomes. (© Mark Pain)

Sergio García, in
blistering form, plays
himself out of trouble.
(© Mark Pain)

A study in concentration: Luke Donald's putter served him well at The K Club. (© Mark Pain)

American heavyweights Jim Furyk and Tiger Woods trying to make their putters work. (© Mark Pain)

Robert Karlsson gives Tiger Woods a run for his money in the last day's singles. (© Adrian Dennis/AFP/Getty Images)

Scott Verplank at the 4th in the singles. He later scored a hole in one and beat Padraig Harrington but still lost the Ryder Cup. (© Jamie Squire/Getty Images)

A face in the crowd: former US President and golf nut Bill Clinton enjoys singles day at the Ryder Cup. (© Darren Jack)

Elin Nordegren watches her husband, Tiger Woods, on his way to another American defeat. (© Darren Jack)

dominoes left the players howling with laughter, as did Billy Foster, Darren Clarke's caddie, after he waved a toy horse above his head when posing with his colleagues.

The loudest cheer of the opening ceremony, however, was reserved for when the fourballs pairings were announced. Lehman, as visiting captain, went first and surprised nobody by naming Woods and Furyk. Woosnam countered with his own heavyweight pairing of Montgomerie and Harrington. Then came the unpredicted. Lehman named Cink and rookie Henry, while Woosnam plumped for the long-hitting partnership of Casey and Karlsson. There were more surprises in the third pairing from the American camp, with Toms being paired with rookie Wetterich, the latter having taken a liking to the Palmer Course, driving the ball long and straight all week in practice. Against them would be the two Spaniards, Olazábal and García. Finally, bringing up the rear would be another mighty clash, with Mickelson and DiMarco playing against Westwood and Clarke.

Afterwards, a more familiar Woosnam was at his bullish best. 'My boys knew who they would be playing, and they are up for it,' he announced. Still, he had made some interesting choices and omissions. It was a brave move to leave out three of his best players – Henrik Stenson, David Howell and Luke Donald – from the first morning's play. Howell had partnered the current World Matchplay champion Casey to success two years before, Donald had won 2½ points out of 4 and Stenson was in form, having won two European Tour events in 2006.

Olazábal and García, meanwhile, had become close over the preceding week. 'Olly might have been around for a long time, but his enthusiasm has been incredible,' Woosnam revealed. 'Keeping him off the golf course has been the biggest problem. Sergio's been around now for a while, and he's such a fantastic player. They are just going to work beautifully together.'

Being a Ryder Cup captain does mean making brave decisions, however, and few have been braver than leaving out the world's ninth, eleventh and thirteenth highest-ranked players. 'When you've got nine players in the world's top twenty-five, it isn't easy telling players they are not playing,' the Welshman admitted. 'But I had to make a choice.' The good thing about Woosnam was that nobody was going to question him or his experience when it came to the fourballs. Woosnam had won more fourball points than any other player in Ryder Cup history. 'My motto as a player was never be scared of anybody,' he explained. 'It honestly didn't matter to me who I was playing, even somebody like Tiger.'

Paul McGinley provided a good example of how to accept bad news. 'I will be supporting the team as well as practising and preparing, so if I am required in the afternoon, I will be ready,' he said. 'And if not, I will be cheering on in the afternoon, too.' Luke Donald, who unlike McGinley was in form, was a little less upbeat. 'I am a little disappointed, as I would have loved to have played, but the aim of the game is to get 14 points as a team, and Woosie has a tough job,' he responded. 'At some Ryder Cups in the past, the team has shaped up pretty easily – you could predict what was happening – but this one is a lot harder. It's a nice situation for Woosie, but it is also tough, as he has to leave someone out.'

Montgomerie, meanwhile, was up for the challenge of leading the European charge against America's big guns. 'The first morning of a Ryder Cup is very important, because you try and build up momentum,' said the Scot. 'I have done a lot of leading in this event. It has almost become my role here. Whether I play again after that, I don't care. To start the thing off is great. Padraig is a great partner, and I wanted to play with him again. We will try our best to lead off in style.'

Woosnam was in no doubt about Montgomerie's importance. 'Monty always seems to raise his game for this tournament,' he said. 'He stands on that first tee, and he changes into a different person. He's playing both for himself and all his teammates. As for that first game, there had been a lot of talk about Tiger and Jim Furyk playing together after what they did in last year's Presidents Cup. They're a very strong partnership, and, obviously, it's going to be a very big boost for us if we can beat that pairing. But if we don't, there's still three more matches to go.' Montgomerie's partner Harrington expected an onslaught from a wounded Tiger after he and the Scot had beaten Woods and Mickelson in the 2004 cup. 'That maybe puts them on their guard a bit,' said the Irishman. 'Tiger has a point to prove, and he has a good partner in Jim Furyk, so it is going to be very difficult. I feel myself and Monty are going to have to bring out our best games. That said, I don't think anybody on the team would not relish the chance to play with Monty in a Ryder Cup. He's one of the best players in the world in the Ryder Cup format. He excels, and when you play with him you let him be the captain of the pairing. He's definitely the one leading the ship.' Since first teaming up in the second session of fourballs at The Belfry in 2002, the pair had won three of their four matches.

Tom Lehman also acknowledged the importance of day one. 'It's crucial to get a lead,' he admitted. He then added, 'It's been a long time coming. I've been looking forward to this for some time. I am sure Woosie has too. As for the opening pairings, I wanted to meet strength with strength.' Woods certainly saw it that way. 'We've got two of Europe's best,' acknowledged the world number one. 'Hopefully, we'll be able to get the momentum started.'

His more experienced partner David Toms was ready and willing to make the new partnership work. 'I'm going to go out and play my game and try to make a lot of birdies, and hopefully he's going to do his part, and I'm going to help him out,' said Toms. 'Brett is an exciting type of player, and I need to play some steady golf and let him play his go-for-broke style and hope it works well for us.'

Phil Mickelson also recognised the importance of the last match of the first session, in which he and DiMarco were due to face Westwood and Clarke in what was sure to be an emotional confrontation. 'It's going to be a difficult match,' Mickelson conceded. 'Not just because Lee and Darren are such incredibly talented players, but because of the emotions that will be involved.'

And so the stage was set. After many years of waiting, Ireland was finally going to see a Ryder Cup begin on home soil. Anticipation and expectation were evident in abundance. The crowds were flocking to

The K Club in numbers and, over the course of the weekend, would demonstrate that they were in voice like never before. Meanwhile, the teams must have spent an uneasy, sleepless last night before the tournament finally got going, hoping and praying that their dreams were about to come true. For America, defeat was unthinkable, especially as it would be their third in succession for the first time in the history of the competition. For Europe, a hat-trick of wins would be as sweet as any moment they had experienced in the Ryder Cup before. And it would all begin with a clash of golfing titans. Few people dared predict with any confidence which team would emerge the eventual winners. Europe might have been hot favourites a week or so before the cup began, but cometh the day, it appeared to be a close call.

THE OLD SAYING GOES THAT ALTHOUGH THE RYDER Cup cannot be won on the opening day, it can most certainly be lost. By the end of day one, neither team had lost the cup, but Europe held a 2-point advantage and had struck most of the psychological blows.

The competition began with a decision by tournament referee Andy McFee to impose the preferred-lies rule. Both captains agreed that, with all the rain that had fallen during the week, lifting, cleaning and placing of the balls would make it a fairer contest. The start of play was almost postponed, too, after another gale hit Straffan during the Thursday night, felling nine trees close to the course. The decision to play on was made by John McHenry, The K Club's director of golf, just three hours before the first tee-off time.

The day ended with a concerned Tom Lehman and a satisfied Ian Woosnam. For all the stick he had received prior to the start of the cup, the Welshman had played all 12 of his team, seen every single player contribute a score and had witnessed his side amass a decent first-day lead. By fielding all of his players, Woosnam became the first European captain since John Jacobs back in 1981 to hand every member of his team a game on the opening day. Ten Americans saw first-day action, the unfortunate Vaughn Taylor and Scott Verplank being the odd men out, and seven out of the eight matches were concluded on the 18th green, which proved how close the contest was on that first day.

The Irish crowd, numbering close to 50,000, indicated the way they would behave throughout the tournament by affording US captain Tom Lehman a standing ovation as he made his entrance to the first tee to lend support to his American pairing. Lehman, gracious throughout the three days, smiled and bowed his head. He then called for a team huddle with assistant Corey Pavin and his first pairing.

The enormity of it all even got to the seasoned announcer Ivor Robson on the first tee. Robson had been making such utterances for many a year, but after calling for order, the Scot made a confusing announcement. 'This morning's matches are foursomes,' he said. It was pointed out to him that they would, in fact, be fourballs, and the Ryder Cup was off and running.

It was America who took first blood in the battle of the heavyweights as the morning fourballs got under way. Two years before, Montgomerie and Harrington had shattered US plans to hit the opposition hard early on, beating the American number-one pairing of Woods and Mickelson. It had been a significant statement of intent from the Europeans. Once again, it was the visitors who drew first blood, but this time it was Woods, with new partner Furyk, who won the day's first point and thus his revenge for 2004.

But Woods had Furyk to thank for much of the round. The world number one began the 2006 Ryder Cup by depositing his first drive straight into the water, forty yards off the ideal line. It was the first of thirteen times the water would claim a ball on day one. For most of the outward nine, Woods struggled, but Furyk took the fight to the European pairing, establishing an early lead. Montgomerie and the out-of-sorts Harrington squared matters up at the 5th and took the lead for the first and only time at the 7th, but Woods then came to the party, producing birdies at the 8th, 11th and 12th to hand his pairing a three-stroke lead. Although Montgomerie and Harrington clawed their way back to just one stroke down at the 16th, the dependable Furyk reached the 18th in two to seal victory. It was the first time in seven years that America had scored the first point in the Ryder Cup. One-nil to America, then, but unlike at Oakland Hills, the early lead was anything but crucial.

'I was really struggling, and it was lucky for me that I had such a solid partner as Jim,' admitted a gracious Woods afterwards, the world number one having found himself three over par after the first nine holes. 'I also didn't warm up too well at all.' Regardless of his poor start, he had just scored a point on the opening day for the first time in nine years of trying.

In match two, Europe were tipped to win and perhaps should have done after establishing a big lead. In the end, the new combination of World Matchplay champion Paul Casey and rookie Robert Karlsson were relieved to get a half, despite playing against American wild card Stewart Cink and rookie J.J. Henry.

Karlsson had enjoyed a sensational season but had never experienced anything like the reception he received when he made his entrance onto the first tee. Normally cool and calm, the Swede admitted later that the occasion had got to him. 'It was an unbelievable feeling,' he said. 'It was really, really emotional.' Casey felt the same way. 'I have thought about what the reception would be like ever since the end of the last Ryder Cup,' he revealed. 'I've been wanting to be here at The K Club for so long, and now that we're here, I can tell you the reception was everything and more.'

An eagle by Casey at the par-5 4th was the highlight of the front nine as Europe reached the turn three-up, although what happened at the 7th proved to be the most bizarre action of the day. When Karlsson stepped up to play his second shot, he knew that those who had already played the hole had struggled to clear the water. On the advice of his captain, Karlsson went for broke, took a club more than his predecessors and watched, initially in horror, as his ball sailed over the green and landed on top of a 15-foot television platform, coming to a standstill beside a bemused cameraman. But the Swede got lucky. By rights, his ball should have shot miles past the green. Instead, he received a free drop, made his par and went on to win the hole. 'The green was hard, so it was just as well the TV tower stopped the ball,' Karlsson admitted. 'Then I got a good drop. Those sort of things happen, I guess, in golf.'

Woosnam was able to laugh at the advice he had given his Swedish player. 'I only gave one piece of advice out there, and then that player ended up on a TV tower,' he admitted. 'After that, I thought it better to keep my mouth shut.'

After going three-up at the 9th, the big-hitting European duo appeared to be home and dry, but America hit back with two consecutive birdies at the 11th and 12th, thanks to Henry, before Cink squared the match at the 14th. When another Henry birdie at the par-4 15th gave America the lead for the first time, Europe seemed to have completely lost momentum, but a Casey birdie at the par-5 16th levelled things, and that was how the match finished. Europe were on the scoreboard with a ½ point, but America still held the lead.

Next up was the human whirlwind that is Sergio García. To say that García loves the Ryder Cup is a huge understatement. A brilliant strokeplay golfer, the 26-year-old Spaniard has failed to win a major championship yet, but in the Ryder Cup – rather like his illustrious predecessor Seve Ballesteros – he comes alive. The ultimate team player, García's infectious enthusiasm lifted all 11 of his cup colleagues in 2006 and especially his Spanish teammate José Maria Olazábal, who had the pleasure of partnering him in the Friday morning fourballs. It was Olazábal who had been Ballesteros's partner, of course, the two having formed a great Ryder Cup pairing. Now, in his first match since watching the Americans trample on his line at Brookline seven years previously, he had found another partner who was destined for Ryder Cup greatness.

The Spanish partnership faced the reliable David Toms and rookie Brett Wetterich. García began as he meant to continue, sinking a long birdie putt at the 1st to give Europe an early lead. Olazábal got in on the act at the 9th with a birdie at the par-4 to hand Europe a two-hole lead at the turn. A Wetterich birdie at the 10th reduced the deficit, and when Toms sunk a 40-foot putt at the 11th, America were on the verge of levelling things. García had other ideas, making his putt to halve the hole, and when Wetterich and Toms both found the water at the 13th, the game was all but up. García birdied the par-4 15th to draw Europe three holes ahead, and a half at the 16th ended the issue. In total, García sank six birdies in sixteen holes. Olazábal added a further two.

'It was wonderful to watch Sergio play,' his admiring partner Olazábal explained afterwards. 'He was just awesome. He has all the tools that any golfer could ever wish for, and when he uses them like he did here he makes the game look easy.' Obvious comparisons between García and Ballesteros, who was known for his amazing powers of recovery, were made. 'It's a little less stressful playing with Sergio,' Olazábal countered. 'When you see your partner splitting every fairway, somehow you feel more relaxed. Is there a secret to the Spaniards? No, there is no secret. First it was Seve, now it is Sergio.' He was too modest to add his own name. A generation apart, the two players had not previously been that close. 'But we've felt closer in recent years,' Olazábal explained. 'He's matured a lot, and he's become close to his countrymen. You could see that out there today. We understood each other out there.'

Their captain was certainly impressed with his young matador. 'Sergio lifts his game in the Ryder Cup,' explained Woosnam. 'He has got that Spanish spirit. He is in top form.' García was equally effusive about his morning partner. 'We gelled beautifully,' he said. 'He played nicely, and José Maria came into his own at the holes where I struggled a bit, and I was able to help him out at times. It helps greatly to play with someone of José Maria's experience. He's a good friend of mine, and he made things very simple for me. He's easy to play with.'

The final fourball match of the morning's play was charged with emotion from the moment Darren Clarke received a hero's welcome from the huge, partisan, raucous but fair Irish crowd. The day began alarmingly for Clarke after he forgot to set his wake-up call and overslept. Other Ryder Cups have been preceded by sleepless nights, but not this one for Clarke. Once up, he had his great friend and playing partner Lee Westwood with him to steady his nerves and keep his understandable emotions in check. And in a nice touch, Phil Mickelson and Chris DiMarco both made a point of hugging Clarke at the first tee.

Both pairs needed the win to give their team the edge at the first lunch break, but it was Europe who took the first hole and the early lead after Clarke sank a birdie putt. It followed what, because of the circumstances, was the shot of the day. A poor first drive would have been understandable amid all the emotion. Instead, Clarke smacked his drive and watched as the ball landed dead centre in the fairway at the end of the dogleg, some 320 yards away from the tee. The roar Clarke received for that shot alone was as if he had just won the Ryder Cup. 'I don't know how, but I got it down there somehow,' explained Clarke. 'I never had any doubts, though. Live by the sword, die by the sword.'

America squared the match at the 4th, went behind again at the 10th, levelled terms at the next hole and fell behind once more at the 16th, after another Clarke birdie. This time there was no way back for the US big guns, who never took the lead in the match. It was left to Clarke, the man of the moment, to hole the putt on the 18th to win for Europe and hand them a 2½–1½ lead. Not since Kiawah Island in 1991 had America entered the first day's lunch in the lead, and this year was no different. Clarke fell into the arms of Westwood then his caddie Billy Foster and teammate Paul Casey, who had just finished his fourballs match. Clarke then hugged his defeated opponents before shedding a few tears and steadying himself again.

The enormity of Clarke's achievement was not lost on anyone. Even Amy Mickelson, wife of the vanquished Phil, gave him a congratulatory hug when it was all over. 'You know, if I can have Phil Mickelson and Chris DiMarco hug me on the first tee . . . well, that's what the Ryder Cup is all about,' admitted Clarke later. 'It's not about animosity. It's about a match that we both want to win among friends. The first tee shot was always going to be tough, but after that you get back into it. It's my job. At the end, I had emotions I hope you won't ever have to feel. Nothing that happens here will help with regard to the healing process. Only time can do that. But I'm proud to be part of this team, proud that I was able to contribute as I knew I could and proud of the American opposition, too. They have welcomed me with open arms, which has been very supportive.'

His birdie at the first hole left his partner Westwood searching for superlatives. 'How do you do that after the reception he got, when his eyes were filled with tears?' he asked. 'That was just amazing. I was nearly crying. I looked at Billy [Foster], and he was nearly crying. That made me worse. I couldn't look at Darren.'

His friend appreciated Westwood being there. 'It was fantastic to go out there and play with Lee,' added Clarke. 'We are great friends. We know how each other ticks. He doesn't say much unless I misbehave and lose my head, but I was all right today. It was nice to get a point for Woosie. I never had any doubts about my decision to come here and play. The reception from the crowd was unbelievable, and to go on and win a point was very special.'

Casey then spoke of his teammate's importance to the team. 'Clarkey's playing a great role behind the scenes,' said the Englishman. 'He's one of the senior figures and talks a lot to the other players. He's one of our rocks. He's having a cracking time and really appreciating all the support he's getting, not only from the team but from outside the ropes.'

So far, so good for Europe and for their captain. 'How good was that for starters?' Woosnam asked. 'Four thrilling matches. Just what the fans have waited for. It was a brilliant effort by Colin and Padraig to take Woods and Furyk down to the 18th. I had a hunch from the start of the week that Paul and Robert would enjoy playing together, but you have to take your hat off to Stewart and J.J. They were three-down at the turn and then one-up with three to play, so my guys did well to get the ½. The front nine from Sergio and José Maria was pure magic. I also know that Darren and Lee thrive in tight, tense situations. Everyone knows how much they enjoy playing with each other, and it was obvious again out there. No quarter was given from start to finish, and all four pairs can be proud of the way they played this morning.'

It would be more of the same in the afternoon foursomes, as former US President George Bush joined Michael Jordan and Boris Becker in the galleries. In the first match, the Irish pairing of Padraig Harrington and Paul McGinley took on Chad Campbell and Zach Johnson. With sensational home support, their greater Ryder Cup experience and a firm friendship, the Irish pair were firm favourites to win the encounter but lost the first hole when they three-putted. They squared at the 3rd and took the lead at the 6th, but they were unable to force their advantage home as Campbell and the impressive Johnson levelled the match at the 9th. When the Irish went two-up with three to play, after winning at the 11th and 15th, it looked enough to win the rubber, but the Americans took the 16th and the 18th with a birdie to sneak a ½ point.

The second foursome match followed in a similar vein to the first. Captains Woosnam and Lehman were prepared to mix up their pairings, and Howell and Stenson, neither of whom had played that morning, took on Cink and Toms. Both Americans had seen action before lunch but with different partners. Europe fell behind at the 2nd to a birdie but answered with wins at the 3rd and 4th. America levelled again at the 5th, but Europe took a single-hole lead once again at the 10th, which they held on to until Howell drove into the lake at the 15th. The Englishman almost made amends for his mistake by holing from 20 feet to win it at the 18th, but his putt lipped out, and both pairs had to settle for a halved match.

It was honours even in match number three of the foursomes as well. Woosnam wisely decided to award Clarke a well-earned rest after the emotion-filled roller-coaster of a morning the Northern Irishman had experienced. Lee Westwood, however, was asked to come out again to partner Montgomerie. Strangely, for all their Ryder Cup experience, they had never played together as a team before. Facing them were Mickelson and DiMarco, who had lost to Westwood and Clarke just a few minutes earlier in the fourballs. This time the Americans made a better fist of it, taking the first hole in a topsy-turvy encounter in which neither pair ever managed to put real daylight between themselves and their opponents. Having levelled at the 2nd, Europe went one-up at the 4th thanks to a birdie but lost the lead at the next hole. Europe took the 13th, but Westwood's tee shot at the par-3 14th plugged in a bunker. When America took the lead at the 16th and held on to it at the 17th, it was looking bleak for the experienced Europeans, but Montgomerie duly delivered when faced with a pressure-filled six-foot putt to win the final hole. 'How many times have we seen him hole that left-to-right putt coming back,' said a smiling Ian Woosnam. 'He's done it so many times. It usually comes down to Monty, doesn't it? What a man to have on your team.' Montgomerie conceded that his partner had made the denouement possible after the Scot had left Westwood with a putt from the far edge of the green. 'Lee's was a fantastic putt, since he hadn't had one since the 5th,' Montgomerie admitted. 'He said to me, "Thanks, Monty. I've got a bloody thirty-yard putt with a six-foot swing." But he still gave me a chance to hole it.' Westwood, incidentally, was now unbeaten in his last six Ryder Cup foursome matches.

The final foursomes match-up saw Woods and Furyk, the victorious heavyweight American pairing from the morning, take on the young European pairing of García and Luke Donald, the latter beginning his 2006 Ryder Cup campaign. Two years before, Donald and García had proved to be a successful pairing on the Englishman's Ryder Cup debut. García had been playing like a man possessed in the build-up to the tournament, and Donald had started the final day's play at the recent US PGA Championship sharing the top of the leaderboard with Woods. They were both young enough and brash enough, therefore, not to be fazed by the world's number one and number three.

And so it proved. Woods once again started the match looking like a pale shadow of the man who dominates strokeplay golf around the world. Europe took full advantage of this, gaining a two-shot lead by the 5th. Furyk was carrying his more illustrious partner at that point, ensuring the European youngsters didn't extend their lead even further. Having taken the 13th, America made it all square when Woods, finally finding his form, hit a four-iron approach shot to within two feet at the 14th. At this juncture, America were heavily favoured to see the young upstarts off, but nobody likes playing against Woods more than García. The Spaniard placed his approach shot on the 17th to within three feet, and the Europeans finished the job off by winning the 18th as well to win by two holes, after Furyk struck his second shot straight into the water. 'I did everything I shouldn't have done,' was Furyk's analysis of his final contribution of the day.

The victory maintained García's 100 per cent foursomes record in the Ryder Cup. He had played seven and won seven, three with Donald, two with Jesper Parnevik and two with Westwood. Of those seven games, he had beaten Woods in three of them. 'It's always nice to beat Tiger,' he admitted afterwards. Donald, meanwhile, had now played three foursomes and had won all three of them in García's company.

Furyk's last-hole mistake handed Europe their first outright win of the afternoon to give them a 2½–1½ foursomes win and an overall 5–3 lead after the first day's play. It was the first time in the history of the Ryder Cup in its present format that a session of foursomes or fourballs had ended in three halved matches. It was also the first time that the USA had not won a single foursomes match, as well as the fifth Ryder Cup in succession that Europe had led after the first day's play. It might only have been 2 points, but it was clear that America had been outplayed in both the fourballs and foursomes.

'It underlines what I have been saying all along,' said Woosnam that night. 'I have twelve fantastic players, and I'm very pleased with every single one of them. What a day's golf it has been. What a feast for the spectators. I would have been happy with a 1-point lead. I don't want to get ahead of myself, because we all know what a game golf can be, but I thought all my team were exceptional. I'm very proud of them.'

Montgomerie, the unofficial European leader on the course, was happy with the way the first day had shaped up. 'It's very pleasing that everyone contributed,' he said. 'It makes everyone feel as if they've done something meaningful, and we've only played the first day. We would definitely have taken a 2-point lead before the start of the day's play. We did very well this afternoon. We didn't lose a single match. That could be significant. As for me, I felt OK on the first tee this morning. In fact, the best I've felt at a Ryder Cup. I've done it a few times now. But I had, without doubt, the noisiest and best reception I've ever had in all the years I've been involved with the Ryder Cup. It made the hairs on the back of my neck stand up.'

The excitable García explained why he had played so well in yet another Ryder Cup. 'I just love playing in the Ryder Cup,' he said. 'I honestly don't think I could live without it. I guess that drives me to try even harder. Today I felt goosebumps running down my back, especially at the 16th. The noise out there made me shiver.'

McGinley knew how important a first-day lead was. 'We have the advantage again,' he said. 'And we have the momentum. Having momentum is very important in the Ryder Cup. Not losing a game in the afternoon was also very important.' For McGinley, who had not been selected for the morning fourballs, his halved match had been a minor triumph, a point noted by his friend and playing partner. 'Paul played some lovely golf,' said Harrington. 'He hit a lot of good shots when we really needed it, and that's exactly what you would have wanted from him. It was disappointing not to win, but the American boys finished well, and I certainly do not begrudge them the ½ point. They finished birdie, birdie, birdie when that was asked of them.'

Ian Woosnam promised he would be sinking a beer in relief that night, before planning how his dozen golfers could extend their first-day advantage. 'Anything can happen in golf, especially when it comes to the Ryder Cup.' He was, quite sensibly, remaining cautious. Europe had given America a sound first-day beating, but they only held a 2-point lead.

Tom Lehman, meanwhile, was his usual honest self as he assessed the day's play and Europe's early advantage. 'It was a fine line out there between 0 points, ½ a point and 1 point,' he summed up. 'It came down to the fact that they holed a couple more decisive putts than we did. They made them when they needed to, and we didn't. If I look at the positives, I will say that a lot of the guys played well.' Not all, though. Lehman must have been disappointed that his two big-gun pairings of Woods and Furyk and Mickelson and DiMarco only returned 1½ points out of 4. 'I know they are very disappointed they didn't win more points,' Lehman conceded. 'I'm sure tomorrow they'll be a lot more positive. We're going to go back to the team room now and decide that tomorrow won't be a repeat of today.'

Except, of course, it was. And by the end of Saturday's play, Europe were in touching distance of winning the Ryder Cup once again.

SEVEN

EUROPE PILE ON THE PRESSURE

THE TWO CAPTAINS ANNOUNCED THE MAKE-UP OF the Saturday morning fourballs on the Friday night. Lehman decided to stick with the Cink and Henry combination after they had fared so well the day before against Casey and Karlsson in the fourballs. They discovered that they were to face the same European pairing again on day two. Next up would be Mickelson and DiMarco, given the chance to make amends for their defeat by Clarke and Westwood. The bad news for them was that their opponents would be the confident Spanish duo of García and Olazábal. Fourballs match number three would see the Woods–Furyk partnership continuing. Against them, rather fittingly, would be Clarke and Westwood. It was Woods, of course, who played his part in persuading Clarke to make himself available for Ryder Cup selection. And the Northern Irishman had expressed a desire to face his good friend. His wish would come true on the Saturday morning, more evidence that the 2006 Ryder Cup was going to be special for Clarke. Scott Verplank would finally get an opportunity to play in the competition in the last fourball match-up of the day, partnering Zach Johnson. Against them would be a new pairing of Harrington and Stenson.

'It's pretty clear that we must have a good day today,' Tom Lehman pointed out before Saturday's action got under way. And that meant starting well. A couple of wins in the first two fourballs would even up the scores and perhaps even begin an American surge. But it was not to be on a morning when Europe continued to ease away.

In the first encounter, amid a rich contrast of sunshine and heavy showers, Casey and Karlsson experienced an almost identical match to the one they managed to halve the day before against the same opposition. Just as on the Friday morning, the Anglo–Swedish pairing grabbed a lead, which they held for fifteen holes, but were then powerless as rookie Henry shot an exquisite eagle at the 16th and then a birdie at the 17th to be standing on the 18th tee one ahead. And just like the day before, having seen a lead transformed into a deficit, Europe salvaged a ½ point at the death when Casey, showing the steely nerve that had won him the World Matchplay so comprehensively the week before, sank a two-putt birdie at the par 5 after Henry missed a chance to win the match. Tom Lehman reacted to that missed putt by falling dramatically to his knees. He knew how important the lost point might be.

Casey is as short as his partner is tall, which made their back-slapping celebrations look somewhat comical. It may have been just a ½ point gained, but Casey's putt was crucial and set the tone for the day. 'It was nice to have a putt like that,' a relieved Casey admitted afterwards. 'I thought Robert and I probably played better golf than we did yesterday. I also knew that snatching the full point away from the Americans at the last would really hurt them and mean a lot to our team. That was the goal down the last, and, fortunately, I had the opportunity to do that. I have three-putted that 18th green many times, and I knew that J.J. had a difficult two-putt. I had a tough putt coming back up the hill there, and I was happy to make it. It just shows how close matchplay is and how good our opponents were. We played them for two days running, and I thought they were tremendous competitors.' Karlsson appreciated having someone like Casey alongside him. 'It was great to have a partner like Paul on the last hole,' the Swede said. Cink, incidentally, became the first American player in Ryder Cup history to halve three consecutive matches. The only other player to achieve this feat was Spain's Ignacio Garrido in 1997.

Karlsson was quite clearly enjoying his first Ryder Cup experience, especially in the European team environment. 'The atmosphere is just great,' he said. 'García is talking a lot and entertaining us all. He's like a big heap of energy swirling around the room. Darren and Colin and Padraig have all helped me in preparing for the atmosphere out on the course. Pretty much everyone has done their part in supporting me as a rookie. As for the crowd, well, it's unbelievable. I had tears in my eyes when I arrived at the first tee yesterday. It was a great reception from the crowd, and the course is fantastic.'

J.J. Henry was another golfer with a broad smile on his face. The rookie had more than earned his spurs after playing well on the Friday and again in the Saturday fourballs, especially with his late surge, which almost gave his pair a win. 'As well as I played yesterday, I was really excited to come out today and hopefully continue,' he said. 'I struggled for most of the round but really dug deep on the 16th to square the match and then hit two or three pretty good shots after that. We battled against Robert and Paul for two straight days and had two great matches. It was up and down all the time. We'd go down early, make a comeback, take a lead, then see it end up all square. It was neat to be a part of it all. We didn't win, unfortunately, but we didn't lose, either.'

The illustrious pairing of Mickelson and DiMarco, despite their standing in world golf, never stood a chance in the second match. Like Toms and Wetterich the day before, the Americans were caught in bright Spanish headlights and succumbed to Messrs García and Olazábal by the same score line in defeat, three and two. The game was long gone by the time the two pairs made it to the 16th, but if the Americans still harboured vain hopes of a comeback, what happened next just about summed up their morning. A stupendous and audacious second shot played from trampled ground landed in a greenside bunker and was the highlight of another full round of highlights from the more junior of the two Spaniards. His follow-up recovery, to just 18 inches from the hole, secured the victory. For Olazábal, the win was a little piece of history. By securing another point with García, he had moved to 10½ fourball points in his cup career, equalling the record held by his captain. He won 5½ of these with Ballesteros, 2 with García, 1½ with Miguel Angel Jiménez, 1 with Costantino Rocca and a ½ point with Ignacio Garrido.

This time it was García's turn to praise his more senior partner. 'José played amazing today,' he said. 'I don't think he missed a single fairway. He was awesome.'

Olazábal, as one of the older members of the European team, was rested for the afternoon foursomes, allowing him more time to prepare for the next day's singles. He was, nevertheless, very pleased with his morning's work and was happy, once again, to have shared his round with García. 'Sergio drove the ball long and straight,' Olazábal said. 'Whenever you play with a guy like that, it makes you so relaxed. When you know you're playing with a guy who's not missing a shot, you're pretty much watching the scenario from the best seat in the house. I knew I could count on him at pretty much every hole.' Olazábal was asked what kind of an influence García had on the older guys in the team. 'Well, he's young,' replied the Spaniard, with an affectionate smile. 'He has a young spirit, and he's full of energy. He loves this event because of the whole atmosphere, the crowds and the team element. You know, myself, Darren, Monty, we've been through that period of our lives. The energy levels are not quite as high as they used to be. It's always good to have young guys like Sergio and Luke and Paul [Casey] in the team. Maybe Sergio, because he comes from the south of Europe, expresses his emotions a little bit more, but they're all keeping me young. This morning it was great in an event like this to shut down the big guns on your opponent's team. But there's a lot of golf still to be played. As long as we keep our heads, it should be great news for us.'

Next up came the match of the day, although, in truth, it never really turned out to be competitive. While Woods remained strangely out of sorts, the force remained with Clarke. Ironically, after the Northern Irishman had received the nod from his captain that he would be a wild-card selection for the European team, one of the first text messages he received had come from Woods. 'Congratulations,' it read. 'I look forward to seeing you at The K Club.' Clarke, despite his recent trauma, still possessed the good humour to reply, 'You won't be saying that when I kick your butt.' On the Saturday morning, this is exactly what Clarke and Westwood did to Woods and Furyk, thumping the Americans three and two. In doing so, they beat Woods for the third time and gained their sixth Ryder Cup point together, lifting the pair into joint second place in Europe's all-time most-successful partnerships alongside Nick Faldo and Ian Woosnam.

The match had begun in a joyous, playful mood. When the European pair were called to the tee, Westwood gave his emotional partner a pat and declared, 'This is it.' They set off together, cheered all the way to the first tee. Behind the players, Billy Foster, Clarke's caddie, called over to Steve Williams, Woods' famous bag man. Laughing, Foster handed the New Zealander Williams his blue European bib and accepted Williams' red American one in exchange. Both hung their respective bibs around their necks and picked up each other's bags as they made their way to the tee. The sight of Williams carrying Clarke's bag and Foster in charge of Woods' bag provoked some early merriment to ease the obvious tension. The fun for Woods did not last long, though.

Clarke had declared a wish to play Woods because he had wanted the challenge of facing the best golfer in the world, as well as a friend who had been there for him during the previous few months. By early afternoon, he had another reason, and it turned out to be a very good one for Europe. To say that Woods displayed more poor form was to understate just how ragged his golf was in the 2006 competition, at least in the pairings. On the Friday, his hapless partner Furyk had spent much of the day carrying Woods. Twenty-four hours later and the second fourball match that Woods played in almost became a threeball. The man with five straight tournament wins to his name during the summer, including the Open and the US PGA, endured one of his most humiliating experiences ever on a golf course.

Woods had a nightmare at almost every hole. Hole one: Woods

overshot the green, and a Furyk putt saved the day with a half. Hole four: Woods sent his iron shot into the rough by the edge of the green, then duffed his chip shot. Hole five: a miscued Woods drive into the rough on the right prompted him to stand motionless on the tee for 20 seconds, staring down the fairway, before he performed a dozen practice swings. By the time he left the tee, shaking his head, his expression was as leaden as the skies above, and the other three golfers were 100 yards down the fairway. Hole seven: Tiger found the rough and then struck his approach shot over and beyond the green. Hole nine: he drove into the rough on the left-hand side and then proceeded to miss a five-foot putt, causing his shoulders to slump. 'You'd better get your clubs out, Michael,' shouted a wag from the crowd as Michael Jordan, a talented amateur golfer, passed by, a huge unlit cigar protruding from his mouth. Hole 12: Woods missed a seven-foot putt that would have won the hole. Hole 15: Woods drove straight into the water. In the 16 holes it took Clarke and Westwood to put the supposedly better Americans out of their misery, Woods failed to score a single birdie. Over the same distance, Clarke landed four, Furyk three and Westwood two.

Clarke, who was still receiving the kind of applause normally reserved for the Open champion designate walking towards the 18th green, and Westwood capitalised on Woods' poor play to the full. Two-up after the 5th, they increased their lead to three holes at the 11th, after Clarke's five-foot putt for birdie, and four holes thanks to Westwood's birdie at the par-3 14th.

The American pair rallied to win the 15th, after Furyk, still playing better than his high-profile partner, birdied. And they looked destined to win the 16th and reduce the European lead to two with two to play after Furyk birdied again. But Clarke, fittingly, chipped in from the green-side rough, some 20 feet from the pin, to wrap matters up and further endorse his wild-card selection. He jumped for joy and exchanged high-fives with Westwood, before Woods, not for the first or last time at The K Club, hugged him at length. Michael Jordan then joined Woods on the back of a golf buggy as they were transported back to the clubhouse for a quick spot of lunch and a change of clothing in time for the commencement of the afternoon foursomes. Woods' Ryder Cup record now stood at 9 out of a possible 24 points.

'I felt for Tiger,' Clarke admitted afterwards. 'He's such a good friend of mine, but he had an off day. I wanted him to play well, to play at his best, because you want to beat the best when they are playing good golf, but he found it tough out there. It happens to us all. I think, because Tiger's standards are so high, that a lot is always expected from him. It's then highlighted more whenever he doesn't achieve the standards we all know he's capable of. Both he and Jim didn't make it happen on the greens.'

Clarke then found out that he was to sit out the afternoon foursomes, which was fine by him. 'I've played five times before in a Ryder Cup, and it can be very, very draining. This year, because of the strength in depth of the team, Woosie has been able to rest some players, and hopefully we'll reap the benefits of that tomorrow. Besides, it's pouring down with rain out there right now. I'd rather have a nice lunch and sit here than try and make four-footers all afternoon.'

Jim Furyk was honest enough to give his verdict on why the Ryder Cup was beginning to drift away from the American team yet again. 'We look constipated,' he said. 'That's how our guys look, and I'm sure when they look at me, they see the same thing. Every two years, when the time comes, whether we're at home or in Europe, it's like we're all constipated. We just get too tight. Any other week, and that includes the Presidents Cup, we have more fun. Guys are on the range talking, joking, loose. But when it's Ryder Cup, everybody's mood seems to change. It's like we're going to work instead of going to the golf course. I don't know if that's why we haven't done better. It's got to be part of the reason.'

After Woods' performance on the Saturday morning, Tom Lehman was asked if he would contemplate the impossible and drop his star player for the afternoon foursomes. 'I don't know how you can bench the best player in the world,' Lehman answered. 'That's just impossible. Tiger is Tiger. He's the best golfer I've ever played with or against. You can't keep him down. Our team draw so much confidence from him. There's not a person in our team who doesn't look at Tiger and feel better because he's there.'

Clarke was pleased to have proved, yet again, how right his captain was to have picked him and Westwood as the team's two wild-card players. 'People said we were a gamble, but the people who were most sure we weren't were the two of us,' he said. 'We know each other's games so well, and we enjoy each other's company so much.'

Westwood, who had spent Friday and Saturday shaking his head in wonder at how Clarke was continually able to defy his emotions, summed up the reason why his friend and partner had wrapped it up at the 16th. 'He's one for the drama, though, isn't he?' he said, laughing. 'It's like a big stage to him.'

America at last found something to be cheerful about in the final fourball match of the morning. Verplank and Johnson's two-and-one victory over Harrington and Stenson kept their team in the competition. Defeat would have given Europe an almost unassailable 5-point lead after just three sessions. The star of the show turned out to be Johnson, who hit seven birdies in total during the round. His best, and most important, was his sixth at the 15th when he responded to Harrington having chipped in by sinking a 20-foot putt to maintain the status quo. Mind you, his 15-foot chip-in at the 17th to win the match was pretty special too. Johnson had shown the older and supposedly better players in the American team how to play in the Ryder Cup, just as Henry had done in his two fourball encounters.

'He played absolutely fantastic all day long,' admitted a magnanimous Stenson. 'We tried everything we could. We went close at 13 and 14, then Padraig chipped in at 15. Then Zach rolled his birdie putt in from 20 feet, and he chipped in on 17. It was disappointing losing our game, but sometimes you can only take your hat off and say, "Well done."'

Verplank was also full of admiration for the rookie. 'I didn't play very well until the last couple of holes,' he admitted. 'Then I started hitting better shots to try and help Zach out and make sure we would win the match. Zach didn't need much help, though. He was all-world. He woke me up last night and said, "Dude, we're playing." He told me all the ground rules, and I just said, "Hey, whatever you want to do." It was important to him that he hit first. We laughed out there and had some fun. We smiled and told jokes. We were pumping each other up and encouraging each other. There was a lot of positive energy flying around between us. It didn't get any better than being on that first tee and listening to the raucous cheers when the European pair, especially Padraig, made their entrance. Zach had a twinkle in his eye, and so did I. There's nothing like going to someone's house and giving them a fight.'

The rookie was keen not to take all the glory. 'It was a team effort, regardless of what anyone says,' he insisted. 'At the 17th, the captain said, "You know what, they have chipped in some, now it's your turn." So I did.'

Ironically, Lehman had planned to play Verplank in the afternoon foursomes but decided to replace him with Johnson after seeing his rookie fare so well in the morning. Verplank was honest enough to admit his disappointment at the decision. 'I sat out all day yesterday, and I scored 1 point today with the only chance I got,' he responded. 'Tom came up to us at the 13th and told Zach he would be playing again after lunch. And I said, "Well, am I playing this afternoon?" He said no. Then I said, "We're going to win this match. I'd like to play." I would be lying to you if I said I wasn't disappointed and didn't feel like I should have another chance. But I'll get one tomorrow in the singles, and hopefully the guys this afternoon can turn it around and we'll still have a chance of winning this cup. That's what we're all here for.'

Johnson received more plaudits from Chris DiMarco, who was eating his lunch with the rest of the team, hoping that the last fourball match would swing America's way. 'To have something to cheer about over lunch was great,' the New Yorker admitted. 'Zach has motivated the whole team. I know Tiger and Jim were both watching that, and it has motivated them to go out and play well this afternoon. Zach is a phenomenal putter and a tremendous competitor. He got off to a great start. When he came back to the clubhouse, I told him, "You did it. You were awesome. We needed you. You're the man. Eat some lunch and then go out this afternoon and do it again." I thought J.J. played great too. Our rookies are doing us proud.'

In typical fashion, DiMarco remained upbeat about his team's chances. 'We're just four good matches away from taking a 1-point lead into tomorrow,' he said. 'Anything can happen. They are playing good, but we just need to show some red on the scoreboard and get some motivation. I'll admit, it's tough when you look at the scoreboard and you see all those blue numbers. Yesterday afternoon, for example, there were only six or seven red numbers out of seventy-two holes. So, when you're not getting the numbers up on the board, it's hard to get the momentum going. When you are putting the numbers up, as Europe have been doing, it's easy to show emotion. Believe me, there were four or five times yesterday when I thought that I had made a putt. I was about to go ballistic, and then it lipped out and took all the wind out of my sails.'

Despite defeat in the final fourballs match of the morning, Ian Woosnam was more than happy to have edged a further point ahead of America to lead 7½–4½. 'That was another great morning's work,' he announced. 'It remains the case that I don't want to get too far ahead of myself, so we'll have to take it shot by shot this afternoon and see how the foursomes go, but the team spirit is brilliant, and it's going well.

'Paul and Robert really enjoyed going out there first this morning. Who wouldn't with that reception on the first tee? They had a great match with Stewart and J.J., just like yesterday. They were ahead early on again and played good, solid golf, but Stewart and J.J. came back at them. Paul's putt at the last was fantastic.

'I'm told that José Maria has joined me with 10½ fourball points, the most in Ryder Cup history by any individual on either team. At least I haven't lost my record yet. When you have two guys like José Maria and Sergio, who are absolutely brimming with confidence and spirit, you know they only have winning on their minds. You could see how much they enjoyed it out there, despite all the rain, and you can't ask for more than 2 points out of two fourball matches. Phil and Chris didn't do much wrong. In fact, they played great. They just were unfortunate to meet the Spanish duo out there.'

There was more. 'What can you say about Darren and Lee together?' Woosnam asked the assembled media. 'They are writing their own place in Ryder Cup history. That's six wins as a partnership in the fourballs and the foursomes. All four guys in this match played great golf, and Tiger and Jim contributed so much to a very special encounter.

'Finally, Henrik and Padraig swapped birdies with Scott and Zach right from the start, and, I'll tell you, there was great golf from those four guys in weather conditions that were very, very difficult. It could have gone either way.'

Woosnam's American counterpart was grateful for the first and last fourball results but knew his job was getting tougher. 'I'm really proud of the way Stewart and J.J. played this morning, while the last match was phenomenal,' he said. 'Zach Johnson was just out of this world. Boy, he just did everything he had to do. The Europeans played great, but the last game was perfect. Our team really needed that result.'

He remained upbeat about his team's chances, as all good captains should, but admitted his players needed to start holing their putts in order to produce a comeback before it was too late. 'I know we're now down by three, but there's still a lot of golf left to be played,' he insisted. 'We need a committed effort this afternoon, and we need good things to happen. You never can tell. Sport is funny like that. Things can shift and change, and before you know it, the match has a whole new complexion. I didn't need to inspire any of my players for this afternoon. They already know what has to be done.'

The afternoon foursomes were even more memorable than what had gone before, not least because they produced a hole in one to win a match. At the end of the session, it was business as usual for

Europe, the team winning the foursomes and extending their lead even further to hand themselves a golden opportunity to win the Ryder Cup.

García and Donald were first up. They faced another heavyweight American pairing in Phil Mickelson, who was enduring another nightmarish Ryder Cup, and David Toms, who was unfortunate enough to have already met García in the first morning's fourballs. Once again, the result was never really in doubt. With García's irons and Donald's impressive putting skills, the Americans did well to cling on for as long as they did. At one stage, after a couple of long putts from Toms, they even drew level, but not for long. While García and Donald played textbook foursomes, Mickelson and Toms were playing catch-up golf. It probably did not help Toms when his drive at the 11th ended up hitting a woman spectator on the head, drawing blood and resulting in an ambulance trip to the hospital. She was fine but missed out on the pièce de résistance. Toms went on to drive into the water at the 15th, and the 16th hole just about summed it up for the desperate Americans, as they watched the smiling, joshing European youngsters make a par-4 from an impossible position. García was facing a truly horrible lie and an intimidating carry over the River Liffey but somehow managed to send his team's ball, together with large clumps of dirt, to within about 20 feet of the pin. It was a magnificent shot under the circumstances, but there was still plenty of work to be done. It was no trouble to the Englishman, though. Donald stepped up and sank the putt, celebrating by dropping to his knees. 'It always looked like a four,' announced Donald later, his tongue firmly in his cheek.

Donald had not stopped smiling ever since he and García had been serenaded to the 16th green by 10,000 Irish fans singing '¡Olé!, ¡olé!, ¡olé!, ¡olé!' in true football style. The noise had then gone off the Richter scale when Donald had sunk his 20-footer. 'What an arena to sink a putt in,' Donald exclaimed. 'The roar at the 16th was probably the loudest I have ever heard in my life.'

The records kept on tumbling for García. He had joined Woosnam (again) as the only European player under the present format to have won both fourball and foursome matches at the same Ryder Cup. García had also matched the record of his fourballs partner Olazábal for most consecutive unbeaten Ryder Cup matches by a European. Adding his four 2006 wins to the five unbeaten matches he had secured at Oakland Hills in 2004, García was now undefeated in nine matches in a row. He had also won all eight of his foursome matches in the Ryder Cup. He and Donald had created yet more European Ryder Cup history by winning four consecutive foursome matches together.

The Europeans sent out two more of their big guns next. After halving their game against Mickelson and DiMarco the day before, Montgomerie and Westwood were asked to try again in the Saturday foursomes, this time against Chad Campbell and rookie Vaughn Taylor, who had been selected to contribute to the American cause at long last. It must have been hard for Taylor to enter the fray having not played for a day and a half, but he coped well with the noise and the pressure as he and Campbell took the game to the opposition. With the match all square going down the last, the Europeans found themselves in a difficult position after Taylor hit the Americans' second shot onto the front of the green. Montgomerie, who had sunk the pressure putt to halve his foursomes match on Friday, again rose to the challenge, this time directing a 250-yard second shot to within 20 feet of the 18th hole, even though the water was a real threat. To play such a shot at any time is impressive; to achieve it when he knew he had to epitomised Colin Montgomerie's efforts when it comes to the Ryder Cup. Westwood then finished the job off. The ½ point gained by Montgomerie saw him move alongside Seve Ballesteros into third place in the all-time list of Ryder Cup points won, with 22½, while Westwood's tally was now 14½.

Vaughn Taylor was just relieved to have finally played. 'It was good to get out there at last and experience playing in a Ryder Cup,' said the rookie. 'It was great to score a ½ point, and I definitely feel better now for tomorrow's singles. I sat out the longest in the team because I was a little bit rusty, but Tom asked if I was ready last night, and I told him I was.'

The third foursomes match saw Paul Casey paired with fellow Englishman David Howell to face two of the better Americans, based on the evidence of their 2006 Ryder Cup form so far. The names of wild card Stewart Cink and rookie Zach Johnson had not come to prominence before the start of the tournament, especially in a team that included such players as Woods, Mickelson and Furyk, but Cink had halved all three matches to date, while Johnson had scored 1½ points out of 2. Both Casey and Howell had come up against Cink already, although with different partners. This time there would be no halves. The English pairing ran away with it, as was to be expected from two of the world's top players. By the time they had reached the 14th, they were standing at five holes to the good. If they could avoid losing the hole, the match was won.

Casey came up with the best way imaginable to avoid defeat at the par 3. The day before, Ian Woosnam had instructed Robert Karlsson to use a longer iron at the 7th, the end result seeing the ball land on a TV platform. This time the little Welshman told Casey that everyone had been using a three-iron at the 14th. Casey thought otherwise. Taking a four-iron from his bag, he sent the perfect drive airborne and watched as the ball landed ten feet in front but in line with the hole and trickled towards its final destination. If it had been asked to travel an inch further, the ball would not have made it. As it was, it staggered over the lip of the cup, having travelled exactly 213 yards, to record a hole in one. The roar from the gallery was such that it would not be surprising if it was heard in Dublin, some 17 miles away. And if Darren Clarke's emotional drive was the shot of Friday's play, all bets were off following Casey's ace for Saturday's number-one spot.

A stunned Casey threw his four-iron high and away into the air, stuck both arms out and shouted in acclaim as first his caddie and then partner Howell rushed over to give him high-fives. It was left to Casey's caddie Craig Connelly to make the exultant walk to the green to retrieve his employer's ball from the cup. Even this piece of action was welcomed with a massive cheer.

Casey's was the fifth ace in Ryder Cup history. Peter Butler scored the first at the 16th at Muirfield in 1973. Nick Faldo followed suit at the 14th at The Belfry in 1993 in a tied match against Paul Azinger. Costantino Rocca came next at Oak Hill in 1995, when he aced at the 6th en route to beating Davis Love III and Jeff Maggert; the Italian was partnered by Sam Torrance that day. And the last player to achieve a hole in one prior to Casey was Howard Clark, who scored his at the 11th at Oak Hill in 1995 on his way to beating Peter Jacobsen in the singles.

Although four Europeans had achieved such a feat before, this was the first time a hole in one had closed out a match. Cink grinned at his opponent, shrugged his shoulders as if to say, 'Well, we can't do anything about that,' and accepted the gracious half conceded by Casey and Howell. By doing so, the Americans also scored a 'one' at the 14th, without ever having to drive a ball.

The European pairing would have won the match without Casey's remarkable shot. In that sense, his ace made little difference, and, in fact, it would have been better used that morning when he and Karlsson could only halve their fourball match with Cink and Henry. But the symbolism of the event meant a great deal. Whatever America tried did not seem to be working; whatever Europe attempted was a success, and now they were knocking the ball in from the tee. Was there no stopping the men who were fittingly decked out in blue?

It had not been a bad couple of weeks for Casey. After having picked up a cool £1 million cheque and the title of World Matchplay champion six days earlier, he had now just scored an ace in the Ryder Cup in front of the most appreciative crowd in the world. And after three games, he remained unbeaten in the 2006 Ryder Cup. No wonder he shook his head in sheer wonderment for many a minute after winning the match.

'Woosie told me the guys in front had used a three-iron,' Casey revealed afterwards. 'So I picked a different club. It was a four-iron.

I hit it very, very hard, and it only just made it. It's fair to say, that was nice. I knew it was pretty close, but when the crowd reacted at the back of the green it was a bizarre moment. Actually, it was really surreal to be shaking hands and saying thanks very much on a tee, as opposed to on a green. But it was a fantastic moment, too. That's my first hole in one in an international tournament. It was just one of those days.' His happy partner concurred. 'It was a wonderful moment,' said David Howell. 'Paul will go down in history as the first person to win a [Ryder Cup] match with a hole in one. I rather enjoyed watching him do it.'

It was always going to be difficult to follow that up, and so it proved for the all-Irish pairing of Paul McGinley and the strangely off-colour Padraig Harrington. It hardly helped, either, that they were up against Furyk and Woods, with the latter hell-bent on making amends for his poor morning display. Woods played much better this time round, while Furyk's putting improved as well, as exemplified by a 40-footer on the 15th to go three-up with three to play. The Irish couple did well to hang in for as long as they did, but the pressure was too much, and they fell by a score of three and two. 'We were disappointed to lose, but the bottom line was that we were playing the number one and the number three in the world out there,' McGinley explained. 'Both were on their game this afternoon, and when it's like that you're going to have a tough day. We battled well, but we were up against a pretty formidable combination.' No matter, McGinley had still enjoyed an experience he had dreamt of all his life, and he recalled some advice Jesper Parnevik had given to him before the Irishman made his Ryder Cup debut in 2002 at The Belfry. 'There are two ways of dealing with adrenalin,' he said, explaining how he was able to play with the knowledge that the whole of Ireland was behind him. 'You can go with the emotion and ride it. Or you can try and keep yourself very calm and collected. It's whatever you choose, and Padraig and I fed off the crowd. You've got to go with it. You ride the emotion but try and keep yourself calm and collected at the same time. We had wonderful support from the Irish people. It was just fantastic.

What a thrill to be able to play in front of your home supporters and have them that passionate.'

The foursomes ended with Europe winning by a margin of 2½–1½ for the fourth session in a row. It was the first time in the history of the Ryder Cup that America had lost all four sessions and the first time that every one had been won by the same score line. Taken individually, each session had given Europe a slender lead; with the four added together, that slender lead became a gaping chasm. Just as on the Saturday morning, a final win for the Americans had turned a desperate situation into a merely worrying one and gave them a sliver of hope for the following day's singles. Defeat would have given Europe a 6-point lead, needing just 3 out of the 12 available on the final day. Even a halved match would have put Europe an unassailable 5 points ahead. But America finished off the Saturday proceedings striking the final blow. They were 4 points in arrears, and the situation looked bleak, but they were still, just about, in the Ryder Cup.

'Our team does not feel that this is over,' warned Tom Lehman that night, as he surveyed the wreckage of the first two days and put on a brave face in readiness for the final day's singles, in which America would be asked to win 8½ out of a possible 12 points on offer. 'We know that we have to play our very best golf, but we feel that we can do that.'

At Brookline in 1999, America had entered the final day 10–6 down, and although the invading antics on the 17th green at the Leonard versus Olazábal match might have dominated the news that day, the fact remained that the American team, under the influential leadership of Ben Crenshaw, produced one of the greatest sporting comebacks of all time. Lehman was hoping for a repeat performance. 'It's a similar situation to seven years ago. Everyone had to look inside in 1999. Everybody had a responsibility to win. There was no margin of error. What made '99 so special, what made it so possible, was that the first six matches all got going so well, so early. We'll be looking to do the same again. I felt my team played with a great deal of heart out there today. They hit a lot of great shots but obviously didn't get the result we wanted. I tip my hat to Europe. They've played a remarkable short game. But we're not out of it yet.'

Lehman's number-one player agreed. 'It's a tough situation,' admitted Tiger Woods. 'We're down not just overall but in each match after five or six holes. It's imperative we get off to a quick start in the morning, just like we did in '99. The Europeans are playing great. They're not going to give it to us. We've got to go out there and beat them.' Colin Montgomerie had his own plans, though. 'We want to go out and win all five sessions for the first time ever,' he said. 'We've never done it before, and we have a golden opportunity to do so tomorrow. It's not about trying to get the 4½ [points] needed to win the Ryder Cup. It's about approaching tomorrow as a fresh new day, with each of us trying to focus on winning our singles match. If we do that, the scoreboard will take care of itself.'

Ian Woosnam was still in a cautious mood on the eve of the final day's play and what could prove to be his greatest moment in golf. 'We've worked hard together,' he said. 'We've put some good pairings up. But let's not get too excited too quickly. You know how strong the Americans are in singles.' Even the European captain, though, was prepared to make one concession when pressed. 'In strength and depth, this is the strongest team we've ever had,' he admitted. 'We came here as a team, we've played here as a team and tomorrow we intend to do more of the same.'

When Woosnam and his counterpart revealed their 12 singles choices, they made for interesting reading. Woosnam faced a no-brainer to start with. It had become almost a Ryder Cup certainty that Colin Montgomerie would start off the Sunday's proceedings. At 10–6 up, the last thing Europe wanted was America to get an early start and gain momentum. Monty was there to make sure that didn't happen, just as he had been in 2002. Two years later, he had started his singles midway down the order of play, which had given him the chance to sink the winning putt. His opponent that day at Oakland Hills was David Toms. It would be Toms again at The K Club.

Next up was García, who had played second in the singles in 2004, when he had beaten Mickelson, and in 2002, when he had lost to Toms. The young Spaniard was in a position to score a maximum 5 points out of 5. His opponent was to be Cink, a wild card but one of the American team's better performers in Ireland.

Third on the European singles list was the man of the moment Paul Casey, who faced stiff opposition from Jim Furyk. The American had barely broken into a smile all week. He was a tough competitor, and he was evidently not enjoying being part of a losing team. The World Matchplay champion would need to continue to be at his best if he was going to prevail against the world number three.

The good news for Robert Karlsson was that he would not have to wait too long in the clubhouse, the Swede having been picked for match number four. The bad news was that his opponent was Tiger Woods. The world number one had shown better form on the Saturday afternoon and, despite playing poorly by his standards, was the joint-top scorer on the American team with 2 points. Someone was going to have to pay for his rather average stay at The K Club, and that someone appeared to be Karlsson. Still, if the Swede needed any encouragement, he only had to look back to the World Matchplay at Wentworth the week before when he had made it to the semi-finals. Woods had been unceremoniously dumped out in the first round.

Match number five paired Luke Donald with Chad Campbell. Campbell had fared reasonably well so far, but in Donald he faced a young opponent playing his best golf, and one who was slightly aggrieved to have played only twice on the first two days. Like a good team player, Donald had made no issue of it, but he was evidently keen to make a further statement of intent on the final day.

Tom Lehman then decided to bury his four rookies in the middle of the pack. Next up came J.J. Henry in the sixth match. His opponent was Paul McGinley. The Irishman had played better than his form coming into the event would have suggested, and with a large home crowd behind him, he was expected to give his opponent a hard time. But Henry had impressed everyone on his Ryder Cup debut. A close match was expected.

Darren Clarke was selected to follow his friend from south of the Irish border in the seventh match. It was a fitting decision: Clarke would follow his great mate and, looking at the make-up of the six previous singles matches, have a chance of securing the point needed to win the Ryder Cup. It would almost be asking too much for that to come true in Ireland, at The K Club and in front of so many thousands of his fellow countrymen after the most tragic and traumatic few weeks of his life, but the possibility was there. Zach Johnson, who had fared so well in the morning fourballs on Friday, was to be Clarke's opponent, and he would find it tough to beat not just one of the most competitive golfers in the world but a man with so many people rooting for him.

Henrik Stenson was picked to play eighth in the singles and faced a battle with another rookie. Vaughn Taylor, despite his belated invitation to come out and play in the Ryder Cup during the Saturday afternoon's foursomes, had shown remarkable character to help secure a ½ point. He would need to show more against the Swede, who would be determined to end his first Ryder Cup on a high.

Likewise David Howell, who had featured in just two out of a possible four matches in two days but had done little wrong in securing 1½ points out of 2, partnering first Stenson and then Casey. He had lost to Jim Furyk in his debut singles match at Oakland Hills two years before. He did not want a repeat result this time round, especially against rookie Brett Wetterich, who had not been picked since playing in the Friday morning fourballs alongside David Toms.

Ian Woosnam must have been hoping that he would not require singles matches ten, eleven and twelve to deliver crucial victories in the search for the 4 points needed to retain the trophy and 4½ points to win it outright, but if this was to be the case, he could rely on three global heavyweights in José Maria Olazábal, Lee Westwood and Padraig Harrington. The Spaniard was matched up against Mickelson, who had once again failed to live up to his star billing, securing just a ½ point out of a possible 4. Olazábal would not have been fazed by the threat from the left-hander, either. On the Saturday morning, he and García had dismissed Mickelson and DiMarco with ease in the fourballs.

Chris DiMarco was another big name who had left his form behind at home. He, too, had won only a ½ point and was not even selected to play in the Saturday afternoon foursomes. The man with the biggest heart and deepest wounds in the American team had one final chance to salvage something from this Ryder Cup, but standing in his way was Westwood, who had already defeated DiMarco and Mickelson in the first morning's fourballs, playing alongside Clarke, and who was once more showing some of his best form.

Finally, Padraig Harrington brought up the European rearguard in a singles encounter against American wild card Scott Verplank, who no doubt wanted to prove his captain Lehman wrong for having dropped him from the Saturday afternoon's foursomes. It was a clever move by Woosnam. If the destiny of the 2006 Ryder Cup was to come down to the 12th and final singles match, Verplank would not just have to beat Harrington, but approximately 50,000 screaming Irish fans as well. The man who was born just a few miles up the road in Dublin would have the weight of a whole nation behind him. It would make for a sensational finale but one that Woosnam was not expecting to face.

His American counterpart had other ideas. 'We have a chance to carry momentum all the way through the line-up, and then with the last few guys, we have a chance to close it out if we get the chance,' explained Lehman. 'I've tried to get the right order here, where some of our best guys can get us going, and then the other guys can feed off that.

'Do I have a feeling about tomorrow? I have a feeling that our team is going to play incredibly inspired golf. No matter who they are playing against, they are going to lay it on the line and give it all they've got. They are going to make our team proud, they are going to make their wives proud and they are going to make their country proud.'

Ian Woosnam was not prepared to claim victory just yet. 'It could still go wrong,' he warned. 'I'll be talking to my players about this. We've got to take every day individually. Some of my players were there in 1999. We're not intending to make that same mistake again. Tomorrow is another day. I will say that I'm very pleased with the draw. But my players still have to go out and finish the job.'

The Welshman did allow himself a moment to think about realising his dream of Ryder Cup victory. 'You know, I've won a major tournament. I've won many tournaments around the world. I think this, though, will be the most satisfactory thing I've ever done in my life if we pull it off. It's all right playing for yourself, because there's only one person to let down. When you're looking after 12 guys, it's a different thing altogether. I'll probably retire after this. I think I'll need a year to recover.'

With McGinley and Clarke at six and seven in the singles, had Woosnam considered that fate might lend a hand? 'I've never believed in fate,' he said. 'I believe in how you play and in the guys' talent, and I'm sure that talent is going to show itself tomorrow and get us those 14½ points we need. Can Darren win it for us? I honestly hadn't thought about it. At the end of the day, all I want us to do is reach that magic winning number.'

Others in the team, though, had thought about it. Colin Montgomerie, the team's talismanic on-course leader, had not been the closest player to Clarke over the years, but he had been through the emotional mangle himself back in 2004, following his high-profile divorce and slump in form. He recognised what the Northern Irishman had already achieved by playing so well in the first two days of the 2006 Ryder Cup. Now he wanted one final wish to come true. 'Darren Clarke's won two out of two so far,' announced the Scot. 'Let's hope to hell that he can make it three out of three tomorrow and finish off what's been a fantastic tournament for him.'

The whole of Europe, and especially the whole of Ireland, was holding its collective breath.

EIGHT

EUROPE IN DREAMLAND

THE WHOLE OF IRELAND WOKE UP ON THE SUNDAY morning full of anxiety and expectation. However, it had poured down all night long, and there was a concern that the start of the deciding day's play might be postponed. Luckily, the sheets of rain turned into a light drizzle and, as morning turned into afternoon and then a glorious dusk, ultimately sunshine. A rainbow even made a welcome appearance late on. It was one of those days.

On the Friday, Europe had worn bright Irish-green jerseys. On the Saturday, they turned to European light blue. On the final day, their captain had the final say. Ian Woosnam, a proud Welshman, decided his team should wear the red of the Principality. When Colin Montgomerie, a Scot for one hundred and three weeks of every two years but a European for one week during every Ryder Cup, made what appeared to be a victory walk from the practice area to the first tee, he was breathing the fire of a Welsh dragon. His task against American David Toms was very clear. Start the European ball rolling, get some momentum going and unlock the door for the rest of his teammates to burst through. Somehow, everyone knew that things would turn out just fine.

If only Monty could play like he does at the Ryder Cup at any of the sport's majors, he would not still be searching for that one elusive major title, and he probably would have bagged a whole lot more as well. Like Sergio García, Montgomerie comes alive at the Ryder Cup, especially when asked to lead off in the singles. It was a huge responsibility, despite Europe's seemingly unassailable lead, and he was just the man to take it on his shoulders.

The night before, his indomitable spirit had shone through. When asked if he was concerned that the 10–6 lead going into the final day was the same as the one Europe had blown at Brookline in 1999, Montgomerie was quick to make a forthright point. 'It wasn't 10–6 then, it was 10–9,' he insisted. He went on to say that there was little chance of a European victory in three of that year's singles matches, because under the captaincy of Mark James, Jean Van de Velde, Andrew Coltart and Jarmo Sandelin had not played on either of the first two days. 'This time it's very different,' he added.

And so it was. He received the loudest roar of his life when his name was announced to the spectators in the first-tee grandstand. He and Toms halved the first two holes, before Montgomerie went one-up at the short 3rd after hitting to within four feet to set up a birdie-two. He led for the rest of the match. Toms bogeyed the par-5 4th, while the Scot struck from the rough to within four feet again to score another birdie and take a two-hole lead. Toms hit back at the 5th to reduce the arrears. He then had to shake his head and smile at an outrageous slice of fortune for his opponent at the 11th. Montgomerie drove into the bunker on the outer corner of the dogleg of the par 4. It left him with 150 yards to the hole. His second shot seemed to be heading straight for the water, but it hit the large stones which support the green above the lake. Even then, the ball looked odds-on to rebound into the water. Instead, it inexplicably bounced high into the air, landed on the edge of the green and spun to within 12 feet of the pin. Montgomerie went on to make his par when moments before Toms had looked certain to draw the match level. Then Montgomerie, playing good golf considering it was such an intense atmosphere, hit to eight feet at the par-3 14th to set up his third birdie of the day and go two-up. To his credit, the man from Louisiana fought all the way, and his birdie at the 17th meant he was just one hole down at the 18th. With the match in the balance, Montgomerie drove into one of the final hole's greenside bunkers. Toms, meanwhile, was on the par-5 green in two. It meant that the Scot had to get up and down to secure the full point. From the sand, he faced the full width of the green and a pin cut close to the back of the putting surface next to the lake. To have to contemplate that shot at such a crucial stage of the match, knowing that a European win would prevent the American plan of dominating the top half of the singles' scoreboard, would have tested the strongest of minds. But Montgomerie, an old hand in these situations, chipped to within eight feet of the pin. With his opponent just four feet from the hole, Montgomerie sunk his putt to halve the hole and win the match.

This time there was no repeat of the emotional scenes at Oakland Hills when Monty, having just sunk a putt to win the Ryder Cup, fell into captain Bernhard Langer's arms. Instead, a smiling Montgomerie blew his cheeks out in relief after winning an incredible sixth Ryder Cup singles match, shook hands warmly with a gracious Toms and hurried to join his captain to watch the rest of the day's action unfold. Montgomerie later revealed what Toms had said to him: 'David told me, "Let's hope we have another game in Louisville in two years' time."' In eight Ryder Cups, Monty had never lost a singles match, halving just two. He joined Neil Coles, Arnold Palmer, Billy Casper and Lee Trevino as the most prolific singles-match points gatherers in Ryder Cup history – it was an impressive little group to be added to. He had done his job again. Europe, with blue showing at the very top of the singles leaderboard, were now on 11 points and needed just 3 more to retain the cup.

Second up was Sergio García, and on the form he had shown on the previous two days, Stewart Cink was not expected to live with him. Few observers thought that the Spaniard would not make it 5 points out of 5 at the 2006 Ryder Cup, and 9½ out of 10 in back-to-back cups. But Cink, who had quietly impressed on the first two days, had other ideas. Playing to an incredibly high standard, especially with his putter, Cink went two-up after the first two holes with two birdies, while García could only record pars. The

Spaniard hit back at the 3rd with a birdie-two at the par-3 hole to suggest the early exchanges had been nothing more than a hiccup for the young favourite. Cink, however, refused to read the script. One of Tom Lehman's wild-card selections, he picked up two more birdies at holes four and five to race to a three-hole lead. García's score was one-under after five holes, but already he had fallen way behind. Under such pressure, and possibly finally tiring after all the emotional energy he had generated – for his playing partners and for the rest of the team – García began to weaken. A bogey at the 6th gave Cink the chance to make par and race to a four-hole lead. Another Spanish bogey at the 7th meant that the American was now, incredibly, five holes to the good. Not even Cink could keep this up. He finally scored a bogey at the 8th to allow García a hole back. When García then won the 11th with a birdie, the American lead had been reduced to three holes. It was still substantial, but García was beginning to pump his fists and get the crowd going. He could smell the beginnings of an unlikely comeback. Cink could not. At the short 12th, he sunk a fifty-foot putt to re-establish a four-hole lead. From then on, not even a glimmer of a chance was offered to García. Cink ended the issue with a birdie, to equal his opponent's, at the par-4 15th, winning the match four and three.

The golf played in this encounter was of the very highest standard. García had recorded a score of two-under after fifteen holes but was thrashed by Cink, who had racked up a six-under-par score and had forced the Spaniard to endure some of the treatment he had been meting out to the opposition all weekend. More importantly for America, they had registered a red singles point high up on the scoreboard, and the Ryder Cup score line now stood at 11–7.

'Stewart's putter melted,' an astonished García later admitted. 'I've never seen anything like it. He starts birdie, birdie on me. Then I get a birdie back, and I'm thinking, "Here we go." And then he goes birdie, birdie again. So I'm playing pretty decent golf in tough conditions, and I'm one under par through five and three-down already. He holes a 50-footer at 12, a 40-footer at the next and then rolls in a 15-footer at the 15th. So, Stewart, thank you very much, and see you in two years.'

Cink had been a man on a mission. 'It was a dream match for me today, because I felt like I had something to prove after going 0–2 in my first two Ryder Cup singles matches,' he admitted. 'I really wanted to go out there and give it 100 per cent. I knew it was going to be tough against Sergio, because he's one of the top two or three players on the European team, and he'd played great golf all week. I made a really wonderful start, and he didn't have an answer. It's hard to get back into a matchplay round of golf when you fall a number of holes behind. Today was the best matchplay experience of my life.'

Next came a real clash of the heavyweights. Jim Furyk was hell-bent on ending his Ryder Cup on a personal high, but his playing opponent was one of the stars of the 2006 tournament and one of the stars of the summer in world golf. Paul Casey had made the very most of his second Ryder Cup appearance and was still on a tremendous high after having scored a hole in one the previous afternoon to win his foursomes match outright. And his confidence was in evidence when he birdied the 1st and 3rd to take an early two-stroke lead. Casey's six at the par-4 4th allowed Furyk to halve the deficit, but the Englishman, maintaining his World Matchplay-winning form, then went on another mini-surge. He birdied the 5th and 7th, while Furyk could only par, and when the American scored a bogey at the par-3 8th, Casey found himself four holes to the good. This commanding lead remained until the 11th, when Furyk scored his second birdie of the round to knock Casey's lead back to three. At the 16th, Casey scored a birdie-four at the par 5. Furyk responded with an eagle-three to reduce Casey's advantage to two holes with two to play. The American, fighting as obstinately as he could, even birdied the 17th, but so too did Casey, and he took the match two and one. The leaderboard now had two blue blocks in the first and third spaces, and the score read Europe 12, USA 7.

For Casey, it was a final triumph after three days of glory. And to cap it all, he had climbed up to 17th in the world rankings and now topped the European Order of Merit – not to mention the fact that he was £1 million better off after his victory one week before. Being part of a winning European team at the Ryder Cup, he insisted later, meant more than any of the rest. 'What's better: £1 million or winning the Ryder Cup?' he asked. 'Now that's a no-brainer. The Ryder Cup wins every time.'

Time, and points, were fast running out for the Americans. If they were going to pull off a victory, they would have to ensure Europe failed to get the two wins that they needed from the remaining nine matches. If they had succeeded, it would have been one of the greatest comebacks in the history of sport.

At least they still had Woods to come. A pale shadow of his usual self during the fourballs and foursomes matches, the best player in the world was not even his best in singles matchplay, as his first-round exit at Wentworth the week before had proved. But the world's best golfer was intent on rounding off his Ryder Cup with a win. Victory might not amount to much in the final picture, but it would help restore some of his injured pride. Woods had taken a barrage of criticism over the previous two days, and he was determined to make a final statement, if nothing else.

Under such circumstances, Robert Karlsson should be applauded for standing up to the onslaught and taking on the world number one. Indeed, the Swede even took the first hole with a classic birdie to the American's par. Although Woods struck back at the next hole to make matters all square, Karlsson managed to keep the red of America and Woods off the scoreboard until the 4th, when a birdie from Tiger gave him a lead that was maintained for the rest of the match. Woods moved to two-up after another birdie at the 5th, but Karlsson struck back at the 6th to haul back his illustrious opponent to a one-hole lead. Then came a moment of high farce.

All week, the Woods expression had remained stony. It was little wonder. He had not played well, and he could tell that he was not contributing enough in an American team that looked set to lose the Ryder Cup yet again. But even he could not keep a straight face at the 7th. Steve Williams, Woods' caddie, went to dip his towel in the water with a view to cleaning his employer's nine-iron. Instead, he slipped on the rocks, almost fell in and let go of the club. He watched in horror as the iron disappeared into the murky depths of the lake. Had it been the final round of a major, Woods might have told Williams to dive in to retrieve the club. Instead, the world number one broke into a chuckle.

'Stevie slipped on a rock,' Woods explained later. 'It was either him or the nine-iron. He chose the nine-iron.' Tiger did get his iron back, but it took until the 15th for the pair to be reunited. Woods admitted he could have done with it at the 11th. 'I had a perfect number, 127, on 11,' he said. 'I had to go with just a tiny little eight-iron instead. It worked out OK, though, because I still made the birdie.' By the time a frogman had retrieved the nine-iron and had delivered it to the American, Woods was back to a two-hole lead, and when Karlsson found water at the 16th the Swede conceded. America had made it two wins each on the day and 12–8 in the overall standings. They needed another 6½ points from the remaining 8 on offer. Former US President Bill Clinton had joined the large throng of fans by now, arriving from an overnight flight from America, and he squelched his way around the course in the hope that his influence would provoke a sensational American revival.

Although the fifth singles match, between Luke Donald and Chad Campbell, followed, it was the ninth encounter, between David Howell and rookie Brett Wetterich, that provided the next point. The American rookies J.J. Henry and Zach Johnson, and to a lesser extent Vaughn Taylor, had done their team proud. Unfortunately, Wetterich, the fourth American rookie, would not be able to look back on the 2006 Ryder Cup with too many fond memories. Having not played since losing his Friday morning fourballs match with David Toms, Wetterich held Howell for the first three holes but fell behind at the par-5 4th to the Englishman's birdie. The man from Swindon was in front from them on. He went two-up at the 7th after the American double-bogeyed the par 4, saw his lead reduced at the

9th when Wetterich scored a birdie and secured his only winning hole of the round, and then returned to a two-hole cushion at the 11th with another birdie. After that, American resistance fell away. Although Wetterich managed to par the next three holes, Howell, playing brilliant golf, recorded further birdies at the 12th, 13th and 14th to take an unassailable five-stroke lead and the match five and four. It would prove to be the biggest winning margin of the day. Europe now stood on the brink with 13 points to America's 8. One more win would retain the trophy. Another ½ point after that would win the Ryder Cup outright for an unprecedented third successive time.

Luke Donald was given the opportunity to win the all-important 14th point and ensure America would not be returning home with the famous old trophy. He had enjoyed a very satisfying Ryder Cup so far, in the very good company of Sergio García in the foursomes. He had also been the one player on either side who had enjoyed having the crowd create a special chant just for him: 'Luuuuuke'. Now he had the chance to shine on his own and to gain revenge on the same American opponent who had beaten him two years before at Oakland Hills in the singles. The young Englishman was not about to disappoint. It took 11 holes for Donald to finally get his nose in front of a stubborn Chad Campbell, although the European stalwart had plenty of chances to take an earlier lead had his putter been a fraction more accurate. Ten holes of par golf had been played by both opponents when Donald finally scored a birdie. Campbell, meanwhile, slumped to a bogey. Worse still for the American, Donald recorded a par at the 12th, while Campbell double-bogeyed. With the scoreboard now resplendent in blue, save for a few small pockets of red resistance, it must have been very hard for Campbell to respond. To his credit, after another double-bogey at the par-4 13th, he hit successive birdies at the 15th and 16th to fall just one hole behind with two to play. However, Campbell's resistance was to end there. A bogey handed the 17th hole to Donald, who wrapped it up with a par putt to win by a score of two and one.

'It really wasn't about revenge, even if Chad had beaten me quite comfortably in 2004,' Donald insisted. 'Our main aim was to win the singles. We had won all the fourballs and foursomes, and we wanted to go out there and show that we didn't just want to reach 14½ points, but to get as many points as we possibly could. I wouldn't say it was easy out there for me, because it wasn't, but it made it a lot easier to play seeing all that blue on the board. That had a great effect on me, as did the crowd. I can hardly find the words to express myself when it comes to talking about the crowd. The noise on the first tee this morning was unbelievable. It made us all shake. It was just a brilliant feeling.'

Donald's victory ensured that the Ryder Cup was retained by Europe, but being the man who ensured at least a draw for the team was not the same as being the man who won the trophy outright. With a 4-point lead entering the final day's singles, no member of the European team would have been happy with just a draw, even if it did mean the Ryder Cup would remain on this side of the Atlantic.

The race to win that ½ point boiled down to two men: Henrik Stenson and, tantalisingly, Darren Clarke. Although Paul McGinley's match had followed Donald's, he and J.J. Henry were involved in a tight tussle that would go all the way to the 18th. That left it open to Clarke, playing in the seventh singles match, and Stenson, competing in the eighth, although neither was aware that he could potentially make history.

In the end, the Swede got there before the Northern Irishman, but it was only the slightest of disappointments to the large and passionate Irish crowd. Facing Vaughn Taylor, it should have been a mismatch for Stenson on the basis of world rankings, although the Ryder Cup has never respected such things. It was the American rookie who drew first blood by winning at the 1st with a birdie-three, a lead he would hold until the 6th when he could only record a double-bogey, while Stenson scored his first birdie of the round. From then on in, it was all one-way traffic. Stenson went one-up at the 7th with a second successive birdie, then two-up at the 9th after

Taylor bogeyed the par 4. Another Taylor bogey at the par-3 12th extended the Swede's lead to three holes, and a further American bogey at the par-3 14th meant that Stenson, four-up with four holes to play, could not lose the match.

Meanwhile, in the game in front of Stenson and Taylor, Darren Clarke was taking on Zach Johnson in a match that was a tight affair, at least initially. The Ulsterman, having received the now expected roar of approval from the crowd at the first tee, took four holes to take the lead with a birdie at the par-5 4th, only for the American rookie to respond with a birdie at the par-4 5th to draw the score level again. Johnson could then only hit a bogey at the next hole, and when he lost the 7th as well he found himself two-down. It became apparent that a special win was going to occur when Clarke sank a wicked 30-feet, right-to-left-swinging putt for a birdie at the 10th, thus extending his lead to three holes. In doing so, Clarke visibly relaxed, while Johnson grew despondent. A birdie at the par-3 12th handed Clarke a four-hole lead. It was not just any old birdie, though. His tee shot was a poor one. No matter. From off the edge of the green, he directed his ball straight into the hole from fully 70 feet away. Behind the green, no less than ten feet further on, was a lake. It was the most outrageous and wonderful putt witnessed at the 2006 Ryder Cup. He lit up a second cigar of the day and walked purposefully to the next tee.

It was looking increasingly likely that Clarke would be the man to strike that winning Ryder Cup putt after all, but a combination of Clarke losing the 13th hole, after scoring a bogey, and Stenson increasing his lead over Taylor in the match behind handed the opportunity to the Swede. At the 15th green, Stenson sank his putt to halve the hole, beat Taylor four and three, and win the Ryder Cup outright.

Clarke was literally a couple of minutes away from winning his match, and if Stenson had known, he might have bided his time to allow Clarke the chance to complete an incredibly emotional three days with a fairy-tale ending. In truth, it did not really matter. The European team had come to do a professional job. Stenson exemplified this, and he took the chance to end it when it was presented to him, holing his putt from six feet away. If the Swede's celebrations were relatively muted, it was only because he had no idea that his putt had just won Europe the Ryder Cup.

Moments later, Zach Johnson conceded a four-foot putt to Clarke at the 16th hole to confirm a three-and-two win for the Northern Irishman. The 16th had been described by captain Woosnam as 'the greatest par 5 in Ireland'. It was also about to witness the greatest-ever golfing scenes on the Emerald Isle. For all his proud record in the Ryder Cup, it was Clarke's first-ever singles win in the competition. It could not have come at a more fitting time. With the victory secured, and the deafening noise of the appreciative Irish crowd packing the biggest grandstand at the Palmer Course, Clarke was finally able to let go of his emotions, and the floodgates opened. Back at home, his two young sons, bereft of their mother, watched on television as their father revealed his true state of mind.

The first man to get to Clarke was his loyal friend and caddie, Billy Foster. As they bear-hugged one other, the tears began to flow and their shoulders shook. Next came European captain Ian Woosnam. Clarke had to stoop to rest his head on his captain's shoulder, but Woosnam took him into his arms and patted his head as the Irishman shed more tears. American captain Tom Lehman had remained dignified throughout the Ryder Cup, and even then, moments after he had seen his two-year dream shattered, he had the good will to approach Clarke, hold his head close and tell him how proud he was of him.

Clarke was now unconcerned if the whole world shared in his emotions. Waving to the crowd, his eyes red and raw with tears, he pumped his clenched fist airborne and looked, momentarily, to the heavens. Woosnam's wife Glendryth was next to hug Clarke, followed by the excitable García and Casey. Last, but by no means least, came Tiger Woods. He had won his singles match but was a Ryder Cup loser once again. At that moment, it seemed that none of that had entered his head. All he wanted to do was to embrace his friend from across the Atlantic, share a moment of emotion he knew only too well, having broken down in tears himself after winning the Open in July, and pay his respects. It was a high-class moment from a high-class individual. The 2006 Ryder Cup had created many stories, and many heroes, too, but no story was bigger than that one and no hero bigger than Darren Clarke.

'I expected the welcome to be loud when Darren and I arrived at the first tee, but it felt like 80,000 people were amassed around one tee box,' Johnson recalled later. 'I felt as if I was the away team playing for the world championships. The way Darren played was truly inspirational. We all know what he can do as a player, but he's an even better person. I could have had my A-plus game out there today, and I'm still not sure I could have beaten him. He's a great guy, and the gods were on his side.'

The Ryder Cup had been won, but there were still four remaining singles matches to be decided. The joke doing the rounds at The K Club that day was that the senior Spaniard of the two in the European team had become an honorary Irishman by virtue of his surname. 'O'lazabal', as the locals spelled it, could hear the chants of celebration ringing around the golf course, but he had no intention of throwing away his chance to beat Phil Mickelson, the world number two. Taking an early lead at the 3rd with a birdie, Olazábal lost the advantage at the 5th, regained it at the very next hole and then increased it at the par-3 12th with a birdie. From then on, par golf sufficed, and the pair shook hands on the 17th with Olazábal winning two and one. Mickelson could not hide his disappointment. 'I expected to get more than ½ a point this week,' he admitted. The rest of the world had anticipated more from him, too.

At that stage, those Europeans who had finished their singles matches were gathered in a happy back-slapping throng, willing their teammates on to yet more glory. Olazábal joined them to greet Lee Westwood as he took on Chris DiMarco. There had been many heroes for Europe in the 2006 Ryder Cup, and Westwood was another one. He had spent a sleepless night suffering from a flu bug and had started his singles match running a high temperature. The heavy rain that greeted him early on in his round hardly helped.

Despite his condition, sheer will-power from the Englishman sent him surging ahead. A birdie on the 1st gave him an early lead. A DiMarco bogey on the 2nd increased Westwood's advantage. Another American bogey at the 4th made it three holes to the European. A birdie at the 6th meant that Westwood, flu or no flu, held a four-hole lead. And another birdie at the 7th stretched his advantage to five holes. The score then stayed the same until the 12th, when Westwood understandably started to flag. DiMarco, who would be the last golfer in the world to give up on a lost cause, hit back with a birdie. Buckling, Westwood could then only score a bogey at the 13th as his lead was reduced to three holes. Birdies at the 16th and the 17th by DiMarco meant that the proud American had fought back from five holes down to be just one behind with one hole to play. Scoring a ½ point or not did not make much of a difference to the overall match result, but it mattered to DiMarco. Perhaps too much. Even after splashing his ball into the water, having seen Westwood find the fairway, DiMarco refused to concede, opting to play another ball. Then, having walked towards the green, DiMarco picked up his ball and offered his hand to the sickly Westwood. It was another hard-earned point for Europe.

This Ryder Cup, for all its stiff competition and rivalry, had been played with great sportsmanship, a fact that could not have been better exemplified by what occurred next in the penultimate game still alive between Paul McGinley and J.J. Henry. The Irishman had enjoyed a two-hole lead up to the 8th hole, but the American rookie pegged McGinley back to all square at the 10th and went on to win the 11th. McGinley made it all square again at the 13th. It then remained level right down to the final hole, the Irishman finding the par-5 green in two. The match was there to be won, but McGinley had heard all the celebrations, playing the final few holes with a beaming smile on his face, and clearly wanted to get on with the party. The result of his match did not really matter in the greater context of the Ryder Cup, and so he conceded a 25-foot putt to Henry to finish the match level, demonstrating great camaraderie and support for his opponent in the process. 'It was a gesture done in the right spirit,' McGinley explained.

J.J. Henry was more taken aback by McGinley's generosity than by the sight of a male streaker who briefly invaded the green in celebration before being escorted away by the Irish *Garda*. 'Well, I think it shows really what the spirit of this competition is all about,' Henry said, referring to McGinley, not the streaker. 'What a gentleman Paul is.'

There was now only one final match to be decided. Padraig Harrington had enjoyed a wonderful week, witnessing how well the Ryder Cup had been staged and supported in his home country and being part of a European team which had yet again crushed America. But his personal contribution, at least on the course, had been disappointing. It would continue in this vein against American wild card Scott Verplank, who upped the ante to win four and three at the 15th, having traded birdies with the Irishman early on. The match might have been a dead rubber, but, in keeping with a memorable Ryder Cup, it still offered the spectators a moment of unforgettable drama.

The day before, Paul Casey had scored a hole in one at the 14th. Late on the Sunday afternoon, Verplank followed suit at exactly the same hole. He already knew that his team had lost the competition once again, but his joy in scoring an ace at the Ryder Cup was evident for all to see. Harrington, showing his good nature, not only exchanged high-fives with Verplank, but then attempted to halve the hole by duplicating Verplank's feat. It was not a bad effort, either. The Irishman's iron shot deposited the ball some 12 feet from the hole. 'I hit a nice-looking shot,' Verplank explained later. 'It never left the flag, but to go in was pretty lucky. I turned round to Padraig and said, "Well, it's your shot now." He actually hit a beautiful shot there to go close to the pin.'

Verplank's win was only America's third outright victory of the day, alongside Stewart Cink's and Tiger Woods'. Together with Henry's half, generously conceded by McGinley, they managed only 3½ points, having started the day requiring 8½ to win back a Ryder Cup they used to win with ease. Europe's 8½ points meant that for the first time in the history of the competition they had won all five of the sessions played. Not even the great American team of 1981 had won all five. It represented the biggest-ever margin of victory in the singles for the European team. The overall winning margin of 9 points, courtesy of an 18½–9½ final score line, also equalled the best-ever European result, secured just two years previously at Oakland Hills. It might have been a 10-point winning margin had McGinley not been so sporting, a point Woosnam jovially highlighted later on. 'I'll be having a word with Paul later about that,' the captain said. 'It could have been the record.' It did not really matter. Europe had won the Ryder Cup in emphatic style and for the first time ever on three successive occasions. It was quite a way to score a hat-trick.

One of the biggest parties ever witnessed in golf began right away. Everyone in Ireland was invited, and everyone in Ireland seemed to be in attendance, standing on the lawn outside the clubhouse as Europe's players began to celebrate. When they emerged onto the clubhouse balcony, the deafening cheer they received was the loudest of the week. Champagne was sprayed liberally over the fans and players, who also helped themselves to copious swigs from the jeroboams and magnums on offer. Woosnam led the party. He had already accepted some bubbly from Ian Botham, his great friend and England cricket legend, near the 18th hole, and now he proceeded to down half a bottle of champagne in full view of an adoring Irish public who had taken to the Welshman and made him one of their own. Darren Clarke, meanwhile, held a pint of Guinness high up in the air before sinking the lot to more cheers and applause. Woosnam, for good measure, followed suit, downing a pint of the black stuff in one attempt. If he was concerned about having to make a valedictory speech at the closing ceremony shortly afterwards, he was most certainly not showing it. Billy Foster had watched his master and his captain, and decided to go one better, downing two pints of Guinness at the same time. Only teetotaller Padraig Harrington refused to drink from the bowl of success. Thank goodness the other 11 were not required to play another set of singles the following day.

Thirty minutes later, rather miraculously, the victorious European Ryder Cup team emerged from the alcoholic mayhem. Drunk with success, rather than with Guinness and champagne, they were resplendent in pink jackets, which were worn as a mark of respect to Heather Clarke. The colour pink was chosen to promote breast-cancer awareness to a worldwide audience. Laughing and joking with the good-natured and sporting American team, they made their way back onto the stage next to the 1st tee for the closing ceremony.

Tom Lehman made the first speech. 'I tip my hat to you all,' the US captain said, turning round and looking at the European team. 'I doubt there has been a Ryder Cup team in history that has played any better.'

Woosnam, having told his rival captain how proud he should be of himself and his team, then got a little carried away with himself when he announced, 'This has been the greatest week in history.' It would seem that he had forgotten to use the words 'Ryder Cup' before 'history', but, at that moment, he would have been forgiven for anything. It was left to the Irish Taoiseach Bertie Ahern to present the trophy to Woosnam, who held it high in one hand to great acclaim from both his teammates and the crowd.

Later, Lehman would be even more gracious. 'More than anything, I feel like our team gave it all we had,' he said. 'It was the one thing we wanted from the very start. We didn't want to leave anything behind. We wanted to play with heart and courage, and I feel like we've done that. So many matches went down to the wire, and it was tight for the most part, but I guess the European team just played better. They played a phenomenal golf tournament. From top to bottom, they played extremely well. At times, their golf was inspired. Around the greens, in particular, they were magical. I've always felt that in the past they have chipped and putted well in every Ryder Cup. But this time it was truly exceptional. I was just amazed at their short game. Every time we made a mistake, they made us pay for it.'

He also had plenty of praise for the mainly Irish crowd in the galleries. 'I don't think I can recall one episode on the golf course between players or fans or anybody that was anything less than perfectly sportsmanlike. The players played tough and they played hard, but they showed respect to each other. The fans were emotional and passionate and excited, but they too showed respect to the players. I thought everything about it was just right.'

He refused to accept that the competition was in danger of becoming too one-sided: 'We have extremely talented players on our tour. I'm continually impressed by the calibre of play and the heart and courage these guys have. All things work in cycles. There will come a time when we'll be sitting here and saying to the Europeans, "You know, this is in danger of getting into trouble, because the American team is so on top."'

Phil Mickelson had endured a wretched time on the golf course but remained philosophical afterwards. 'I felt like we had chances in every match to win and to get some momentum, but things didn't go our way,' he said. 'I look back on the matches, and it all seemed to come down to the greens. It's going to make me work harder on my putting in the off season, because I didn't make anything this week, and that was very frustrating. On a high note, I really enjoyed the captaincy that Tom Lehman put forth. He was an incredible captain, in that we all had so much fun. He was a great leader, and he gave us direction, providing us with every opportunity to play well. I'm sorry we didn't play better for him.'

Chris DiMarco also expressed his disappointment about his personal contribution. 'I didn't play well,' he was honest enough to admit. 'I was very excited going out with Phil. I felt we had a great partnership at the Presidents Cup and we were going to go out and do some damage this week. We just never got any momentum going.'

David Toms explained what it was like fighting against the crowd and a scoreboard that was covered in blue. 'Any time you hear the roar for the other side early on, you look up and see the board. It went blue, blue, blue all over the place. We had a tough feat today, but I thought we stood a chance. We liked the match-ups, but, in the end, they played too well for us.' He also felt that the US team needed to play on Ryder Cup courses more in order to improve their lot: 'The Europeans play at The K Club all the time. They play at The Belfry all the time, too. We seem to go to major championship venues once every eight years, and that makes it more difficult.'

Jim Furyk clearly loathed losing out once again. He sat quietly, and with his own thoughts, as he watched his European conquerors go wild beside the 18th green. Later, he had no answers as to why a team as good as the American dozen he had just played in had fallen so far short. 'Earlier in the week I was quoted as saying that I felt like we approached the Ryder Cup too tight,' he said. 'That we didn't play loose, and that our team had a different look on their faces when the gun went off in the first round for the Presidents Cup than it did in the Ryder Cup. A lot of us made a big effort to ensure that didn't happen this week. I wish we could have played better for our captain. Everyone will now want to have some answers. What's the difference between 18½ points and 9½? I don't think there's a guy in the US team who can give that answer right now. But it's definitely going to have to be a point of reflection in the future. Next year we'll send 12 guys to the Presidents Cup, and hopefully they can take care of business there. But come Ryder Cup time, it will be on everyone's minds. We're going to have to take care of business in two years' time as well, but before we do we're going to have to figure out what the big difference is between the American team who play so well at the Presidents Cup and the one who doesn't at the Ryder Cup.'

Over in the other camp, everyone from Europe wanted to have their say. 'It's all very emotional,' admitted the victorious captain. 'I just can't say enough about my team. They played absolutely fantastic golf. And the crowd has never been as good. They made history. This is the pinnacle of my life. When I was made captain 18 months ago, I said that any victory would be fantastic. But to walk away with the same record as Bernhard Langer is unbelievable. I've been worrying about this for 18 months, because it's an unbelievable responsibility to be captain. I've had some criticism in the past few months as well, but that's gone and in the past. I had so many players in the team who were all winning tournaments. We have such strength in depth, we could have put two teams out there this week. I think the future of the Ryder Cup is going to look great for Europe. I can hand it on to Nick Faldo now to make it four in a row.'

Faldo appreciated the kind of golfers he would be inheriting. 'Can I have 12 wild cards and simply take this whole team over?' he asked, grinning. 'Just give them a cat's lick, some deodorant and clean shirts, and then let's just start all over again in a couple of years' time.'

An emotional Colin Montgomerie looked back on an incredible three days of dramatic golf and realised he had entered the twilight of his Ryder Cup career. 'I'm going to really miss this when it's gone,' he admitted. 'This was my eighth Ryder Cup now, and I don't know if I'm due a ninth. The atmosphere was truly amazing. If you were at all shaky, there was no way you would have managed to hit a ball off that first tee on any of the three days. If it were not for a difficult Sunday at Brookline in 1999, it would have been six European wins out of six. Now that's fairly dominant.'

Montgomerie's respect for his captain was plain to see. 'The one thing a team needs is to be able to respect their captain, and we had 12 members of our team who respected Ian both as a person and as a captain,' he added. 'We wanted to win for him, and that's what we do on this team. I don't hole a putt for me, I hole it for Ian. We're going to have a good party later on.'

Darren Clarke reiterated the point about his captain. 'I can't remember ever being part of a Ryder Cup team, and this is my fifth Ryder Cup, where all 12 guys played so well,' he said. 'Woosie's been great with us all, but his only real dilemma was who to rest and who to play. You can see from the result that he chose wisely. He's been a great captain. All the players agree on this. He's done everything absolutely perfectly, and the score line reflects this.'

They were queuing up to praise Monty, too. 'Monty is simply a leader, both on and off the course,' explained Lee Westwood. 'He's proven today to be an inspiration when going out first.'

An ecstatic Sergio García added his own excitable take on the big Scot. 'There's nothing sweeter than beating the Americans. America may have Walt Disney, but we've got Monty,' he announced.

Montgomerie heard this and blushed. 'I was just delighted to be part of this team, never mind where I played,' he added. 'Woosie thought it was good I went out first. I'm probably the quickest player on the team, and it was important I got off to a good start and got some blue on the board early, which I did from the third hole onwards, never allowing it to get back to all square. I'm very proud to have been part of the 12 here, and to have equalled the record score from Oakland Hills. We never thought that would be possible again for many, many years, and yet we've done it the very next time. Tom Lehman's father came up to me at the 17th and said that this was the best European team that had ever been assembled. I'd have to agree with him on that.'

David Howell and Paul Casey were in the midst of a fierce battle to win the European Order of Merit. At The K Club, this was the last thing on their minds. 'At the Ryder Cup, individual results and Order of Merits just become irrelevant,' said Howell. 'We're just 12 guys, and we're all playing for Europe and trying to achieve the same thing. I was as pleased as punch to play with Paul yesterday in the foursomes. It's all about the team, and I think the Europeans do it better than anybody.'

Casey agreed. 'I haven't won a major or an Order of Merit, but I definitely haven't experienced anything like winning a Ryder Cup,' he said. 'Nothing compares to this. To share it with 11 other players and all the backroom staff is a very, very special thing. This is sporting history, and it will give me many wonderful memories.'

Luke Donald admitted that when he had woken up on the Sunday morning he had reminded himself of his fellow players on the European team and could not imagine how America could bounce back. 'It was hard to see,' he admitted. 'We had so much confidence as a team. I think we truly believed that they would have to do something spectacular to come back and win today. The team spirit has been great all week. We knew we had 12 players all on form. For us not to have got the 4½ points we needed would have been very tough to take, especially with this crowd behind us.'

The man who holed the winning putt remained modest and a team player even after it was all over. 'Everybody went out today to try and do the job in the matches, and I was no different,' Stenson explained. 'Holing the winning putt on that hole or not, it didn't really matter. What mattered was that one of us holed the winning putt. It was a magnificent team performance, and it just happened to be that way. I'm just very pleased to have been part of this team and am proud of the way we played this week.'

Padraig Harrington had not enjoyed the best of Ryder Cups from a personal point of view, but he was still happy to have won the competition in his home country. 'My biggest emotion is sheer relief,' he admitted. 'I really wanted to win the Ryder Cup in Ireland. We'd won the last two Ryder Cups, and I felt the US team would be really up for this one. This has been a massive occasion for Ireland. It's the first time it's ever happened here. Who knows when the next time will be? So, yeah, it's a big deal for us. All the European guys are very proud to have won, but it's even more special for the Irish boys to have won it in Ireland.'

Harrington's fellow Irishman Paul McGinley was insistent that for all the home advantage and tremendous support, there was another explanation why Europe had triumphed. 'There's one reason why Europe won, and one reason only,' said the Irishman. 'And that's pure talent in this European team. We really thumped them, and I'm very proud of all the rest of the players on the team and of the Irish people and the way they behaved this week.' McGinley's thoughts then turned briefly to Heather Clarke. 'She'd be right in the middle of all this if she was here this week,' he added. 'We miss Heather dearly. As for "Big D", he's been marvellous. We're so proud of the way he's handled everything. We're all one big family.'

Everyone felt the same about Clarke. Tom Lehman paid a special tribute to the big Northern Irishman. 'You hurt us real bad,' he said during his speech at the closing ceremony, causing Clarke's eyes to well up once more. 'But we are so glad you were on the team.'

Tiger Woods was more succinct. 'Inspiration in itself,' was how he would later describe Clarke. 'His play was remarkable, considering the loss he's had recently and the things he and his family are going through. For him just to be here is one thing. To go out there and play as well as he did was absolutely remarkable. That's what I kept telling him, that you're one hell of a player. In the whole scheme of things, it puts things in perspective real quick when you lose people so close to you. It's changed his life, and it's made it tougher, but it's also drawn him closer to his kids, and that's something that's going to get even better for him in the future.'

Ian Woosnam was keen to get his team off to the post-match function, but he had a final point to make. 'Every single player and member of the staff involved in the European team have dedicated this victory to Heather Clarke,' he announced. The statement was greeted with an immediate round of applause from his 12 merry men.

Darren Clarke struggled to put into words what he had just experienced. It had been an incredibly emotional past three days, and yet he had scored a maximum 3 points from three games. 'The emotion's been huge,' he admitted. 'The support I've had from my teammates, from their wives, from the American team, the American wives, all the captains, vice-captains and assistants has been fantastic. The crowd have been very, very touching. The reception they gave me on Friday morning, and again today, will be something I cherish forever. It's meant a great deal to me that people have showed how much they cared about Heather.

That and the fact that I was able to contribute to the team and score some points. I think, maybe, Heather was looking down on me.'

It had been a quite remarkable Ryder Cup. Europe had boasted so many heroes, from their brave rookies to the triumvirate of young Englishmen Howell, Donald and especially Casey, from the joy of Irishmen McGinley and Harrington to the strength of Westwood, from the charisma of the Spaniards García and Olazábal to the on-course leadership of Montgomerie and the resolute defiance of captain Woosnam and his staff. But when it came down to it, the 2006 Ryder Cup had been Darren Clarke's. His incredible and emotional story was one which had resonance far beyond the boundaries of sport.

CONCLUSION

THE EUROPEAN PARTY, AS HAS BECOME THE TRADITION, went long, hard and loud into the night before stuttering and staggering to a climax just before dawn broke over The K Club. There was never any doubt that the winners of the 2006 Ryder Cup were up for the biggest party of their lives. The scenes up on the clubhouse balcony that evening, even before the official closing ceremony got under way, suggested things might get rowdier yet. Man of the moment Darren Clarke and captain Ian Woosnam had already begun a personal drinking contest involving both champagne and Guinness, and they challenged each other to bring it on again later that night, much to the amusement of the assembled media from around the world. One look at the distinctive differences in body size made Clarke the hot favourite to win that particular brand of matchplay. A cocktail of euphoria and Irish delight provided all the intoxication the Europeans required. But a drop or two of champagne did not go amiss.

To their eternal credit, and in keeping with the sportsmanship and friendship they had shown throughout the week, the Americans also joined in. 'We were in the American team room, and they were in ours,' revealed Clarke, bleary-eyed on the morning after the night before. 'There was drinking, there was singing and, yes, Tiger was enjoying himself as much as anyone. Everyone had a go at the karaoke machine.' The Northern Irishman added that the respect between the two teams and the strength of their relationship was 'just what it should be'. Interaction between the 24 opposing players was even better at the end of the tournament than it had been at the beginning. 'This was the best Ryder Cup I have ever played in terms of the spirit between the two teams,' Clarke added.

Woosnam left the proceedings at 3 a.m., which, for him, was surprisingly early. Then again, he had already downed more than most could handle in a whole night as he stood celebrating on the clubhouse balcony earlier in the evening. 'I was going to go at two but finally went an hour later,' he explained, his head still throbbing from the morning-after hangover. 'My room was two floors up, but I could still feel the floor rocking. I've nothing left to achieve now, and I almost feel like retiring. I've already spoken to Sam [Torrance], and he said he felt the same. I feel 50 years older. There were times when I wasn't eating properly, and I had a churning in my stomach. It was not until the last couple of hours when I saw all the blue on the scoreboard that I finally felt some relief.'

The European players would wake from their deep, satisfied sleeps to read glowing headlines in the British and Irish newspapers. The Americans, in contrast, were subjected to the most damning of reactions by their own media. 'We have entered into the realm of embarrassment and humiliation,' shrilled the *Boston Globe*. 'Americans should have been issued with a blindfold at the gate on Friday and a last cigarette before the singles matches began on Sunday,' said the *Washington Post*. 'The United States were absolutely squashed.'

ESPN.com went further still: 'Underdog . . . we lose. Favourite . . . we lose. On home soil . . . we lose. On foreign turf . . . we lose. With hard-ass Hal Sutton as captain . . . we lose. With caring, ultra-organised Tom Lehman . . . we lose. With Woods playing five matches . . . we lose.'

'This isn't soccer or cricket,' added *Fox News*. 'We're supposed to win this thing on a semi-regular basis.' And Gene Wojciechowski, an ESPN columnist, came up with a novel idea. 'From now on, the losing Ryder Cup team has to clean up after the winning team when it's done partying,' he suggested. If such a deal had been struck at The K Club, the Americans would have been cleaning up for a very long time.

In truth, Tom Lehman had done little wrong, and a great deal right, but even he could not change a very evident fact: Europe were, by some distance, the better team. They were immediately installed as favourites to win a fourth back-to-back Ryder Cup in 2008 in Louisville, and the team possessed players who would surely go on and repeat their Ryder Cup success at the four major championships over the forthcoming years.

This was certainly the hope of Woosnam, when he finally emerged from one of the hardest-drinking nights of his colourful life. 'European golf is looking very strong,' he said. 'Hopefully, they will turn this success into more success at the majors. They just have to believe in themselves.'

Lehman was more concerned about where American golf went next. 'I think when you've lost again, you need to sit down and think about everything and figure out the entire Ryder Cup universe and ask, "What can we do better?" I'm not too sure we left many bases uncovered, but, at the end of the day, you've still got to put the ball into the hole, and that part didn't work out too good.'

Having the kind of team spirit Europe clearly possessed certainly helped. 'If you could bottle that and distil it back home, it would be awesome,' admitted an honest Stewart Cink.

His captain knew his own Ryder Cup story, both as a player and a captain, had run its course. 'It was a thrill that I know will never happen again, but it's been two years I wouldn't trade for anything,' Lehman concluded, before flying back to his Arizona home for a well-earned rest and a period of recuperation with his wife Melissa and his young family.

For Clarke, his immediate priorities lay a little closer to his Sunningdale home. By Monday afternoon, approximately 24 hours after the wave of emotion had hit him on the 16th green at The K Club, he was back outside the school gates in Surrey to collect his two sons, eight-year-old Tyrone and younger brother Conor. Meanwhile, most of the other Ryder Cup players were already preparing for the WGC-American Express Championship, to be played at The Grove, near Watford – such is the ever-moving nature of international golf. Tiger Woods was the defending champion, and it would be little surprise if he emerged from another disappointing Ryder Cup to defend his title successfully. Even in defeat, Woods remains a sporting icon, as underlined by the huge crowds that flocked to see him promoting a new computer game in London's Leicester Square on the Monday afternoon.

Clarke, though, had no intention of joining his fellow golfers for Tuesday practice. Instead, he was going to ensure Conor had a memorable sixth birthday. 'It's Conor's birthday,' he explained. 'He knows he is going to have a party, but he has no idea how huge it is going to be.' If it was half the size of the European party at The K Club, the lad would never forget becoming a six year old.

Colin Montgomerie, meanwhile, revealed one of the European team's secret tactics, one that certainly seemed to have done the trick. 'It was Ian Woosnam's idea,' said the Scot, by way of explanation. 'Every time one of us was about to tee off at the 1st, Woosie, or one of his assistants, would be there to say, "You're a great champion." We all feel a bit of self-doubt on the first tee at the Ryder Cup, so being reminded that you can play a bit doesn't do anyone any harm. We also talked ourselves into believing that our 12 was better than the American 12.

'I saw it as a huge honour to be asked by Woosie to go out first in the singles on the Sunday. It meant so much that he should think that I was the man for the job. Now I aim to make it nine Ryder Cups at Valhalla under Nick Faldo's captaincy. I'll do everything in my power to make sure I get there.'

Bernard Gallacher, the former European captain, had no doubts about Montgomerie's impact on the US line-up for the final day's singles matches. Gallacher believed the reputation of his fellow Scot made the American captain doubt even his best player: 'Tom Lehman thought, "No, I'm not going to put Tiger at number one, because Monty will be there, and that will be a dodgy one." They wanted a win out of Tiger, and so they avoided Monty. Monty is just a dream.'

Sandy Lyle, another European heavyweight, even suggested that it was time for America to look for help from elsewhere. The Scot, who harbours hopes of one day being European captain himself, said that he felt that Europe's opposition should become North America, incorporating Canada, after they had lost eight times in the last eleven competitions, five times out of the last six and the last three times in a row. 'We're enjoying this, and long may it continue,' said the former Open and Masters champion. 'Europe is getting stronger and stronger. We're on a roll. You might say it is time for Canada to join the American team to make them a little stronger. Or we could have a handicap system.'

Ian Botham, who joined his good friend Ian Woosnam for the post-match celebrations, agreed. 'I'm so pleased for my mate Woosie, and I'm so pleased for the European team,' said the former England cricket all-rounder. 'We've got some great players out there, and I can't see America winning this for a while. We're just too good for them.' A British columnist, meanwhile, asked if there were any good Nicaraguan golfers out there to help make up an Americas team.

Mark James, the European captain who saw victory turn into defeat on that unfortunate Sunday at Brookline in 1999, joined in with the plaudits for Woosnam. 'Woosie barely put a foot wrong all week,' he stated. 'He was spot on as a captain. He did everything that could have been asked of him. He had a gut feeling that Darren Clarke and Lee Westwood, his wild cards, were the right men for the job, and he was totally vindicated. The whole team will have been inspired by Darren's performance. I don't know how he did it. I certainly couldn't have. Sergio García also had a huge influence on the team. Tom Lehman didn't do anything wrong. His team were just outclassed.'

Goodness knows how Thomas Bjørn must have felt as he watched a European team, led by a captain he had so publicly criticised, trounce the opposition and Lee Westwood, who was given the wild-card selection the Dane felt should have been his, conclude the three days with 4 points out of a possible 5 and an unbeaten record. Fortunately, he and Lee Westwood are good friends and will remain so. Besides, Bjørn will have felt motivation in spades. Which European golfer will not have after witnessing one of the greatest Ryder Cups in history and perhaps – in terms of the crowds, the passion, the standard of play and the raw emotion – the best of the lot?

Certainly not Bjørn. Nor the colourful Ian Poulter, who was part of the victorious team in 2004 and who had just missed out in 2006 after finding his best form too late. Not Justin Rose, who is finally making a significant mark on the American Tour. Not Nick Dougherty, the forgotten youngster who has slipped behind his contemporaries Casey and Donald. Not Graeme McDowell, the Northern Irishman, who will surely be a strong contender to make the European team next time. The list could go on. If any European golfer is not bursting to be there in Valhalla in 2008 after what occurred at The K Club, then they are in the wrong job.

And what of the class of 2006? No wonder the man with one of the biggest smiles on his face on the Sunday night in County Kildare was 2008 European captain Nick Faldo. If he could have brought forward the next Ryder Cup by two years, he would have played it right there and then. He could leave Ireland comforted by the thought that in García, Casey, Donald, Howell, Stenson and Harrington, he has half a dozen young men who are still likely to improve, while Westwood, McGinley and Karlsson will be very keen to stay in the team. The 2006 Ryder Cup may have represented Olazábal's last Ryder Cup as a player, although surely a European captaincy berth will be kept warm for the Spaniard for the future; while Colin Montgomerie, another future European captain, will be hell-bent on making it to his ninth tournament, where, more likely than not, he will be asked to be the first out of the trenches one final time.

And then there is Darren Clarke. He has no plans to disappear, either, but his life will never be the same again, whatever happens in the future. The chances are that if he shows anything like the mental fortitude he revealed during one weekend in Ireland in September 2006, he will almost certainly win quite a few more golf tournaments in the years to come. He will need a lot more time for his wounds to heal, but he can go about his business knowing that he did everything his late wife would have asked of him and more. Whatever the future holds for him, what happened at The K Club will never leave the big Northern Irishman, nor anyone else who was privileged enough to witness one of the great and truly emotional sporting stories of recent times. Europe were crowned as Ryder Cup victors yet again in 2006. It was also the year when the biggest occasion in golf became Darren Clarke's Ryder Cup.

RYDER CUP STATISTICS

Past Results

Year	Site	USA	Europe/ GB&I/GB	Winner
2004	Oakland Hills CC, Bloomfield Township, MI	9½	18½	Europe
2002	The Belfry, Sutton Coldfield, England	12½	15½	Europe
1999	The Country Club, Brookline, MA	14½	13½	USA
1997	Valderrama GC, Sotogrande, Spain	13½	14½	Europe
1995	Oak Hill CC, Rochester, NY	13½	14½	Europe
1993	The Belfry, Sutton Coldfield, England	15	13	USA
1991	The Ocean Course, Kiawah Island, SC	14½	13½	USA
1989	The Belfry, Sutton Coldfield, England	14	14	Draw
1987	Muirfield Village GC, Dublin, OH	13	15	Europe
1985	The Belfry, Sutton Coldfield, England	11½	16½	Europe
1983	PGA Ntnl GC, Palm Beach Gds, FL	14½	13½	USA
1981	Walton Heath GC, Surrey, England	18½	9½	USA

Year	Site	USA	Europe/ GB&I/GB	Winner
1979	The Greenbrier, WV	17	11	USA
1977	Royal Lytham St Anne's, England	12½	7½	USA
1975	Laurel Valley GC, Ligonier, PA	21	11	USA
1973	Muirfield, Scotland	19	13	USA
1971	Old Warson CC, St Louis, MO	18½	13½	USA
1969	Royal Birkdale GC, Southport, England	16	16	Draw
1967	Champions GC, Houston, TX	23½	8½	USA
1965	Royal Birkdale GC, Southport, England	19½	12½	USA
1963	East Lake CC, Atlanta, GA	23	9	USA
1961	Royal Lytham St Anne's, England	14½	9½	USA
1959	Eldorado CC, Palm Desert, CA	8½	3½	USA
1957	Lindrick GC, Yorkshire, England	4½	7½	GB
1955	Thunderbird CC, Palm Springs, CA	8	4	USA
1953	Wentworth GC, Wentworth, England	6½	5½	USA
1951	Pinehurst CC, Pinehurst, NC	9½	2½	USA
1949	Ganton GC, Scarborough, England	7	5	USA
1947	Portland Golf Club, Portland, OR	11	1	USA
	No matches played due to Second World War			
1937	Southport and Ainsdale GC, England	8	4	USA
1935	Ridgewood CC, Ridgewood, NJ	9	3	USA
1933	Southport and Ainsdale GC, England	5½	6½	GB
1931	Scioto CC, Columbus, OH	9	3	USA
1929	Moortown GC, Leeds, England	5	7	GB
1927	Worcester CC, Worcester, MA	9½	2½	USA

European Player Records

No.	Total Matches	R.C. Records W-L-H	Singles W-L-H	Foursomes W-L-H	Fourballs W-L-H	Total Points Won

Jimmy Adams (1947–49–51–53)

| 4 | 7 | 2–5–0 | 1–2–0 | 1–3–0 | 0–0–0 | 2.0 |

Percy Alliss (1929–31–33–35–37)

| 5 | 6 | 3–2–1 | 2–1–0 | 1–1–1 | 0–0–0 | 3.5 |

Peter Alliss (1953–57–59–61–63–65–67–69)

| 8 | 30 | 10–15–5 | 5–4–3 | 4–6–1 | 1–5–1 | 12.5 |

Peter Baker (1993)

| 1 | 4 | 3–1–0 | 1–0–0 | 0–1–0 | 2–0–0 | 3.0 |

Seve Ballesteros (1979–83–85–87–89–91–93–95)

| 8 | 37 | 20–12–5 | 2–4–2 | 10–3–1 | 8–5–2 | 22.5 |

Harry Bannerman (1971)

| 1 | 5 | 2–2–1 | 1–0–1 | 1–0–0 | 0–2–0 | 2.5 |

Brian Barnes (1969–71–73–75–77–79)

| 6 | 25 | 10–14–1 | 5–5–0 | 2–4–0 | 3–5–1 | 10.5 |

Maurice Bembridge (1969–71–73–75)

| 4 | 17 | 6–8–3 | 1–3–1 | 3–5–0 | 2–0–2 | 7.5 |

Thomas Bjørn (1997–2002)

| 2 | 6 | 3–2–1 | 1–0–1 | 0–2–0 | 2–0–0 | 3.5 |

Aubrey Boomer (1927–29)

| 2 | 4 | 2–2–0 | 1–1–0 | 1–1–0 | 0–0–0 | 2.0 |

Ken Bousfield (1949–51–55–57–59–61)

| 6 | 10 | 5–5–0 | 2–2–0 | 3–3–0 | 0–0–0 | 5.0 |

Hugh Boyle (1967)

| 1 | 3 | 0–3–0 | 0–1–0 | 0–1–0 | 0–1–0 | 0.0 |

Harry Bradshaw (1953–55–57)

| 3 | 5 | 2–2–1 | 1–1–1 | 1–1–0 | 0–0–0 | 2.5 |

Gordon Brand Jr. (1987–89)

| 2 | 7 | 2–4–1 | 0–1–1 | 0–2–0 | 2–1–0 | 2.5 |

No.	Total Matches	R.C. Records W-L-H	Singles W-L-H	Foursomes W-L-H	Fourballs W-L-H	Total Points Won

Gordon Brand, sen. (1983)

| 1 | 1 | 0–1–0 | 0–1–0 | 0–0–0 | 0–0–0 | 0.0 |

Paul Broadhurst (1991)

| 1 | 2 | 2–0–0 | 1–0–0 | 0–0–0 | 1–0–0 | 2.0 |

Eric Brown (1953–55–57–59)

| 4 | 8 | 4–4–0 | 4–0–0 | 0–4–0 | 0–0–0 | 4.0 |

Ken Brown (1977–79–83–85–87)

| 5 | 13 | 4–9–0 | 2–2–0 | 1–4–0 | 1–3–0 | 4.0 |

Richard Burton (1935–37–49)

| 3 | 5 | 2–3–0 | 0–3–0 | 2–0–0 | 0–0–0 | 2.0 |

Jack Busson (1935)

| 1 | 2 | 0–2–0 | 0–1–0 | 0–1–0 | 0–0–0 | 0.0 |

Peter Butler (1965–69–71–73)

| 4 | 14 | 3–9–2 | 2–3–0 | 1–4–0 | 0–2–2 | 4.0 |

José Maria Cañizares (1981–83–85–89)

| 4 | 11 | 5–4–2 | 2–1–1 | 2–1–0 | 1–2–1 | 6.0 |

Paul Casey (2004)

| 1 | 2 | 1–1–0 | 0–1–0 | 0–0–0 | 1–0–0 | 1.0 |

Alex Caygill (1969)

| 1 | 1 | 0–0–1 | 0–0–0 | 0–0–0 | 0–0–1 | 0.5 |

Clive Clark (1973)

| 1 | 1 | 0–1–0 | 0–0–0 | 0–0–0 | 0–1–0 | 0.0 |

Howard Clark (1977–81–85–87–89–95)

| 6 | 15 | 7–7–1 | 4–2–0 | 0–4–0 | 3–1–1 | 7.5 |

Darren Clarke (1997–99–2002–04)

| 4 | 17 | 7–7–3 | 0–2–2 | 3–3–0 | 4–2–1 | 8.5 |

Neil Coles (1961–63–65–67–69–71–73–77)

| 8 | 40 | 12–21–7 | 5–6–4 | 4–8–1 | 3–7–2 | 15.5 |

Andrew Coltart (1999)

| 1 | 1 | 0–1–0 | 0–1–0 | 0–0–0 | 0–0–0 | 0.0 |

No.	Total Matches	R.C. Records W-L-H	Singles W-L-H	Foursomes W-L-H	Fourballs W-L-H	Total Points Won
Archie Compston (1927–29–31)						
3	6	1–4–1	1–2–0	0–2–1	0–0–0	1.5
Henry Cotton (1929–37–47)						
3	6	2–4–0	2–1–0	0–3–0	0–0–0	2.0
Bill Cox (1935–37)						
2	3	0–2–1	0–0–1	0–2–0	0–0–0	0.5
Fred Daly (1947–49–51–53)						
4	8	3–4–1	1–2–1	2–2–0	0–0–0	3.5
Eamonn Darcy (1975–77–81–87)						
4	11	1–8–2	1–3–0	0–1–1	0–4–1	2.0
William Davis (1931–33)						
2	4	2–2–0	1–1–0	1–1–0	0–0–0	2.0
Peter Dawson (1977)						
1	3	1–2–0	1–0–0	0–1–0	0–1–0	1.0
Luke Donald (2004)						
1	4	2–1–1	0–1–0	2–0–0	0–0–1	2.5
Norman Drew (1959)						
1	1	0–0–1	0–0–1	0–0–0	0–0–0	0.5
George Duncan (1927–29–31)						
3	5	2–3–0	2–0–0	0–3–0	0–0–0	2.0
Syd Easterbrook (1931–33)						
2	3	2–1–0	1–0–0	1–1–0	0–0–0	2.0
Nick Faldo (1977–79–81–83–85–87–89–91–93–95–97)						
11	46	23–19–4	6–4–1	10–6–2	7–9–1	25.0
John Fallon (1955)						
1	1	1–0–0	0–0–0	1–0–0	0–0–0	1.0
Niclas Fasth (2002)						
1	3	0–2–1	0–0–1	0–0–0	0–2–0	0.5
Max Faulkner (1947–49–51–53–57)						
5	8	1–7–0	0–4–0	1–3–0	0–0–0	1.0

No.	Total Matches	R.C. Records W-L-H	Singles W-L-H	Foursomes W-L-H	Fourballs W-L-H	Total Points Won
David Feherty (1991)						
1	3	1–1–1	1–0–0	0–1–0	0–0–1	1.5
Pierre Fulke (2002)						
1	2	0–1–1	0–0–1	0–1–0	0–0–0	0.5
Bernard Gallacher (1969–71–73–75–77–79–81–83)						
8	31	13–13–5	4–3–4	5–6–0	4–4–1	15.5
Sergio García (1999–2002–04)						
3	15	10–3–2	1–2–0	6–0–0	3–1–2	11.0
John Garner (1971–73)						
2	1	0–1–0	0–0–0	0–0–0	0–1–0	0.0
Antonio Garrido (1979)						
1	5	1–4–0	0–1–0	1–1–0	0–2–0	1.0
Ignacio Garrido (1997)						
1	4	0–1–3	0–1–0	0–0–2	0–0–1	1.5
David Gilford (1991–95)						
2	7	3–3–1	1–0–1	1–2–0	1–1–0	3.5
Malcolm Gregson (1967)						
1	4	0–4–0	0–2–0	0–1–0	0–1–0	0.0
Joakim Haeggman (1993)						
1	2	1–1–0	1–0–0	0–0–0	0–1–0	1.0
Tom Haliburton (1961–63)						
2	6	0–6–0	0–2–0	0–3–0	0–1–0	0.0
Padraig Harrington (1999–2002–04)						
3	12	7–4–1	3–0–0	2–2–1	2–2–0	7.5
Arthur Havers (1927–31–33)						
3	6	3–3–0	2–1–0	1–2–0	0–0–0	3.0
Jimmy Hitchcock (1965)						
1	3	0–3–0	0–2–0	0–1–0	0–0–0	0.0
Bert Hodson (1931)						
1	1	0–1–0	0–1–0	0–0–0	0–0–0	0.0

No.	Total Matches	R.C. Records W-L-H	Singles W-L-H	Foursomes W-L-H	Fourballs W-L-H	Total Points Won
Tommy Horton (1975–77)						
2	8	1–6–1	1–1–1	0–2–0	0–3–0	1.5
David Howell (2004)						
1	2	1–1–0	0–1–0	0–0–0	1–0–0	1.0
Brian Huggett (1963–67–69–71–73–75)						
6	24	8–10–6	3–3–1	5–3–2	0–4–3	11.0
Bernard Hunt (1953–57–59–61–63–65–67–69)						
8	28	6–16–6	4–3–3	1–9–1	1–4–2	9.0
Geoffrey Hunt (1963)						
1	3	0–3–0	0–1–0	0–1–0	0–1–0	0.0
Guy Hunt (1975)						
1	3	0–2–1	0–1–0	0–1–0	0–0–1	0.0
Tony Jacklin (1967–69–71–73–75–77–79)						
7	35	13–14–8	2–8–1	8–1–4	3–5–3	17.0
John Jacobs (1955)						
1	2	2–0–0	1–0–0	1–0–0	0–0–0	2.0
Mark James (1977–79–81–89–91–93–95)						
7	24	8–15–1	2–4–1	1–7–0	5–4–0	8.5
Edward Jarman (1935)						
1	1	0–1–0	0–0–0	0–1–0	0–0–0	0.0
Miguel Angel Jiménez (1999–2004)						
2	4	1–3–0	0–1–0	0–2–0	1–0–0	1.0
Per-Ulrik Johansson (1995–97)						
2	5	3–2–0	1–1–0	1–0–0	1–1–0	3.0
Herbert Jolly (1927)						
1	2	0–2–0	0–1–0	0–1–0	0–0–0	0.0
Michael King (1979)						
1	1	0–1–0	0–1–0	0–0–0	0–0–0	0.0
Sam King (1937–47–49)						
3	5	1–3–1	1–1–1	0–2–0	0–0–0	1.5

No.	Total Matches	R.C. Records W-L-H	Singles W-L-H	Foursomes W-L-H	Fourballs W-L-H	Total Points Won
Arthur Lacey (1933–37)						
2	3	0–3–0	0–2–0	0–1–0	0–0–0	0.0
Barry Lane (1993)						
1	3	0–3–0	0–1–0	0–1–0	0–1–0	0.0
Bernhard Langer (1981–83–85–87–89–91–93–95–97–2002)						
10	42	21–15–6	4–3–3	11–6–1	6–6–2	24.0
Paul Lawrie (1999)						
1	5	3–1–1	1–0–0	1–1–0	1–0–1	3.5
Arthur Lees (1947–49–51–55)						
4	9	4–5–0	2–3–0	2–2–0	0–0–0	4.0
Thomas Levet (2004)						
1	3	1–2–0	1–0–0	0–2–0	0–0–0	1.0
Sandy Lyle (1979–81–83–85–87)						
5	18	7–9–2	1–4–0	3–3–1	3–2–1	8.0
Jimmy Martin (1965)						
1	1	0–1–0	0–0–0	0–1–0	0–0–0	0.0
Paul McGinley (2002–04)						
2	6	2–1–3	1–0–1	1–1–0	0–0–2	3.5
Peter Mills (1957)						
1	1	1–0–0	1–0–0	0–0–0	0–0–0	1.0
Abe Mitchell (1929–31–33)						
3	6	4–2–0	1–2–0	3–0–0	0–0–0	4.0
Ralph Moffitt (1961)						
1	1	0–1–0	0–1–0	0–0–0	0–0–0	0.0
Colin Montgomerie (1991–93–95–97–99–2002–04)						
7	32	19–8–5	5–0–2	8–3–1	6–5–2	21.5
Christy O'Connor Jr. (1975–89)						
2	4	1–3–0	1–0–0	0–2–0	0–1–0	1.0
Christy O'Connor, sen. (1955–57–59–61–63–65–67–69–71–73)						
10	36	11–21–4	2–10–2	6–6–1	3–5–1	13.0

No.	Total Matches	R.C. Records W-L-H	Singles W-L-H	Foursomes W-L-H	Fourballs W-L-H	Total Points Won
John O'Leary (1975)						
1	4	0–4–0	0–1–0	0–2–0	0–1–0	0.0
José Maria Olazábal (1987–89–91–93–97–99)						
6	28	15–8–5	1–4–1	7–2–1	7–2–3	17.5
Peter Oosterhuis (1971–73–75–77–79–81)						
6	28	14–11–3	6–2–1	3–6–1	5–3–1	15.5
Alf Padgham (1933–35–37)						
3	7	0–7–0	0–4–0	0–3–0	0–0–0	0.0
John Panton (1951–53–61)						
3	5	0–5–0	0–1–0	0–4–0	0–0–0	0.0
Jesper Parnevik (1997–99–2002)						
3	11	4–3–4	0–2–1	2–0–2	2–1–1	6.0
Alf Perry (1933–35–37)						
3	3	0–2–1	0–0–1	0–2–0	0–0–0	0.5
Manuel Piñero (1981–85)						
2	9	6–3–0	2–0–0	2–2–0	2–1–0	6.0
Lionel Platts (1965)						
1	5	1–2–2	1–1–0	0–1–0	0–0–2	2.0
Eddie Pollard (1973)						
1	2	0–2–0	0–0–0	0–1–0	0–1–0	0.0
Ian Poulter (2004)						
1	2	1–1–0	1–0–0	0–0–0	0–1–0	1.0
Phillip Price (2002)						
1	2	1–1–0	1–0–0	0–1–0	0–0–0	1.0
Ronan Rafferty (1989)						
1	3	1–2–0	1–0–0	0–2–0	0–0–0	1.0
Ted Ray (1927)						
1	2	0–2–0	0–1–0	0–1–0	0–0–0	0.0
Dai Rees (1937–47–49–51–53–55–57–59–61)						
9	17	7–9–1	5–4–0	2–5–1	0–0–0	7.5

No.	Total Matches	R.C. Records W-L-H	Singles W-L-H	Foursomes W-L-H	Fourballs W-L-H	Total Points Won
Steven Richardson (1991)						
1	4	2–2–0	0–1–0	0–1–0	2–0–0	2.0
José Rivero (1985–87)						
2	5	2–3–0	0–2–0	1–1–0	1–0–0	2.0
Fred Robson (1927–29–31)						
3	6	2–4–0	0–3–0	2–1–0	0–0–0	2.0
Costantino Rocca (1993–95–97)						
3	11	6–5–0	1–2–0	3–1–0	2–2–0	6.0
Jarmo Sandelin (1999)						
1	1	0–1–0	0–1–0	0–0–0	0–0–0	0.0
Syd Scott (1955)						
1	2	0–2–0	0–1–0	0–1–0	0–0–0	0.0
Des Smyth (1979–81)						
2	7	2–5–0	0–2–0	1–2–0	1–1–0	2.0
Dave Thomas (1959–63–65–67)						
4	18	3–10–5	0–4–1	3–2–2	0–4–2	5.5
Sam Torrance (1981–83–85–87–89–91–93–95)						
8	28	7–15–6	2–3–3	3–7–0	2–5–3	10.0
Peter Townsend (1969–71)						
2	11	3–8–0	0–3–0	2–2–0	1–3–0	3.0
Jean Van de Velde (1999)						
1	1	0–1–0	0–1–0	0–0–0	0–0–0	0.0
Brian Waites (1983)						
1	4	1–3–0	0–1–0	0–1–0	1–1–0	1.0
Philip Walton (1995)						
1	2	1–1–0	1–0–0	0–1–0	0–0–0	1.0
Charles Ward (1947–49–51)						
3	6	1–5–0	0–3–0	1–2–0	0–0–0	1.0
Paul Way (1983–85)						
2	9	6–2–1	2–0–0	1–2–0	3–0–1	6.5

No.	Total Matches	R.C. Records W-L-H	Singles W-L-H	Foursomes W-L-H	Fourballs W-L-H	Total Points Won
Harry Weetman (1951–53–55–57–59–61–63)						
7	15	2–11–2	2–6–0	0–4–2	0–1–0	3.0
Lee Westwood (1997–99–2002–04)						
4	20	11–8–1	1–3–0	6–2–0	4–3–0	11.5
Charles Whitcombe (1927–29–31–33–35–37)						
6	9	3–2–4	1–2–1	2–0–3	0–0–0	5.0
Ernest Whitcombe (1929–31–35)						
3	6	1–4–1	0–2–1	1–2–0	0–0–0	1.5
Reg Whitcombe (1935)						
1	1	0–1–0	0–1–0	0–0–0	0–0–0	0.0
George Will (1963–65–67)						
3	15	2–11–2	0–3–1	2–3–1	0–5–0	3.0
Norman Wood (1975)						
1	3	1–2–0	1–0–0	0–1–0	0–1–0	1.0
Ian Woosnam (1983–85–87–89–91–93–95–97)						
8	31	14–12–5	0–6–2	4–3–2	10–3–1	16.5

US Player Records

No.	Total Matches	R.C. Records W-L-H	Singles W-L-H	Foursomes W-L-H	Fourballs W-L-H	Total Points Won
Tommy Aaron (1969–73)						
2	6	1–4–1	0–2–0	1–1–0	0–1–1	1.5
Skip Alexander (1949–51)						
2	2	1–1–0	1–0–0	0–1–0	0–0–0	1.0
Paul Azinger (1989–91–93–2002)						
4	15	5–7–3	2–0–2	2–2–0	1–5–1	6.5
Jerry Barber (1955–61)						
2	5	1–4–0	0–3–0	1–1–0	0–0–0	1.0
Miller Barber (1969–71)						
2	7	1–4–2	1–1–0	0–3–0	0–0–2	2.0
Herman Barron (1947)						
1	1	1–0–0	0–0–0	1–0–0	0–0–0	1.0
Andy Bean (1979–87)						
2	6	4–2–0	2–0–0	0–1–0	2–1–0	4.0
Frank Beard (1969–71)						
2	8	2–3–3	0–1–1	0–2–1	2–0–1	3.5
Chip Beck (1989–91–93)						
3	9	6–2–1	3–0–0	1–1–1	2–1–0	6.5
Homero Blancas (1973)						
1	4	2–1–1	1–1–0	0–0–0	1–0–1	2.5
Tommy Bolt (1955–57)						
2	4	3–1–0	1–1–0	2–0–0	0–0–0	3.0
Julius Boros (1959–63–65–67)						
4	16	9–3–4	3–2–1	5–0–2	1–1–1	11.0
Gay Brewer (1967–73)						
2	9	5–3–1	2–1–1	0–1–0	3–1–0	5.5
Billy Burke (1931–33)						
2	3	3–0–0	1–0–0	2–0–0	0–0–0	3.0

No.	Total Matches	R.C. Records W-L-H	Singles W-L-H	Foursomes W-L-H	Fourballs W-L-H	Total Points Won
Jack Burke Jr. (1951–53–55–57–59)						
5	8	7–1–0	3–1–0	4–0–0	0–0–0	7.0
Walter Burkemo (1953)						
1	1	0–1–0	0–0–0	0–1–0	0–0–0	0.0
Mark Calcavecchia (1987–89–91–2002)						
4	14	6–7–1	1–2–1	4–1–0	1–4–0	6.5
Chad Campbell (2004)						
1	3	1–2–0	1–0–0	0–0–0	0–2–0	1.0
Billy Casper (1961–63–65–67–69–71–73–75)						
8	37	20–10–7	6–2–2	8–5–2	6–3–3	23.5
Stewart Cink (2002–04)						
2	7	2–4–1	0–2–0	1–2–0	1–0–1	2.5
Bill Collins (1961)						
1	3	1–2–0	0–1–0	1–1–0	0–0–0	1.0
Charles Coody (1971)						
1	3	0–2–1	0–1–0	0–1–0	0–0–1	0.5
John Cook (1993)						
1	2	1–1–0	0–1–0	0–0–0	1–0–0	1.0
Fred Couples (1989–91–93–95–97)						
5	20	7–9–4	2–1–2	1–5–0	4–3–2	9.0
Wilfred Cox (1931)						
1	2	2–0–0	1–0–0	1–0–0	0–0–0	2.0
Ben Crenshaw (1981–83–87–95)						
4	12	3–8–1	2–2–0	1–2–0	0–4–1	3.5
Jimmy Demaret (1947–49–51)						
3	6	6–0–0	3–0–0	3–0–0	0–0–0	6.0
Gardner Dickinson (1967–71)						
2	10	9–1–0	2–1–0	4–0–0	3–0–0	9.0
Leo Diegel (1927–29–31–33)						
4	6	3–3–0	2–1–0	1–2–0	0–0–0	3.0

No.	Total Matches	R.C. Records W-L-H	Singles W-L-H	Foursomes W-L-H	Fourballs W-L-H	Total Points Won
Chris DiMarco (2004)						
1	4	2–1–1	1–0–0	1–1–0	0–0–1	2.5
Dave Douglas (1953)						
1	2	1–0–1	0–0–1	1–0–0	0–0–0	1.5
Dale Douglass (1969)						
1	2	0–2–0	0–1–0	0–0–0	0–1–0	0.0
Ed Dudley (1929–33–37)						
3	4	3–1–0	1–0–0	2–1–0	0–0–0	3.0
Olin Dutra (1933–35)						
2	4	1–3–0	1–1–0	0–2–0	0–0–0	1.0
David Duval (1999–2002)						
2	6	1–3–2	1–0–1	0–1–0	0–2–1	2.0
Lee Elder (1979)						
1	4	1–3–0	0–1–0	0–1–0	1–1–0	1.0
Al Espinosa (1927–29–31)						
3	4	2–1–1	1–0–1	1–1–0	0–0–0	2.5
Johnny Farrell (1927–29–31)						
3	6	3–2–1	1–2–0	2–0–1	0–0–0	3.5
Brad Faxon (1995–97)						
2	6	2–4–0	0–2–0	0–0–0	2–2–0	2.0
Dow Finsterwald (1957–59–61–63)						
4	13	9–3–1	3–3–0	4–0–1	2–0–0	9.5
Raymond Floyd (1969–75–77–81–83–85–91–93)						
8	31	12–16–3	4–4–0	4–8–0	4–4–3	13.5
Doug Ford (1955–57–59–61)						
4	9	4–4–1	2–2–1	2–2–0	0–0–0	4.5
Fred Funk (2004)						
1	3	0–3–0	0–1–0	0–0–0	0–2–0	0.0
Ed Furgol (1957)						
1	1	0–1–0	0–1–0	0–0–0	0–0–0	0.0

No.	Total Matches	R.C. Records W-L-H	Singles W-L-H	Foursomes W-L-H	Fourballs W-L-H	Total Points Won
Marty Furgol (1955)						
1	1	0–1–0	0–1–0	0–0–0	0–0–0	0.0
Jim Furyk (1997–99–2002–04)						
4	15	4–9–2	3–0–1	1–4–0	0–5–1	5.0
Jim Gallagher Jr. (1993)						
1	3	2–1–0	1–0–0	0–0–0	1–1–0	2.0
Al Geiberger (1967–75)						
2	9	5–1–3	2–0–1	2–1–0	1–0–2	6.5
Bob Gilder (1983)						
1	4	2–2–0	1–0–0	0–2–0	1–0–0	2.0
Bob Goalby (1963)						
1	5	3–1–1	2–0–0	1–0–0	0–1–1	3.5
Johnny Golden (1927–29)						
2	3	3–0–0	1–0–0	2–0–0	0–0–0	3.0
Lou Graham (1973–75–77)						
3	9	5–3–1	1–1–0	1–2–1	3–0–0	5.5
Hubert Green (1977–79–85)						
3	7	4–3–0	3–0–0	0–1–0	1–2–0	4.0
Ken Green (1989)						
1	4	2–2–0	0–1–0	2–0–0	0–1–0	2.0
Ralph Guldahl (1937)						
1	2	2–0–0	1–0–0	1–0–0	0–0–0	2.0
Jay Haas (1983–95–2004)						
3	12	4–6–2	0–3–0	2–3–0	2–0–2	5.0
Fred Haas Jr. (1953)						
1	1	0–1–0	0–1–0	0–0–0	0–0–0	0.0
Walter Hagen (1927–29–31–33–35)						
5	9	7–1–1	3–1–0	4–0–1	0–0–0	7.5
Bob Hamilton (1949)						
1	2	0–2–0	0–1–0	0–1–0	0–0–0	0.0

No.	Total Matches	R.C. Records W-L-H	Singles W-L-H	Foursomes W-L-H	Fourballs W-L-H	Total Points Won

Chick Harbert (1949–55)

| 2 | 2 | 2–0–0 | 2–0–0 | 0–0–0 | 0–0–0 | 2.0 |

Chandler Harper (1955)

| 1 | 1 | 0–1–0 | 0–0–0 | 0–1–0 | 0–0–0 | 0.0 |

Dutch Harrison (1947–49–51)

| 3 | 3 | 2–1–0 | 2–0–0 | 0–1–0 | 0–0–0 | 2.0 |

Fred Hawkins (1957)

| 1 | 2 | 1–1–0 | 1–0–0 | 0–1–0 | 0–0–0 | 1.0 |

Mark Hayes (1979)

| 1 | 3 | 1–2–0 | 1–0–0 | 0–1–0 | 0–1–0 | 1.0 |

Clayton Heafner (1949–51)

| 2 | 4 | 3–0–1 | 1–0–1 | 2–0–0 | 0–0–0 | 3.5 |

Jay Hebert (1959–61)

| 2 | 4 | 2–1–1 | 0–1–1 | 2–0–0 | 0–0–0 | 2.5 |

Lionel Hebert (1957)

| 1 | 1 | 0–1–0 | 0–1–0 | 0–0–0 | 0–0–0 | 0.0 |

Dave Hill (1969–73–77)

| 3 | 9 | 6–3–0 | 3–0–0 | 1–2–0 | 2–1–0 | 6.0 |

Scott Hoch (1997–2002)

| 2 | 7 | 2–3–2 | 0–1–1 | 2–1–0 | 0–1–1 | 3.0 |

Ben Hogan (1947–51)

| 2 | 3 | 3–0–0 | 1–0–0 | 2–0–0 | 0–0–0 | 3.0 |

Hale Irwin (1975–77–79–81–91)

| 5 | 20 | 13–5–2 | 3–1–2 | 6–1–0 | 4–3–0 | 14.0 |

Tommy Jacobs (1965)

| 1 | 4 | 3–1–0 | 1–1–0 | 0–0–0 | 2–0–0 | 3.0 |

Peter Jacobsen (1985–95)

| 2 | 6 | 2–4–0 | 0–2–0 | 2–0–0 | 0–2–0 | 2.0 |

Don January (1965–77)

| 2 | 7 | 2–3–2 | 0–1–1 | 0–2–1 | 2–0–0 | 3.0 |

RYDER CUP STATISTICS

No.	Total Matches	R.C. Records W-L-H	Singles W-L-H	Foursomes W-L-H	Fourballs W-L-H	Total Points Won
Lee Janzen (1993–97)						
2	5	2–3–0	1–1–0	1–1–0	0–1–0	2.0
Herman Keiser (1947)						
1	1	0–1–0	0–1–0	0–0–0	0–0–0	0.0
Tom Kite (1979–81–83–85–87–89–93)						
7	28	15–9–4	5–0–2	7–5–1	3–4–1	17.0
Ted Kroll (1953–55–57)						
3	4	3–1–0	0–1–0	3–0–0	0–0–0	3.0
Ky Laffoon (1935)						
1	1	0–1–0	0–0–0	0–1–0	0–0–0	0.0
Tom Lehman (1995–97–99)						
3	10	5–3–2	3–0–0	1–2–1	1–1–1	6.0
Tony Lema (1963–65)						
2	11	8–1–2	3–0–1	3–0–1	2–1–0	9.0
Justin Leonard (1997–99)						
2	8	0–3–5	0–0–2	0–2–1	0–1–2	2.5
Wayne Levi (1991)						
1	2	0–2–0	0–1–0	0–0–0	0–1–0	0.0
Bruce Lietzke (1981)						
1	3	0–2–1	0–0–1	0–1–0	0–1–0	0.5
Gene Littler (1961–63–65–67–69–71–75)						
7	27	14–5–8	5–2–3	4–3–1	5–0–4	18.0
Davis Love III (1993–95–97–99–2002–04)						
6	26	9–12–5	3–1–2	3–5–1	3–6–2	11.5
Jeff Maggert (1995–97–99)						
3	11	6–5–0	1–2–0	4–2–0	1–1–0	6.0
John Mahaffey (1979)						
1	3	1–2–0	1–0–0	0–1–0	0–1–0	1.0
Tony Manero (1937)						
1	2	1–1–0	0–1–0	1–0–0	0–0–0	1.0

No.	Total Matches	R.C. Records W-L-H	Singles W-L-H	Foursomes W-L-H	Fourballs W-L-H	Total Points Won
Lloyd Mangrum (1947–49–51–53)						
4	8	6–2–0	3–1–0	3–1–0	0–0–0	6.0
Dave Marr (1965)						
1	6	4–2–0	2–0–0	1–1–0	1–1–0	4.0
Billy Maxwell (1963)						
1	4	4–0–0	1–0–0	1–0–0	2–0–0	4.0
Dick Mayer (1957)						
1	2	1–0–1	0–0–1	1–0–0	0–0–0	1.5
Mark McCumber (1989)						
1	3	2–1–0	1–0–0	0–0–0	1–1–0	2.0
Jerry McGee (1977)						
1	2	1–1–0	0–1–0	1–0–0	0–0–0	1.0
Bill Mehlhorn (1927)						
1	2	1–1–0	1–0–0	0–1–0	0–0–0	1.0
Phil Mickelson (1995–97–99–2002–04)						
5	20	9–8–3	3–2–0	2–2–2	4–4–1	10.5
Cary Middlecoff (1953–55–59)						
3	6	2–3–1	1–2–0	1–1–1	0–0–0	2.5
Johnny Miller (1975–81)						
2	6	2–2–2	0–2–0	2–0–0	0–0–2	3.0
Larry Mize (1987)						
1	4	1–1–2	0–0–1	0–1–1	1–0–0	2.0
Gil Morgan (1979–83)						
2	6	1–2–3	0–1–1	1–0–1	0–1–1	2.5
Bob Murphy (1975)						
1	4	2–1–1	2–0–0	0–1–0	0–0–1	2.5
Byron Nelson (1937–47)						
2	4	3–1–0	1–1–0	2–0–0	0–0–0	3.0
Larry Nelson (1979–81–87)						
3	13	9–3–1	2–0–1	4–2–0	3–1–0	9.5

No.	Total Matches	R.C. Records W-L-H	Singles W-L-H	Foursomes W-L-H	Fourballs W-L-H	Total Points Won
Bobby Nichols (1967)						
1	5	4–0–1	1–0–1	2–0–0	1–0–0	4.5
Jack Nicklaus (1969–71–73–75–77–81)						
6	28	17–8–3	4–4–2	8–1–0	5–3–1	18.5
Andy North (1985)						
1	3	0–3–0	0–1–0	0–0–0	0–2–0	0.0
Mark O'Meara (1985–89–91–97–99)						
5	14	4–9–1	1–4–0	1–3–0	2–2–1	4.5
Ed Oliver (1947–51–53)						
3	5	3–2–0	1–1–0	2–1–0	0–0–0	3.0
Arnold Palmer (1961–63–65–67–71–73)						
6	32	22–8–2	6–3–2	9–3–0	7–2–0	23.0
Johnny Palmer (1949)						
1	2	0–2–0	0–1–0	0–1–0	0–0–0	0.0
Sam Parks (1935)						
1	1	0–0–1	0–0–1	0–0–0	0–0–0	0.5
Jerry Pate (1981)						
1	4	2–2–0	0–1–0	1–0–0	1–1–0	2.0
Steve Pate (1991–99)						
2	5	2–2–1	1–0–1	1–0–0	0–2–0	2.5
Corey Pavin (1991–93–95)						
3	13	8–5–0	2–1–0	2–2–0	4–2–0	8.0
Calvin Peete (1983–85)						
2	7	4–2–1	2–0–0	2–1–0	0–1–1	4.5
Kenny Perry (2004)						
1	2	0–2–0	0–1–0	0–1–0	0–0–0	0.0
Henry Picard (1935–37)						
2	4	3–1–0	2–0–0	1–1–0	0–0–0	3.0
Dan Pohl (1987)						
1	3	1–2–0	0–1–0	1–0–0	0–1–0	1.0

No.	Total Matches	R.C. Records W-L-H	Singles W-L-H	Foursomes W-L-H	Fourballs W-L-H	Total Points Won
Johnny Pott (1963–65–67)						
3	7	5–2–0	1–1–0	2–1–0	2–0–0	5.0
Dave Ragan (1963)						
1	4	2–1–1	1–0–0	1–0–0	0–1–1	2.5
Harry Ransom (1951)						
1	1	0–1–0	0–0–0	0–1–0	0–0–0	0.0
Johnny Revolta (1935–37)						
2	3	2–1–0	1–0–0	1–1–0	0–0–0	2.0
Chris Riley (2004)						
1	3	1–1–1	0–1–0	0–0–0	1–0–1	1.5
Loren Roberts (1995)						
1	4	3–1–0	0–1–0	1–0–0	2–0–0	3.0
Chi Chi Rodríguez (1973)						
1	2	0–1–1	0–0–0	0–1–1	0–0–0	0.5
Bill Rogers (1981)						
1	4	1–2–1	0–0–1	1–1–0	0–1–0	1.5
Bob Rosburg (1959)						
1	2	2–0–0	1–0–0	1–0–0	0–0–0	2.0
Mason Rudolph (1971)						
1	3	1–1–1	0–1–0	0–0–1	1–0–0	1.5
Paul Runyan (1933–35)						
2	4	2–2–0	1–1–0	1–1–0	0–0–0	2.0
Don Sanders (1967)						
1	5	2–3–0	0–2–0	0–1–0	2–0–0	2.0
Gene Sarazen (1927–29–31–33–35–37)						
6	12	7–2–3	4–1–1	3–1–2	0–0–0	8.5
Denny Shute (1931–33–37)						
3	6	2–2–2	1–1–1	1–1–1	0–0–0	3.0
Dan Sikes (1969)						
1	3	2–1–0	1–0–0	1–0–0	0–1–0	2.0

No.	Total Matches	R.C. Records W-L-H	Singles W-L-H	Foursomes W-L-H	Fourballs W-L-H	Total Points Won
Scott Simpson (1987)						
1	2	1–1–0	1–0–0	0–0–0	0–1–0	1.0
Horton Smith (1929–31–33–35–37)						
5	4	3–0–1	2–0–1	1–0–0	0–0–0	3.5
J.C. Snead (1971–73–75)						
3	11	9–2–0	3–1–0	2–1–0	4–0–0	9.0
Sam Snead (1937–47–49–51–53–55–59)						
7	13	10–2–1	6–1–0	4–1–1	0–0–0	10.5
Ed Sneed (1977)						
1	2	1–0–1	0–0–0	0–0–1	1–0–0	1.5
Mike Souchak (1959–61)						
2	6	5–1–0	3–0–0	2–1–0	0–0–0	5.0
Craig Stadler (1983–85)						
2	8	4–2–2	2–0–0	1–2–0	1–0–2	5.0
Payne Stewart (1987–89–91–93–99)						
5	19	8–9–2	2–3–0	4–5–1	2–1–1	9.0
Ken Still (1969)						
1	3	1–2–0	0–1–0	0–1–0	1–0–0	1.0
Dave Stockton (1971–77)						
2	5	3–1–1	1–0–1	1–1–0	1–0–0	3.5
Curtis Strange (1983–85–87–89–95)						
5	20	6–12–2	2–3–0	4–4–1	0–5–1	7.0
Hal Sutton (1985–87–99–2002)						
4	16	7–5–4	1–2–1	5–1–1	1–2–2	9.0
David Toms (2002–04)						
2	8	4–3–1	1–1–0	2–0–1	1–2–0	4.5
Lee Trevino (1969–71–73–75–79–81)						
6	30	17–7–6	6–2–2	5–3–2	6–2–2	20.0
Jim Turnesa (1953)						
1	1	1–0–0	1–0–0	0–0–0	0–0–0	1.0

No.	Total Matches	R.C. Records W-L-H	Singles W-L-H	Foursomes W-L-H	Fourballs W-L-H	Total Points Won
Joe Turnesa (1927–29)						
2	4	1–2–1	0–2–0	1–0–1	0–0–0	1.5
Ken Venturi (1965)						
1	4	1–3–0	0–1–0	0–2–0	1–0–0	1.0
Scott Verplank (2002)						
1	3	2–1–0	1–0–0	1–1–0	0–0–0	2.0
Lanny Wadkins (1977–79–83–85–87–89–91–93)						
8	34	20–11–3	4–2–2	9–6–0	7–3–1	21.5
Art Wall (1957–59–61)						
3	6	4–2–0	2–0–0	2–2–0	0–0–0	4.0
Al Watrous (1927–29)						
2	3	2–1–0	1–1–0	1–0–0	0–0–0	2.0
Tom Watson (1977–81–83–89)						
4	15	10–4–1	2–2–0	4–1–1	4–1–0	10.5
Tom Weiskopf (1973–75)						
2	10	7–2–1	2–0–1	3–1–0	2–1–0	7.5
Craig Wood (1931–33–35)						
3	4	1–3–0	1–2–0	0–1–0	0–0–0	1.0
Tiger Woods (1997–99–2002–04)						
4	20	7–11–2	3–1–1	2–5–1	3–5–0	8.0
Lew Worsham (1947)						
1	2	2–0–0	1–0–0	1–0–0	0–0–0	2.0
Fuzzy Zoeller (1979–83–85)						
3	10	1–8–1	0–2–1	0–2–0	1–4–0	1.5

2006 Results

Individual Point Totals

Europe

	Foursomes W–L–H	Fourball W–L–H	Singles W–L–H	Total W–L–H	Matches	Points
Paul Casey	1–0–0	0–0–2	1–0–0	2–0–2	4	3
Darren Clarke	0–0–0	2–0–0	1–0–0	3–0–0	3	3
Luke Donald	2–0–0	0–0–0	1–0–0	3–0–0	3	3
Sergio García	2–0–0	2–0–0	0–1–0	4–1–0	5	4
Padraig Harrington	0–1–1	0–2–0	0–1–0	0–4–1	5	½
David Howell	1–0–1	0–0–0	1–0–0	2–0–1	3	2½
Robert Karlsson	0–0–0	0–0–2	0–1–0	0–1–2	3	1
Paul McGinley	0–1–1	0–0–0	0–0–1	0–1–2	3	1
Colin Montgomerie	0–0–2	0–1–0	1–0–0	1–1–2	4	2
José Maria Olazábal	0–0–0	2–0–0	1–0–0	3–0–0	3	3
Henrik Stenson	0–0–1	0–1–0	1–0–0	1–1–1	3	1½
Lee Westwood	0–0–2	2–0–0	1–0–0	3–0–2	5	4

United States

	Foursomes W–L–H	Fourball W–L–H	Singles W–L–H	Total W–L–H	Matches	Points
Chad Campbell	0–0–2	0–0–0	0–1–0	0–1–2	3	1
Stewart Cink	0–1–1	0–0–2	1–0–0	1–1–3	5	2½
Chris DiMarco	0–0–1	0–2–0	0–1–0	0–3–1	4	½
Jim Furyk	1–1–0	1–1–0	0–1–0	2–3–0	5	2
J.J. Henry	0–0–0	0–0–2	0–0–1	0–0–3	3	1½

	Foursomes W–L–H	Fourball W–L–H	Singles W–L–H	Total W–L–H	Matches	Points
Zach Johnson	0–1–1	1–0–0	0–1–0	1–2–1	4	1½
Phil Mickelson	0–1–1	0–2–0	0–1–0	0–4–1	5	½
Vaughn Taylor	0–0–1	0–0–0	0–1–0	0–1–1	2	½
David Toms	0–1–1	0–1–0	0–1–0	0–3–1	4	½
Scott Verplank	0–0–0	1–0–0	1–0–0	2–0–0	2	2
Brett Wetterich	0–0–0	0–1–0	0–1–0	0–2–0	2	0
Tiger Woods	1–1–0	1–1–0	1–0–0	3–2–0	5	3

Friday Morning Fourballs

Match 1

P. Harrington/C. Montgomerie
T. Woods/J. Furyk   (Won by 1 Hole)

Match 2

P. Casey/R. Karlsson
S. Cink/J.J. Henry   (Halved)

Match 3

S. García/J. Olazábal   (Won 3 and 2)
D. Toms/B. Wetterich

Match 4

D. Clarke/L. Westwood   (Won by 1 Hole)
P. Mickelson/C. DiMarco

Friday Afternoon Foursomes

Match 1

P. Harrington/P. McGinley
C. Campbell/Z. Johnson   (Halved)

Match 2

D. Howell/H. Stenson
S. Cink/D. Toms   (Halved)

Match 3

L. Westwood/C. Montgomerie
P. Mickelson/C. DiMarco   (Halved)

Match 4

L. Donald/S. García   (Won by 2 Holes)
T. Woods/J. Furyk

Saturday Morning Fourballs

Match 1

P. Casey/R. Karlsson
S. Cink/J.J. Henry   (Halved)

Match 2

S. García/J. Olazábal   (Won 3 and 2)
P. Mickelson/C. DiMarco

Match 3

D. Clarke/L. Westwood   (Won 3 and 2)

T. Woods/J. Furyk

Match 4

H. Stenson/P. Harrington

S. Verplank/Z. Johnson   (Won 2 and 1)

Saturday Afternoon Foursomes

Match 1

S. García/L. Donald   (Won 2 and 1)

P. Mickelson/D. Toms

Match 2

C. Montgomerie. L. Westwood   (Halved)

C. Campbell/V. Taylor

Match 3

P. Casey/D. Howell   (Won 5 and 4)

S. Cink/Z. Johnson

Match 4

P. Harrington/P. McGinley

J. Furyk/T. Woods   (Won 3 and 2)

Sunday Singles

Match 1

C. Montgomerie   (Won by 1 Hole)

D. Toms

Match 2

S. García

S. Cink   (Won 4 and 3)

Match 3

P. Casey   (Won 2 and 1)

J. Furyk

Match 4

R. Karlsson

T. Woods   (Won 3 and 2)

Match 5

L. Donald   (Won 2 and 1)

C. Campbell

Match 6

P. McGinley   (Halved)

J.J. Henry

Match 7

D. Clarke   (Won 3 and 2)

Z. Johnson

Match 8

H. Stenson   (Won 4 and 3)

V. Taylor

Match 9

D. Howell   (Won 5 and 4)

B. Wetterich

Match 10

J. Olazábal   (Won 2 and 1)

P. Mickelson

Match 11

L. Westwood   (Won by 2 Holes)

C. DiMarco

Match 12

P. Harrington

S. Verplank   (Won 4 and 3)

223